Working with TILE

Select · Install · Maintain · Repair

By Jim Barrett

CREATIVE HOMEOWNER PRESS®, Upper Saddle River, New Jersey

Manufactured in the United States of America

Editorial Director: Timothy O. Bakke
Art Director: Annie Jeon

Author: Jim Barrett
Editors: Kimberly Kerrigone, David Schiff
Copy Editor: Marilyn Gilbert
Technical Reviewer: Gerald Zakim

Illustrators: James Randolph, Norman Nuding
Photo Researcher: Kimberly Kerrigone
Electronic Production: Annie Jeon, Brian Demeduk

Cover Design: Annie Jeon
Cover Photography: Scott Star

Electronic Prepress: TBC Color Imaging, Inc.
Printer: Webcrafters, Inc.

Current Printing (last digit)
10 9 8 7 6 5

Working with Tile
LC: 92-074900
ISBN: 1-880029-15-4

CREATIVE HOMEOWNER PRESS®
A Division of Federal Marketing Corp.
24 Park Way
Upper Saddle River, NJ 07458
Web site: http://www.chp-publisher.com

PHOTOGRAPHY

American Standard, 88 (bottom right)
Armstrong World Industries, Inc., 136, 137, 138, 167
James Brett, 20 (top), 96, 107, 150, 152
Bruce Hardwood Floors, 148, 149, 156
Cedonosa, 118
Phil Ennis, Phillip H. Ennis Photography, 6, 7, 13 (bottom), 15, 18, 36 (bottom), 39, 61, 83, 98, 105, 108, 119, 128, 129, 165
Epro, Inc., 24, 36 (top), 37 (top), 82
David Estreich & Associates, Architects, 17 (top)
Florida Tile, 13 (top left), 35
The Gura Agency, 38 (bottom left), 62 (top), 62 (bottom)
Lis King, 131
Kohler, 88 (top right), 88 (top left), 88 (bottom left)
Laufen International, 11, 85
Mannington Ceramic, 17 (bottom), 20 (bottom), 38 (top right)
Ro Meade & Candy Resnick, Architectural Accents, Courtesy of the Heritage Foundation, 114
Melabee M Miller, 63, 84, 97, 130, 133, 157
National Kitchen & Bath Association, 13 (top right)
Bill Rothschild, 16, 34 (left), 37 (bottom), 101, 113, 151, 159, 160, 170
Jeremy Samuelson, 116
Everette Short, 125
Holly Stickley, 87
Terra Designs, 10, 21
United States Ceramic Tile Co., 67

DESIGNERS

David Barrett, 232 East 59 Street, New York, N.Y., 160
Brook/Andrews, Atlantic Beach, N.Y., 170
Ginsberg Development Corporation, Hawthorne, N.Y., 159
Debbie Kuntsler, Oyster Bay Cove, N.Y., 16
Ellen Lemer, Culver City, Calif., 148
Jeanne Leonard, Westhampton Beach, N.Y., 113
Vogel & Mulea, Lawrence, N.Y., 37 (bottom)
Lee Napolitano, 55 Woodland Drive, Oyster Bay Cove, N.Y., 34 (left)
Teri Seidman, 136 East 55 Street, New York, N.Y., 101, 151

ACKNOWLEDGMENTS

American Olean
Bergen Brick Stone & Tile Co.
The Gura Agency
Lis King Public Relations

S A F E T Y ▪ F I R S T

Though all the designs and methods in this book have been tested for safety, it is not possible to overstate the importance of using the safest construction methods possible. What follows are reminders; some do's and don'ts of basic carpentry. They are not substitutes for your own common sense.

- *Always* use caution, care, and good judgment when following the procedures described in this book.

- *Always* be sure that the electrical setup is safe; be sure that no circuit is overloaded and that all power tools and electrical outlets are properly grounded. Do not use power tools in wet locations.

- *Always* read container labels on paints, solvents, and other products; provide ventilation, and observe all other warnings.

- *Always* read the manufacturer's instructions for using a tool, especially the warnings.

- *Always* use hold-downs and push sticks whenever possible when working on a table saw. Avoid working short pieces if you can.

- *Always* remove the key from any drill chuck (portable or press) before starting the drill.

- *Always* pay deliberate attention to how a tool works so that you can avoid being injured.

- *Always* know the limitations of your tools. Do not try to force them to do what they were not designed to do.

- *Always* make sure that any adjustment is locked before proceeding. For example, always check the rip fence on a table saw or the bevel adjustment on a portable saw before starting to work.

- *Always* clamp small pieces firmly to a bench or other work surface when using a power tool on them.

- *Always* wear the appropriate rubber or work gloves when handling chemicals, moving or stacking lumber, or doing heavy construction.

- *Always* wear a disposable face mask when you create dust by sawing or sanding. Use a special filtering respirator when working with toxic substances and solvents.

- *Always* wear eye protection, especially when using power tools or striking metal on metal or concrete; a chip can fly off, for example, when chiseling concrete.

- *Always* be aware that there is seldom enough time for your body's reflexes to save you from injury from a power tool in a dangerous situation; everything happens too fast. Be *alert!*

- *Always* keep your hands away from the business ends of blades, cutters, and bits.

- *Always* hold a circular saw firmly, usually with both hands so that you know where they are.

- *Always* use a drill with an auxiliary handle to control the torque when large-size bits are used.

- *Always* check your local building codes when planning new construction. The codes are intended to protect public safety and should be observed to the letter.

- *Never* work with power tools when you are tired or under the influence of alcohol or drugs.

- *Never* cut tiny pieces of wood or pipe using a power saw. Cut small pieces off larger pieces.

- *Never* change a saw blade or a drill or router bit unless the power cord is unplugged. Do not depend on the switch being off; you might accidentally hit it.

- *Never* work in insufficient lighting.

- *Never* work while wearing loose clothing, hanging hair, open cuffs, or jewelry.

- *Never* work with dull tools. Have them sharpened, or learn how to sharpen them yourself.

- *Never* use a power tool on a work-piece—large or small—that is not firmly supported.

- *Never* saw a workpiece that spans a large distance between horses without close support on each side of the cut; the piece can bend, closing on and jamming the blade, causing saw kickback.

- *Never* support a workpiece from underneath with your leg or other part of your body when sawing.

- *Never* carry sharp or pointed tools, such as utility knives, awls, or chisels, in your pocket. If you want to carry such tools, use a special-purpose tool belt with leather pockets and holders.

C • O • N • T • E • N • T • S

INTRODUCTION

When most people hear the word "tile," ceramic tile immediately comes to mind. It's no wonder, since ceramic tile undoubtedly is the most versatile surfacing material used in commercial and residential architecture. Ceramic tile spans the ages—from ancient Egypt in 4,000 B.C. to the tiled heat shields used on NASA space shuttles today. Ceramic tile has long been a mainstay in residential architecture because it is at once an attractive and practical surfacing material that provides excellent resistance to heat, water, abrasion, and ordinary household cleaners. In the home, tile can be found gracing many surfaces: walls, floors, countertops and wet bars, shower enclosures and tub surrounds, bathroom vanities, fireplaces, and more. Outdoors, you will see ceramic tile used for patios, entries and walkways, swimming pools, spas and hot tubs, garden pools and fountains, roofs, garden walls, murals, house signs, and even as decorative accents on the home's exterior walls. A nearly infinite range of colors, patterns, sizes, and surface textures offers limitless design possibilities to fit practically any architectural style, from traditional to contemporary.

Tile, in a broader sense, can refer to any relatively small, thin, geometrically shaped unit used in multiples as a surfacing material. That is, tile does not necessarily have to be ceramic. Resilient (vinyl) floor tiles and wood parquet tiles are two familiar examples. Several types of natural stone, such as slate, marble, and onyx, also come in tile form. They are called gauged stone. Unlike split paving stones, which vary in shape, size, and thickness, gauged stone is cut on a saw to uniform dimensions, and comes in either a polished or rough surface. Cement tiles, which are nearly indistinguishable from their ceramic counterparts, also are available. While the majority of this book is devoted to ceramic tile, the other tile options are also included.

Although some tile jobs are more difficult to execute than others, most are well within the capability of the do-it-yourselfer, thanks to the advent of easy-to-use thin-set mortars and organic adhesives. This book provides much of the information needed to do a top-notch installation that will last for many years. The recommended materials and installation techniques apply to most situations and are standard in the industry.

Every tile job has its own unique set of requirements that depend upon factors such as the substructure and surface to which the tile is being applied, environmental conditions, the degree of use and abuse the tile will receive, and, of course, your personal design goals. Since an incredible variety of tile is available today, visit as many dealers as possible and collect literature so that you are aware of all the options. A good tile dealer can further assist you in choosing the appropriate kind of tile and setting materials for a specific location or for a particular use.

The dealer can also supply other helpful tips on installing the tile once you have selected it. Do not hesitate to take full advantage of the dealer's expertise throughout the planning and installation process. Tile manufacturers also can provide installation advice and recommend specific adhesives and other setting materials for the various lines they carry. In addition, you can write directly to the manufacturer for catalogs, dealer lists, and installation information. Many manufacturers' catalogs not only show you what is available, but also serve as excellent sources for design ideas.

One final word of advice: If, after reading the appropriate section for the type of installation you would like to do, you have any questions on the suitability or condition of the surface you are tiling—or the substructure beneath it—seek the advice of a qualified tile contractor, architect, or building engineer. It is far cheaper to enlist a professional for advice before you start than to hire one to correct any problems after you have finished.

1

CHOICES IN CERAMIC TILE

The earliest forms of ceramic tile date back to prehistoric times. These crude tiles were made of natural clay formed into squares and allowed to dry in the sun. Well over 6,000 years ago, and probably in ancient Egypt, it was discovered that firing the clay tiles in a kiln made them stronger and more water resistant. At about the same time, tile-makers experimented with various mixtures of clays, combined with ingredients such as pulverized gypsum, shale, talc, vermiculite, or sand to make the tile body (called the bisque) even more durable. Glazes were applied to some tiles to further improve moisture resistance, and pigments were added to the bisque or the glazes to provide a variety of colors.

Although the basic methods of making ceramic tile have remained largely unchanged over the centuries, experimentation with different clays, glazes, and other materials, as well as firing temperatures and number of firings, has produced many kinds of tile. There are virtually limitless combinations of sizes, colors, textures and patterns. When shopping for tiles, the available choices can be overwhelming. However, you can narrow your search considerably once you understand the various ways tiles are categorized and the types that are best for your installation.

▶ *The painted tiles in this country kitchen grace the walls, countertops, and range hood, and are repeated as accents on the terra cotta floor.*

▼ *A fountain is the perfect centerpiece for this elaborate patio displaying one tile-setter's artistic talent.*

TYPES OF CERAMIC TILE

Ceramic tile is categorized and subcategorized in many different ways. At the most basic level, tiles may be either glazed or unglazed. Degree of porosity is another major distinction.

Glaze. The color in glazed tiles runs throughout the tile body, which is called bisque. The color can be the natural earth tone of the clay itself or a pigment that has been added to the clay bisque before firing. With glazed tiles, the color is added to surface glaze (usually a mixture of lead silicate and pigments), which is applied to the tile after firing. The tile is then fired again to bond the glaze to the bisque.

Glazed tiles range from a high gloss to a dull matte finish and offer a wider variety of colors, patterns, and surface textures than unglazed tiles.

Porosity. Porosity is classified according to the amount of water the tile will absorb. Nonvitreous tile absorbs 7-percent or more water; semi-vitreous tile absorbs between 3-percent and 7-percent water; vitreous tile absorbs between 0.6-percent and 3-percent water, and impervious tile absorbs less than 0.5-percent water. Generally, the longer the firing time and the higher the firing temperature, the more nonporous (or vitreous) the tile. Vitreous and impervious tiles include ceramic and glass mosaic varieties, as well as porcelain tiles. The latter are made of the same materials as porcelain china and are suitable for walls and floors. Many unglazed machine-made pavers and quarry tiles also are vitreous (see page 16). Nonvitreous tiles include white-bodied, glazed wall tiles; low-fired, red-bodied patio tiles; and pavers for outdoor use.

Water Resistance. Although the glazed surface of any tile is impervious to water, glazed tiles may be less water resistant than unglazed ones, depending on the porosity of the bisque and the thickness of the glaze. Also, water can enter the tile body through grout joints between the tiles. Tile porosity becomes important in the choice of tiles for wet conditions (such as a shower, tub surround, or bathroom floor, and around sinks) because water absorbed by porous tiles can harbor bacteria and will eventually penetrate the surface or substrate beneath, loosening the bond between the tile and substrate. Nonvitreous or semi-vitreous tiles should not be used outdoors in cold climates either, because water trapped in the tile body will alternately freeze and thaw, cracking the tile. Although the local tile dealers generally will not group tiles by porosity, they should be able to provide this information.

When you visit your tile dealer, the ceramic tile probably will be divided into three basic categories: glazed wall tile, floor tile, and ceramic mosaic tile. Within each of these categories, tiles are rated according to their ability to resist various environmental and use conditions: water penetration, abrasion, and impact. The size and thickness of the tile further dictate its suitability for a particular use, as does its surface texture (for example, a slip-resistant texture on floor tiles).

Other tiles that share many of the same characteristics and applications as ceramic tile include brick-veneer (thin sections of brick) and cement tiles. They are included in this chapter for these reasons, and because they require the same setting materials. Various types of natural stone—marble, slate, granite, onyx—also are available in tile form. These, as well as vinyl and wood tiles, are discussed on pages 128-135.

◄ *Painted tiles are arranged to form a pretty spring basket of flowers and a matching floral border.*

► *Ceramic tile is applauded for its water-resistant quality. This bathroom glistens with large square tiles and a sleek black border.*

WALL TILE

This is the most frequently used type of ceramic tile and is available in a wide variety of sizes, colors, and patterns. Most custom decorative and hand-painted tiles fall into this category. Wall tiles typically are 1/4 to 3/8 inch thick, and range in size from 3 inches x 3 inches to 6 inches x 6 inches square, although larger sizes and different shapes are available. Stated sizes are nominal, not exact. The stated size includes an allowance for grout. Typically, wall tiles are thin, lightweight, nonvitreous (porous) tiles coated with a soft glaze, which makes most of them unsuitable for use on floors and countertops. However, some tiles classified as wall tiles also can be used on countertops and on floors in light-duty or "slipper-traffic" areas, such as bedrooms or bathrooms. Wall tiles can be used in wet conditions, such as a tub surround or shower enclosure. In such applications, a waterproofing sealer is sometimes used to protect the grout joints against water penetration. Although some tile catalogs do not identify wall tiles as such, calling them by "designer" names instead, they usually do specify the surfaces and service conditions for which a particular tile is suitable.

Sheet-Mounted Wall Tiles. Sheet tiles are evenly spaced tiles mounted on a backing sheet of paper, plastic mesh, or fabric mesh; or they are joined by small dabs of vinyl, polyurethane or silicone rubber, called dot mounting. They are 12 inches square or larger. Although sheet-mounted wall tiles eliminate the laborious process of spacing individual tiles, thereby simplifying installation considerably, they usually are more expensive per square foot than individual tiles of comparable quality. They also are available in a limited variety of sizes, colors, and surface textures. Some sheet-mounted tiles also can be used on floors and countertops. All require grouting once installed.

Pregrouted Tile Panels. Eliminating the need to grout the joints, pregrouted tile panels go one step further than sheet-mounted wall tiles. The "grout" is actually a flexible polyurethane, polyvinyl chloride, rubber grout, or silicone caulk that does not require sealing and demands less maintenance than ordinary cement-based grouts. The sheets themselves are flexible enough to bend and stretch with normal building movement, and a variety of standard trim pieces are available to complete the installation. Tubes of matching silicone caulk are used to grout the joints between panel edges and trim pieces. Typically, the grout is treated with a special mildew and fungus inhibitor, making these panels suitable for shower and tub enclosures. Because of this chemical treatment, the FDA does not recommend installing the sheets on kitchen countertops or on other food-preparation and serving areas. These rubber grouts are available in white and a wide range of colors.

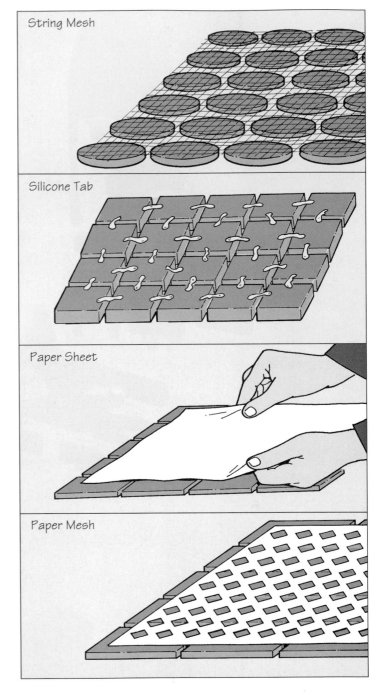

String Mesh

Silicone Tab

Paper Sheet

Paper Mesh

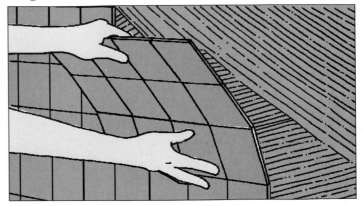

Pregrouted Tile Panels

▲ *The ceramic tiles used here are rustic and rugged, yet warm and inviting. The trim has gently rounded corners.*

▲ *Use a solid-colored tile with white grout to emphasize the grid-like pattern, creating a modern look.*

▼ *As a longer-lasting surface material, painted tiles can provide the same colorful, decorative features as wallpaper.*

MOSAIC TILE

All tiles that are 2 inches square or smaller are considered ceramic mosaic tiles. They are made either of glass or of a fine-grained porcelain clay that is mixed with colored pigments. These dense-bodied vitreous tiles resist water, stains, impact, frost, and abrasion, making them suitable for practically any application. Surface textures range from a smooth, glassy surface for walls to a textured slip-resistant surface for use on floors.

Shapes include squares, rectangles, hexagons, circles, teardrops, clover leafs, and random "pebble" designs, among others. Most ceramic mosaic tiles are mounted on a backing sheet of rubber, plastic, paper, or heavy thread to facilitate application. Because of their small size, these tiles adapt well to contoured or irregular surfaces, such as columns, curved counters, unusually shaped tubs, garden pools and fountains, spas, and curved raised planters.

▶ *A floor benefits from the striking drama created by mosaic tile laid out in a detailed pattern.*

▼ *Not only do mosaic tiles produce an interesting floor pattern, they are dense-bodied tiles that resist water and stains: a perfect choice for the kitchen floor.*

FLOOR TILE

As the name indicates, this group includes all tiles suitable for use on indoor and outdoor floors. Most glazed floor tiles are suitable for use on countertops and other horizontal surfaces subject to impact, abrasion, and heavy use in general. As a rule, floor tiles are too heavy to install on walls. With the proper adhesives, however, they can be used on walls if the walls are designed to support the additional weight.

Floor tiles usually are thicker than wall tiles, ranging from 3/8 inch to 3/4 inch thick. Sizes for square tiles range from 4 to 24 inches square. These dimensions include grout space. Other shapes include rectangular, hexagonal, octagonal, and ogee. Floor tiles fall into three general categories: unglazed quarry tile, unglazed pavers, and glazed floor tile.

Unglazed Quarry Tile. This category often is applied loosely in the industry to any hard, red-bodied clay floor tile of consistent dimensions not less than 3/8 inch thick. Unglazed quarry tile typically is a hard-bodied semivitreous or vitreous tile used for indoor and outdoor floors. The bisque is usually a deep, brick red, although other earth-tone colors are available, depending on the natural clays used. Although most quarry tile has a natural clay color, some manufacturers add pigments to the clay before firing. These range from pastel hues of blue, green, peach, pink, and mauve to off-whites and tans. Glazed quarry tile is offered in a wide range of brighter colors.

Unglazed Pavers. All floor tiles that are not classified as red-bodied quarry tiles are called unglazed pavers, although the terms are sometimes used interchangeably. Pavers range from impervious porcelain varieties to soft-bodied, nonvitreous handmade "Mexican," or "patio," pavers. Pavers that are available in various earth tones generally are referred to as terra cotta tiles and are popular for floors, indoors and outdoors. Today, most terra cotta tiles are imported from Italy, Spain, France, and Mexico.

Machine-made pavers usually are hard-bodied, semivitreous or vitreous tiles that are uniform in dimension and relatively free of surface imperfections. Nominal thicknesses are 1/4 inch to 1/2 inch. These are glazed or unglazed, and the bisque may be natural clay, shale, porcelain, or various mixtures of clay and other ground minerals. Machine-made pavers come in a wide variety of colors, surface textures, and porosities. Some are strong enough to use for driveways and other high-traffic areas. Many are vitreous and are tolerant to freezing and thawing.

Rustic handmade pavers are low-fired, nonvitreous clay tiles, formed by hand in crude wooden frames or hand-

▲ *For a warm, Southwestern feel, install terra cotta tiles on the walls and floor.*

cut from sheets in a cookie-cutter fashion. Most come from Mexico (hence the name Mexican pavers), but some are imported from the Mediterranean countries. These tiles come in various earth-tone shades and often are not of a uniform overall size, thickness, shape, or surface texture. The edges are not always perfectly straight and may be chipped or cracked. The surface may include fingerprints, animal tracks, or similar imprints. While these characteristics are what lend many handmade pavers their charm, special care must be taken in laying out and setting the tiles so grout joints will align properly and the overall tiled surface will be relatively smooth and level. Because handmade pavers or patio tiles absorb water, and will crack under continuous freezing and thawing, they should not be used outdoors in cold climates.

Unglazed pavers and quarry tiles must be sealed when used on interior floors to resist dirt and stains. Some sealers also provide a low sheen to the tiles and enhance their natural color. While some unglazed floor tiles are "factory treated" with a sealer to provide initial protection, you will need to reapply a sealer periodically to maintain that protection. For more on sealing unglazed tile, see page 33. Because unglazed tiles stain easily, the sealers generally are not recommended for use on food-preparation surfaces such as countertops.

Glazed Floor Tiles. These tiles often are listed in manufacturers' catalogs as glazed quarry tile, glazed pavers, or simply glazed floor tiles, depending on the clay used to make the tile. Most floor tiles are made from a red-bodied clay, while wall tiles are white-bodied. Colors range from muted earth tones to bold, bright, solid-color, or patterned tiles.

Generally, you would use glazed floor tiles on interior floors only, because the tile body and glaze on most types will not hold up to outdoor conditions. However, the glaze on floor tiles usually is heavier than that found on wall tiles, providing good abrasion resistance on interior surfaces. Glazed floor tiles are an excellent choice for kitchen countertops, tables, and other horizontal surfaces that are subject to frequent use.

Some glazed floor tiles are more slip-resistant than others. When installing floor tiles in bathrooms or other areas subject to splashed water on the floor, make sure the tile provides a good slip-proof surface underfoot. Some glazed floor tiles have a fine carbide grit incorporated into the glaze to make them extremely slip-proof.

▲ *A modern dining area is enhanced by an oversized checker-board pattern on the floor.*

▼ *The area that surrounds the wood stove is defined by a perimeter of darker glazed tiles that extend out onto the floor.*

CEMENT-BODIED TILE

Cement-bodied tiles are made out of cement rather than clay. There are two basic kinds: Mexican saltillo (pronounced sal-tee'-yo) tile and extruded cement-bodied tile.

Saltillo Tile. These tiles are named after the town in northern Mexico where they are made. The tiles are composed mostly of soft clay and are cured simply by being allowed to dry in the sun. They have a very rustic appearance caused by fingerprints, animal tracks, and "lime pops," small pinholes or cavities that occur when lime leaches from the clay during curing. Saltillo tiles come stained in a variety of earthtone colors. Because they are porous, saltillo tiles require a sealer to help resist staining. In some areas, the tiles are available presealed. Also, because of their porosity, saltillo tiles are not suitable for wet indoor locations.

Extruded Cement-Bodied Tile. This tile is a mixture of portland cement, sand, and a fine aggregate (concrete) that is extruded or cast under pressure, and then steam-cured in a kiln to produce an extremely dense-bodied tile with strong resistance to wear.

Extruded cement-bodied tiles usually imitate quarry tiles, pavers, cut stone, or brick in appearance. The tiles come in a variety of stained colors, which run throughout the tile body. Tiles intended for indoor use are factory-treated with a clear surface sealer, rather than an applied glaze, to give them a semi-glossy appearance. To seal the grout joints, a second coat of sealer is applied after installation. This must be reapplied every year or two to maintain the tile surface. Although much less porous than saltillo tiles, extruded cement-bodied tiles are not recommended for consistently wet indoor locations, such as tub or shower surrounds. Extruded tiles made for outdoor use are treated with a clear penetrating sealer, which also requires periodic reapplication. These tiles are water resistant; but if used outdoors, make sure the type chosen resists freezing and thawing.

Both saltillo and extruded cement-bodied tiles come in most standard "floor tile" sizes, although shapes are usually limited to squares and rectangles. They weigh about the same as ceramic floor tiles or veneer bricks of the same dimensions and are installed similarly.

◀ *Glazed floor tiles are available in a range of colors, from muted earth tones to bright solids and patterns.*

▶ *Extruded cement floor tiles resemble cut stone and pavers. Those used indoors must have a clear acrylic surface.*

BRICK VENEER TILE

Also called "floor bricks," brick veneer tiles include unglazed ceramic tiles that simulate real brick, and actual bricks formed to the thickness of tile. (Some cement tiles, which are discussed following this section, also simulate veneer bricks.) Real veneer bricks and cement-bodied bricks often are used on floors for fireplace hearths. Outdoors, they are used for patios, house sidings, driveways, and other applications in place of conventional bricks as a paving or siding material. Veneer bricks or floor bricks are extruded from a high-quality shale to produce an extremely dense brick suitable for heavy-traffic areas. Some ceramic "simulated-brick" tiles do not have the wear characteristics of real brick or cement brick tiles, so they might not be appropriate for floors and similar applications. Check the manufacturer's specifications to be sure.

Because most brick veneer tiles (real or simulated) are porous, they are not a good choice for interior wet installations, such as tub surrounds or showers. If you use brick tiles for an interior floor, you will need to seal them to prevent staining and to maintain their appearance.

▲ *Used inside the home, floor bricks create a rugged, old-fashioned aura.*

▼ *Use brick veneer tile to extend the patio into the sunroom.*

FIELD TILES

The standard unit of ceramic tile used to cover a surface is called a field tile. Field tiles come in several different shapes, which can be used singly or in various combinations to form a variety of patterns within the tile field. All four edges of a field tile are unfinished, and they do not turn corners.

The most popular size field tile for most wall applications is 4 1/4 inches x 4 1/4 inches. The actual size of these tiles may vary 1/8 inch more or less, as will the thickness, depending on the manufacturer. For this reason, you cannot always mix tiles from different manufacturers; the grout joints may not line up. Differing thicknesses will prevent you from setting tiles on the same plane.

TRIM TILES

All tiles that are not field tiles are referred to as trim tiles. They are used to create smooth, finished edges and corners for specific areas. In tile catalogs, manufacturers usually picture the available sizes and shapes of trim pieces for different tiles in their line.

Angles: Left-Out, Right-Out, Left-In, Right-In. These trim tiles create sharp corners instead of rounded ones.

Aprons. Half-size tiles called aprons are used to fill in narrow areas, such as along the front of a countertop.

Bases. Tiles designed specifically for the floor line, base trims (sometimes called runners) have a finished top edge. They are used in areas where the floor has been tiled, but the wall has not.

Beads. These trims are sometimes called quarter-rounds, and are used to finish off corners and edges. The pieces are narrow, and they turn a rounded, 90-degree angle.

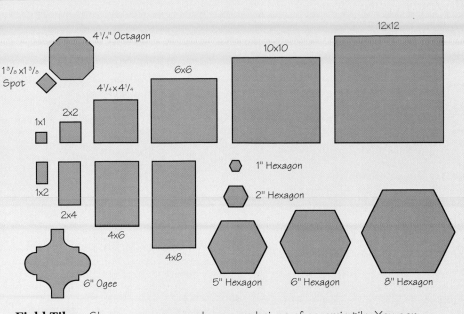

Field Tiles. Shown are common shapes and sizes of ceramic tile. You can use them to create a variety of tile patterns.

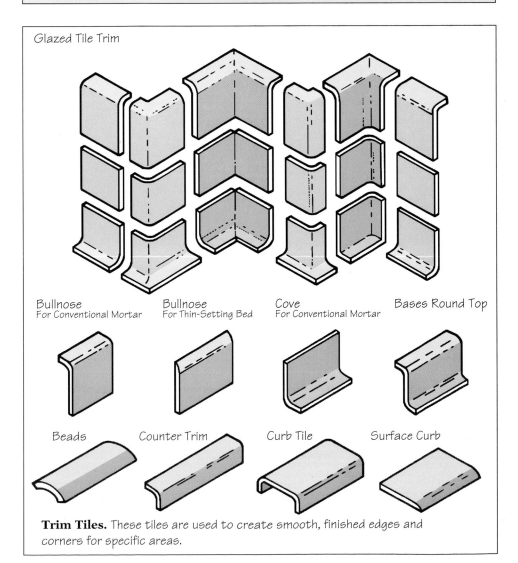

Trim Tiles. These tiles are used to create smooth, finished edges and corners for specific areas.

SPECIALTY TILE

Within the standard wall and floor tile classifications are ceramic tiles made for specific applications.

Decorative. Limited only by the artist's imagination, decorative tiles come in an infinite variety of designs. Large tile manufacturers offer a broad selection of domestic and imported hand-painted tiles, from traditional designs such as Delft or Art Nouveau to contemporary objects d'art. Several large manufacturers even employ a staff of artists to make personalized hand-painted tiles to order, as do small independent artisans and ceramic shops. For example, tiles can be painted to match a china pattern, or with the names of family members on them. Hand-painted tiles are available as individual accents, used to spruce up a kitchen countertop, backsplash, shower enclosure, or fireplace surround, or as a mural covering a large area. Some hand-painted tiles have sculptured surfaces, while others are hand-cut into unusual shapes.

Custom-made hand-painted tiles vary widely in price—from $20 to $100 a piece—depending on whether they are chosen from stock designs or are custom-made to your specifications. However, when used as accents just a few of these tiles are needed to add a distinctive touch to any installation. If hand-painted tiles are too costly, most tile dealers also carry decorator tiles and picture tiles with silk-screened or decal designs at a more affordable price. Do not overlook used building-material dealers as sources for decorative tiles.

Antique. Like other traditional art forms, antique, hand-painted tiles span the centuries and globe. Although some rare examples command prices in the hundreds or even thousands of dollars, others are relatively affordable. All are collectible. In the United States, tile-making got its start in the mid-1800s. Collectible American tiles include Victorian art tiles, arts and crafts tiles, and art deco tiles, among others. Collecting antique tiles is a highly specialized subject, far beyond the scope of this book. However, if you are interested in antique tiles, you will find books in your local library dedicated to this subject. Antiques dealers

▲ *If you want to be really original, design a wall mural an[d] have it custom-made.*

and auctions are typical sources for antique tiles. [ ] best bet for early American tiles is to search out de[ ] who specialize in deco and nouveau pottery. If [ ] cannot find the real thing, most companies special[ ] in imported hand-painted tiles usually inc[ ] a selection of reproduction antique designs [ ] "picture" tiles.

If you are living in an older home that has [ ] surfaces, you may already have a functional colle[ ] of antique tiles, or simply some older tiles that [ ] want identified for replacement purposes. If so, [ ] can contact the Tile Heritage Foundation, *P.O. [ ] 1850, Healdsburg, CA 95448.* This nonprofit, mem[ ] supported foundation is dedicated to the research [ ] preservation of American antique tiles and maintai[ ] nationwide network of tile historians and identif[ ] If you send a quality photo of the tile and a [ ] addressed stamped envelope, the foundation [ ] probably be able to tell you what type of tile it is, w[ ] it was produced, and the company that made it. If [ ] are interested in repairing or replacing a few ant[ ] tiles, there are many small, custom-tile studios ac[ ] the country that specialize in this service. Check [ ] Yellow Pages in your phone book under the hea[ ] *Ceramic Products, Decorative.*

SPECIALTY TILE

Within the standard wall and floor tile classifications are ceramic tiles made for specific applications.

Decorative. Limited only by the artist's imagination, decorative tiles come in an infinite variety of designs. Large tile manufacturers offer a broad selection of domestic and imported hand-painted tiles, from traditional designs such as Delft or Art Nouveau to contemporary objects d'art. Several large manufacturers even employ a staff of artists to make personalized hand-painted tiles to order, as do small independent artisans and ceramic shops. For example, tiles can be painted to match a china pattern, or with the names of family members on them. Hand-painted tiles are available as individual accents, used to spruce up a kitchen countertop, backsplash, shower enclosure, or fireplace surround, or as a mural covering a large area. Some hand-painted tiles have sculptured surfaces, while others are hand-cut into unusual shapes.

▲ *If you want to be really original, design a wall mural and have it custom-made.*

Custom-made hand-painted tiles vary widely in price— from $20 to $100 a piece—depending on whether they are chosen from stock designs or are custom-made to your specifications. However, when used as accents just a few of these tiles are needed to add a distinctive touch to any installation. If hand-painted tiles are too costly, most tile dealers also carry decorator tiles and picture tiles with silk-screened or decal designs at a more affordable price. Do not overlook used building-material dealers as sources for decorative tiles.

Antique. Like other traditional art forms, antique, hand-painted tiles span the centuries and globe. Although some rare examples command prices in the hundreds or even thousands of dollars, others are relatively affordable. All are collectible. In the United States, tile-making got its start in the mid-1800s. Collectible American tiles include Victorian art tiles, arts and crafts tiles, and art deco tiles, among others. Collecting antique tiles is a highly specialized subject, far beyond the scope of this book. However, if you are interested in antique tiles, you will find books in your local library dedicated to this subject. Antiques dealers and auctions are typical sources for antique tiles. Your best bet for early American tiles is to search out dealers who specialize in deco and nouveau pottery. If you cannot find the real thing, most companies specializing in imported hand-painted tiles usually include a selection of reproduction antique designs and "picture" tiles.

If you are living in an older home that has tiled surfaces, you may already have a functional collection of antique tiles, or simply some older tiles that you want identified for replacement purposes. If so, you can contact the Tile Heritage Foundation, *P.O. Box 1850, Healdsburg, CA 95448.* This nonprofit, member-supported foundation is dedicated to the research and preservation of American antique tiles and maintains a nationwide network of tile historians and identifiers. If you send a quality photo of the tile and a self-addressed stamped envelope, the foundation will probably be able to tell you what type of tile it is, when it was produced, and the company that made it. If you are interested in repairing or replacing a few antique tiles, there are many small, custom-tile studios across the country that specialize in this service. Check the Yellow Pages in your phone book under the heading *Ceramic Products, Decorative.*

FIELD TILES

The standard unit of ceramic tile used to cover a surface is called a field tile. Field tiles come in several different shapes, which can be used singly or in various combinations to form a variety of patterns within the tile field. All four edges of a field tile are unfinished, and they do not turn corners.

The most popular size field tile for most wall applications is 4¼ inches x 4¼ inches. The actual size of these tiles may vary 1/8 inch more or less, as will the thickness, depending on the manufacturer. For this reason, you cannot always mix tiles from different manufacturers; the grout joints may not line up. Differing thicknesses will prevent you from setting tiles on the same plane.

TRIM TILES

All tiles that are not field tiles are referred to as trim tiles. They are used to create smooth, finished edges and corners for specific areas. In tile catalogs, manufacturers usually picture the available sizes and shapes of trim pieces for different tiles in their line.

Angles: Left-Out, Right-Out, Left-In, Right-In. These trim tiles create sharp corners instead of rounded ones.

Aprons. Half-size tiles called aprons are used to fill in narrow areas, such as along the front of a countertop.

Bases. Tiles designed specifically for the floor line, base trims (sometimes called runners) have a finished top edge. They are used in areas where the floor has been tiled, but the wall has not.

Beads. These trims are sometimes called quarter-rounds, and are used to finish off corners and edges. The pieces are narrow, and they turn a rounded, 90-degree angle.

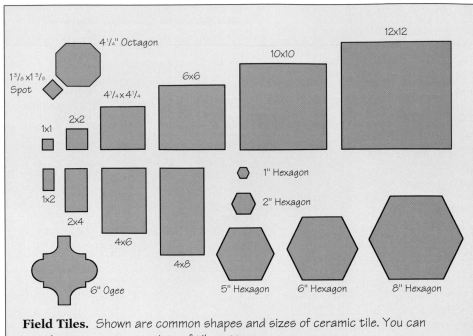

Field Tiles. Shown are common shapes and sizes of ceramic tile. You can use them to create a variety of tile patterns.

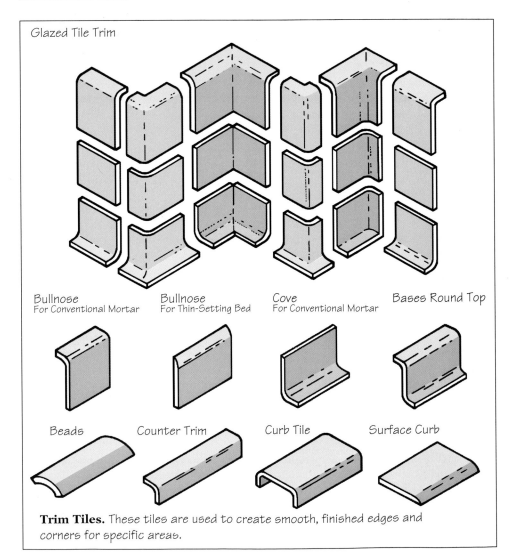

Trim Tiles. These tiles are used to create smooth, finished edges and corners for specific areas.

Bullnose Trims. These are regular field tiles with one curved, finished edge. They finish a course without turning a corner. Often, a bullnose is paired with an apron tile meeting the bullnose at a right angle. The result is a smoothly turned corner and edge. Two types are available: surface bullnose (for thin-set installations) and radiused bullnose (for thick-bed installations).

Countertop Trims or Sink Caps.
These special trim pieces are set on the outside edge of a countertop. The raised lip is designed to prevent drips.

Coves. These pieces are used to turn corners at a right angle. The corner can turn either inward or outward. Cove base turns a corner at floor level; cove itself turns a corner in any course. Special cove pieces have a finished edge; they are used to turn a corner at the top row of a backsplash, for instance. Other cove pieces do not have finished edges. Since the inside surface of a cove piece is hollow, it can compensate for out-of-plumb corners.

Miters. Two miter pieces together create the look of a miter joint in a corner.

Rounds: In- and Out-Corners.
These trim tiles create a rounded corner instead of an angular one.

Swimming Pool Edging.
Designed to cover the coping on swimming pools, this edging requires a thick-set mortar bed.

Window Sill. Window sill tile has a finished edge on one side, and a rounded corner on the other. It covers the sill itself and turns to meet the tile on the wall. Without this trim piece, you would need two tiles: a flat field tile for the sill itself and a quarter-round to turn the corner. Sill trim simplifies the installation.

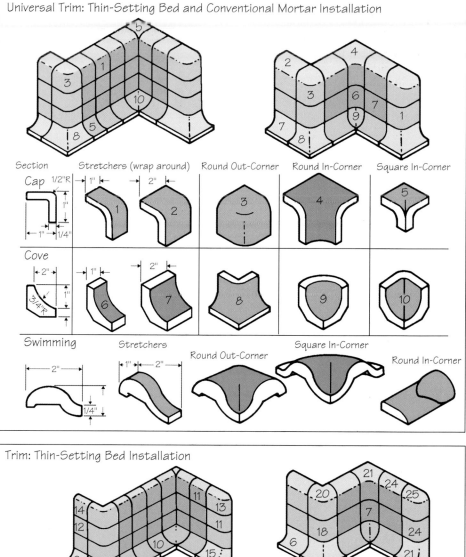

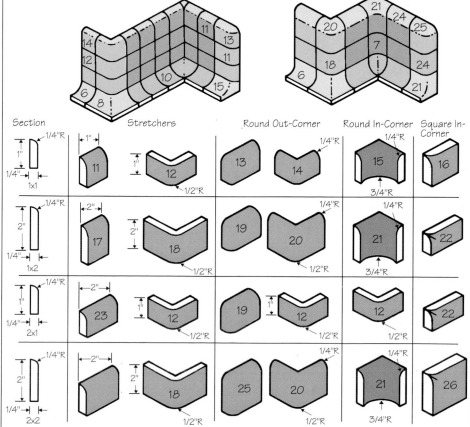

2

TOOLS & MATERIALS

All tile jobs share the same basic method: preparing the surface to be tiled; establishing layout lines to guide tile placement; cutting the tiles; setting the tiles with mortar or adhesive; applying grout to fill the joints between tiles; and, in some cases, sealing the grout joints and tile surface. The following chapter covers the basic tools and materials required to accomplish these steps. Detailed how-to instructions for specific projects are presented in Chapters 3-11.

▼ *Prepare yourself with the necessary tools before beginning any job.*

If you are an active do-it-yourselfer, you probably own most of the tools needed to complete a tile job. Specialized tile-setting tools can be purchased at a local hardware store, home center, or tile dealer.

LAYOUT & PREPARATION TOOLS

The tools you will need include a *2-foot level, steel tape measure, combination square, 2-foot carpenter's square, plumb bob and chalkline, scraper or putty knife, caulking gun, squeegee, and hammer or rubber mallet*. Also, keep several damp sponges, rags, and buckets half-filled with warm water handy for cleaning up as you proceed with the job.

If the surface you are tiling requires more preparation, you may need additional masonry and carpentry tools. Because surface preparation can involve anything from a simple cleaning to a complete rebuilding of a wall or floor, in this book specific surface-preparation tools are listed at the beginning of each project.

CUTTING TOOLS

To make straight cuts in most glazed tile, all you need is a conventional *glass cutter, a short metal straightedge or square, and a short length of coat-hanger wire or thin dowel*. Simply score the glazed surface of the tile with the cutter and straightedge; then place the tile on the wire or dowel with the score mark centered directly above it, and press down on both sides of the tile to snap it.

If you have very many straight cuts to make, a *snap cutter* will speed things along considerably. Snap cutters are available at tool-rental shops. Some tile dealers will loan out their tools if you have purchased the tile from them. These tools come in several sizes and

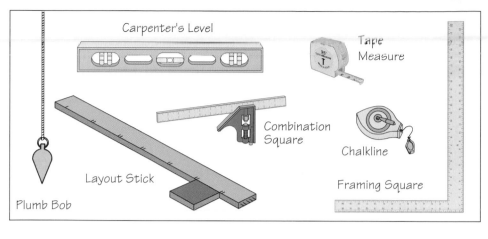

Carpenter's Level
Tape Measure
Combination Square
Chalkline
Layout Stick
Plumb Bob
Framing Square

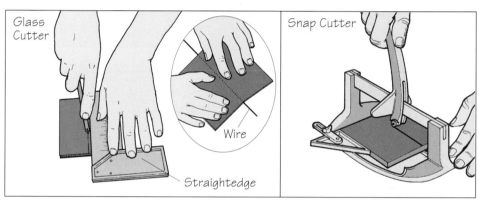

Glass Cutter
Wire
Straightedge
Snap Cutter

variations; but most consist of a metal frame that holds the tile in position, a carbide-tipped blade or wheel to score the tile, and a device to snap the tile once scored. After positioning the tile, draw the carbide blade or wheel lightly across the tile to score it; then press down on the handle until it snaps.

Some snap cutters may not work on very large, thick tiles, such as unglazed quarry tile or pavers. If you have just a few of these tiles to cut, use this variation of the score-and-snap method: Equip a hacksaw with a carbide-grit blade, then cut a groove about 1/16 inch deep in the face of the tile. (Very thick tiles may require a second cut on the back side to get a clean snap.) Place the tile over a wood dowel or length of heavy insulated wire, and press down sharply to snap the tile. If you have many cuts to make, have the tiles cut on a wet saw (a stationary circular saw with a water-cooled carbide-grit blade, used for cutting

hard masonry materials). Most tile dealers have a wet saw and will make cuts for a small fee. You also can rent one at a tool-rental shop. Wet saws should not be used to cut floor tiles that are coated with abrasive carbide grit, since the grit will quickly dull the saw blade. Have your tile dealer cut these, or use the score-and-snap method above.

Caution: Because ceramic tile is brittle, none of the above cutting tools works all of the time. Make sure you buy enough extra tiles to allow for breakage and other mistakes. If you do not want to cut tiles at all, carefully lay out all the tiles in advance, mark the ones that need to be cut, and have the tile dealer cut them for you. Be sure to identify the location of each cut tile with matching numbers or other symbols marked on the back of each tile and on your layout drawing or on the surface to be tiled, so you do not get the cut tiles mixed up.

Cutting Irregular Shapes. Wet saws make clean, straight cuts in tile. They also are used to make irregular cutouts. First, make a series of parallel cuts inside the area to be removed. Then snap off the pieces with *tile nippers or biters*. Tile nippers are used to make curved or irregularly shaped cuts to fit tile around supply pipes, sink cutouts, or other irregular contours. As the name implies, these plier-type tools are used to nip away tiny bits of tile. Working with nippers takes a strong wrist and plenty of patience. To use them, hold the tile glazed side up and take small, 1/8-inch bites with the nippers to break off tiny pieces. Take your time. If you take too large a bite, the tile might break.

If your layout requires a hole in the center of the tile (for supply pipes, etc.), use a *carbide-tipped hole saw chucked in a heavy-duty, variable-speed electric drill.* Hole saws also make clean radius cuts in tile corners. Because carbide hole saws tend to produce heat during cutting, slow speeds (under 500 RPM) are recommended. Submerging the tile in water during cutting also will reduce heat buildup. You can only do this safely with a heavy-duty cordless drill or air-powered drill. This practice is prohibited when you use a corded electric drill, because of the high risk of electric shock.

Smoothing Cut Edges. A *carborundum stone or whetstone* comes in handy for smoothing rough tile edges; you also can use a piece of *metal plaster lath, or even a rough cement brick,* for this purpose.

Tile Spacers. When setting individual ceramic tiles, you must allow space between them for grout joints. To assure even, uniform spacing for grout joints, some tiles (typically wall tiles) have built-in *nubs* molded into the sides of each unit. If the tiles you are using do not have nubs, there are several options. Molded *plastic spacers* can be purchased from a tile dealer.

These small plastic crosses come in various sizes for creating grout joints from 1/32 inch to 1/2 inch wide. Some can be removed (before the adhesive cures) and reused. Others can be left in place and grouted over.

You also can use *cotton cord, dowels, rope, toothpicks, matchsticks, nails, or plywood strips.* All of these must be removed before the adhesive sets.

Another good way of spacing tiles on walls or countertops is to mark the centers of the grout lines (in both directions) on the surface to be tiled. Then, attach 6d finishing nails at each end of the grout lines, and stretch pieces of dampened cotton cord between them to serve as spacers. After aligning the tiles in one direction, remove the cords and nails; then reposition them to establish the perpendicular joints. On floors and other surfaces with wider grout joints, small wood spacers combined with wood battens can be used.

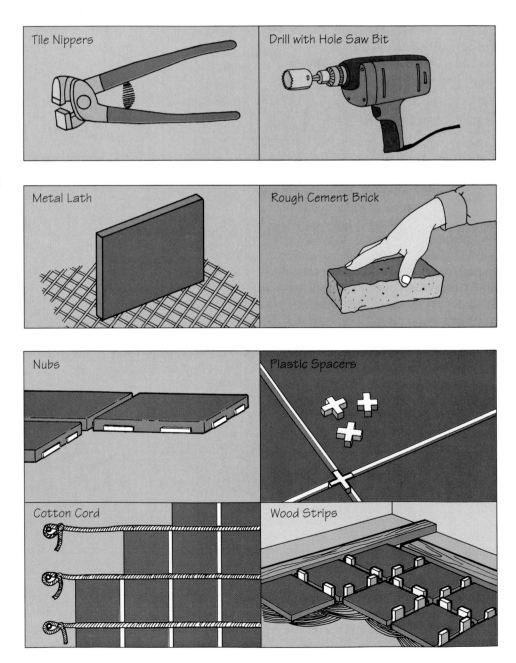

SETTING TOOLS

These include *tools for mixing and spreading the tile adhesive, and tools for bedding and leveling the tiles.* You also will need some material, such as cotton cord, to establish uniform spacing for grout joints.

Mixing the Adhesive. Organic adhesives and some thin-set cement-based adhesives are available in a premixed form, while traditional thick-set mortar, most thin-set adhesives, and two-part epoxy adhesives require mixing. When mixing very large amounts of cement-based adhesives, you will need a *mason's hoe and wheelbarrow or large sheet-metal cement-mixing barge.* When mixing smaller amounts of mortar, thin-set adhesives, or powdered grout (2 to 10 gallons), you can use a *bucket and a mortar-mixing paddle or paint mixer chucked in a heavy-duty electric drill.* Use the mixer at a slow speed of 300 rpm or less. Very small amounts of these materials (less than 2 gallons) can be hand-mixed with an ordinary paint stick or large mixing spoon in a small plastic bucket or paint tray.

Spreading the Adhesive. In most cases, a *notched trowel* is all you need to apply adhesive. Typically, only one side and one end of the trowel is notched. Use the flat side to spread the adhesive evenly, and then immediately use the notched side to comb evenly spaced ridges in the adhesive.

Trowels come with various-size square or V-shaped notches for spreading different adhesives on different tiles. The required notch size is usually specified by the tile or adhesive manufacturer. If you do not want to invest in a trowel, your tile dealer can supply you with an inexpensive, disposable spreader.

Various other mason's tools, such as *floats,* will be needed to level and finish thick-set mortar beds (see page 31).

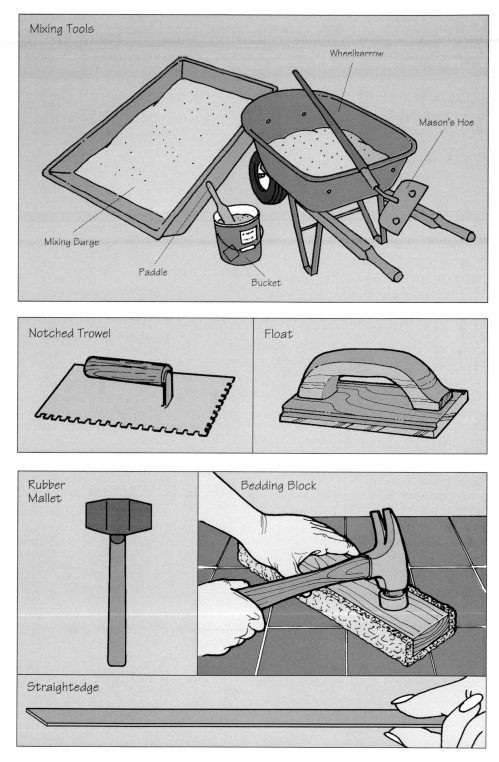

Mixing Tools

Wheelbarrow

Mason's Hoe

Mixing Barge

Paddle

Bucket

Notched Trowel

Float

Rubber Mallet

Bedding Block

Straightedge

Bed and Level Tiles. To bed the tiles firmly into the adhesive, you will need a *hammer or rubber mallet and a bedding block.* To make a bedding block, cut a wood block large enough to cover several tiles at once and cover it with a piece of felt, heavy fabric or scrap carpet.

To use the bedding block, slide the block across the tiles while tapping it lightly with a *hammer or rubber mallet.* During this process, you also will need a *metal straightedge* to periodically make sure that the tiles are even and level, and that the grout joints remain in alignment.

FINISHING TOOLS

Apply Sealant. Unglazed tiles are sometimes sealed before grouting and then afterward to seal the grout joints. A *foam-rubber roller* makes a good applicator for clear sealants.

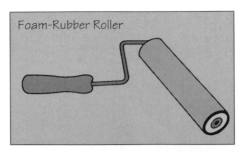

Foam-Rubber Roller

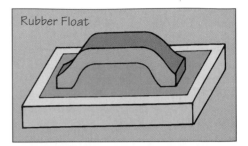

Rubber Float

Apply Grout. Grout usually is applied by spreading a liberal amount across the tile surface and forcing it into the joints with a *rubber float or squeegee*, and then wiping off the excess with the same tool.

A *grout bag* (similar to a pastry bag) is another option for applying grout. This bag has a small fitting on one end to which you can attach nozzles of different sizes to control the amount of grout applied to the joint. After filling the bag, squeeze it to lay a bead of grout directly into the joint. Grout bags work well in situations where cleaning excess grout off the tile surface would be difficult or where the grout might stain the tile surface.

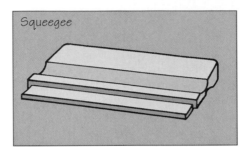

Squeegee

Grout Bag

Drawbacks to using the bag include problems with applying a fast-setting grout and mixing this grout to a consistency that enables it to be squeezed out. Do not allow it to become too thin and watery to achieve a strong hold. After the grout has been applied, and most of the excess has been removed, clean the tiles with a damp sponge.

Striking Tools. Special striking tools are available for shaping or "striking" the grout joints after the grout is applied. However, *dowels, spoons, wooden sticks, and toothbrush handles* can be used.

Caulking Gun. Polyurethane or silicone caulk usually is used to fill gaps or joints where tile meets surfaces of dissimilar materials, such as where the floor meets the wall, or where the tiles abut fixtures, such as a tub. It's cheapest to buy caulk in cartridges and to apply it with a *caulking gun*. To apply, follow manufacturer's instructions.

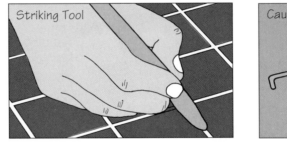

Striking Tool

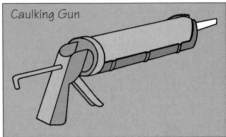

Caulking Gun

Safety Equipment & Procedures

When using any tool to cut tile, wear safety glasses or goggles to protect your eyes. Wear them when working with power tools and when doing jobs such as tear-out work. Because cut-tile edges can be sharp, wear heavy leather or canvas gloves when handling them and also when doing tear-out work.

Most cutting, sanding, and grinding procedures create dust, which can irritate your lungs. Many older building materials, including some resilient tiles, contain asbestos and other carcinogens. Breathing the dust can be unhealthy, so wear a respirator when working with any building materials.

Powdered grouts also may contain toxic substances. A fitted rubber mask with replaceable cartridges provides better protection than a paper or fabric dust mask. The cartridges filter out harmful chemical fumes. Some of these products irritate the skin, so wear chemical-resistant rubber gloves when working with them. Keep plenty of clean rags and the appropriate solvent handy for cleaning up excess materials as you work. Always read and follow label precautions. If you will be doing a lot of work on your knees, such as when setting floor tiles, wear knee pads.

Although ceramic tile can be laid over a variety of existing surfaces, there may be cases when a smooth, rigid surface must be installed.

CEMENT BACKER BOARD

Also called cementitious backer units, or CBUs, cement backer board is a rigid, portland cement-based panel designed for use as a substrate or underlayment for ceramic tile in wet or dry areas. Sometimes the binder material is made of fiberglass-reinforced coatings. Different types are recommended for interior floors, interior walls, and exterior walls.

Next to a thick-bed mortar installation, cement backer board is the best substrate for wet areas because, although it is not waterproof, water will not deteriorate it. Wood, plywood, particleboard, and drywall underlayments deteriorate when exposed to water.

Because cement backer board is a rigid, dense, dimensionally stable product, it does not expand and contract as much as conventional wood subflooring and underlayment materials. The installation of CBUs is similar to that used for drywall.

Backer board is available in thicknesses from 1/8 inch to 5/16 inch. The panels come in standard widths from 32 inches (to fit the end walls above conventional-width bathtubs) to 48 inches and in lengths from 4 to 8 feet.

Backer board can be installed directly over wall studs. In wet areas, waterproof the backer board with a waterproofing material that is compatible with the setting material.

Backer board is fireproof, so you can use it in place of asbestos millboard as an insulating material for wood-stove surrounds. Using it in conjunction with tile may enable reduced clearances between the stove and wall. Check manufacturer's directions and local building codes. See page 113 for specific applications and installations.

WATERPROOF MEMBRANES

Even if you use glazed tiles, water-resistant adhesives and grouts, and a waterproofing sealer over the entire expanse, water can still manage to seep through, weakening the bond between the tile and underlayment and eventually damaging the underlayment and framing beneath. In wet conditions, such as a tub surround, waterproof membranes are recommended between the studs and the substrate to prevent such damage.

Waterproof membranes also work in reverse when tile is installed over concrete floors that are subject to moisture penetration from beneath. They may be required for

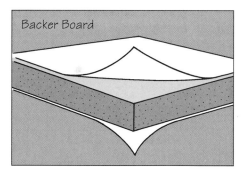

Backer Board

some exterior applications, such as tiling a wooden deck.

Tar paper or building felt have long been used as waterproofing membranes. Other types include chlorinated polyethylene membranes and combination liquid and fabric membranes. Make sure the membrane is compatible with the setting material you are using.

ISOLATION MEMBRANES

Like waterproofing membranes, isolation membranes "isolate" the tile from the underlayment to compensate for differences in expansion and contraction rates of the dissimilar materials. Typically, they consist of chlorinated polyethylene sheets that are laminated between the tile and substrate. Isolation membranes often are required if the existing underlayment shows signs of excessive movement, due to seasonal changes in temperature and humidity, or the settling of the house. Signs include cracks in plaster or masonry, sagging floors, and cracks at joints where two different subflooring materials meet (such as a concrete slab abutting a wood subfloor). If you suspect excessive seasonal movement or a weak substructure, seek professional advice.

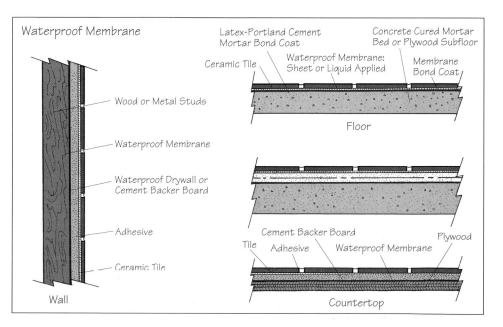

Waterproof Membrane

Wood or Metal Studs

Waterproof Membrane

Waterproof Drywall or Cement Backer Board

Adhesive

Ceramic Tile

Wall

Latex-Portland Cement Mortar Bond Coat

Concrete Cured Mortar Bed or Plywood Subfloor

Ceramic Tile

Waterproof Membrane: Sheet or Liquid Applied

Membrane Bond Coat

Floor

Cement Backer Board

Plywood

Tile

Adhesive

Waterproof Membrane

Countertop

EXPANSION JOINTS

Most of us are familiar with the expansion and control joints used in concrete patios and sidewalks to prevent random cracking due to expansion and contraction. However, few do-it-yourselfers realize that expansion joints are required in some tile installations for the same reason. Expansion joints should be placed around the perimeter of any tile installation, especially where the tile abuts or adjoins surfaces of a different material. They also should be used at corners, in places where a floor meets a wall, or a countertop meets the backsplash. In such situations, perimeter expansion joints should not only be left for the tile, but also for the substrate or underlayment beneath it. For example, when tiling a floor, simply stop the tile

and underlayment about 1/4 inch short of the wall, and fill the joint with a flexible silicone caulk. Prefabricated corner expansion joints made of a rigid PVC material also are available—some with decorative brass inserts.

On interior walls and floors, expansion joints or control joints usually are not needed within the tile field itself, unless the floor is larger than 24 feet x 24 feet, or the wall is longer than 24 feet long (which is uncommon in residential construction). Most homeowners will encounter the need for control joints when tiling large patios or other outdoor areas, where the joints must be installed at least every 16 feet. In such situations, expansion joints in the substrate are generally carried up through the tile and are generally installed

directly over the control joints in an existing concrete patio, or over those in the concrete or mortar setting bed on new installations.

In both interior and exterior applications, control joints should be about four times the width of the expected movement of the tiled surface and setting bed. The joints are then filled with a compressible, foam backer bond breaker rod topped by a urethane caulking material.

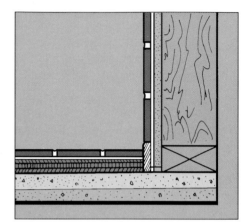

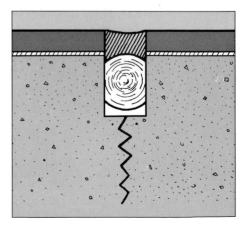

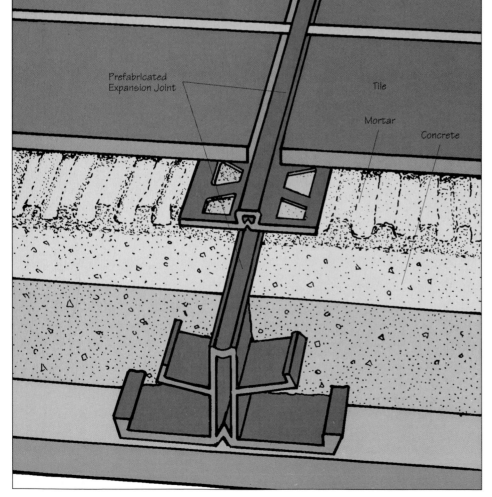

Prefabricated
Expansion Joint

Tile

Mortar

Concrete

MORTAR & ADHESIVES

The traditional method of setting ceramic tile has been to lay the tiles directly in a bed of wet portland cement mortar. This is called a thick-bed or "mud" installation. While some professional tile-setters still use this method today, the development of thin-set, also called dry-set, mortars and organic mastics have made it possible to easily install all types of tile directly over a variety of surfaces. The traditional thick-bed mortar base has its advantages, as it can help level an uneven floor or provide a slope for drainage in a shower. Because they are unaffected by water, thick-bed installations have long been the preferred method for installing tile in wet areas, such as tub and shower enclosures.

THICK-BED

Installing thick-bed mortar requires considerable experience and a variety of tools to do the job correctly. Typically, the tiles must be soaked in water before they can be set in this type of bed. When a thick-set installation is required, most tile-setters will lay down the mortar bed, smooth it, allow it to cure, and then set the tiles over the bed with a "bond coat" of thin-set cement adhesive. In any case, the job is best left to a professional.

THIN-SET

There is a bewildering array of thin-set adhesives on the market—not only different types for various applications, but also different brands that vary in price and quality. A tile dealer can recommend the best adhesive for the job, but it helps to have a basic knowledge of how adhesives are categorized. All tile-setting adhesives fall into three general categories: cement-based adhesives (mortars), organic mastic adhesives, and epoxy-based mortars.

Portland Cement Mortars.

These adhesives actually are forms of cement-based mortar, although they should not be confused with the portland cement mortar used for thick-bed installations. Most of these nonflammable, thin-set mortars come in powder form. Some must be mixed with sand before use, while others come presanded. You also can get them ready to use in premixed liquid form. Powdered forms are mixed with water or a liquid latex additive.

■ *Dry-Set Mortars.* The most common adhesives, dry-set mortars consist of cement combined with additives to retard the curing process. Most of them come in powder form and are mixed with water. They are called dry-set because even though these tiles have a cement base, there usually is no need to presoak them, as is required for a thick-bed installation. Highly resistant to impact, dry-set mortar can be cleaned up easily with water. Once cured, this mortar is not affected by prolonged contact with water, so it can be used in wet installations. It does not form a waterproof barrier, however, so before tiling you will have to install a waterproof membrane.

Typically applied in a layer about 3/32 inch thick, dry-set mortar will cover and level minor surface irregularities; but it is not intended as a setting bed or for leveling very rough surfaces.

Dry-set mortars adhere well to a variety of substrate materials, including relatively smooth, plumb masonry and concrete, insulation board, drywall, cement backer board, cured portland cement beds, ceramic tile, and stone. Some types are suitable for use over plywood. Check the label for appropriate applications.

■ *Latex-Portland Cement Mortars* are a mixture of portland cement, sand, and a liquid latex additive.

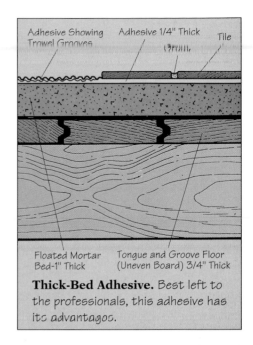

Thick-Bed Adhesive. Best left to the professionals, this adhesive has its advantages.

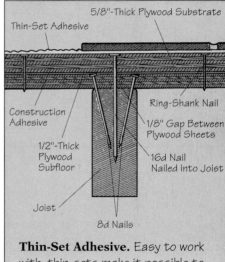

Thin-Set Adhesive. Easy to work with, thin-sets make it possible to install tile over a variety of surfaces.

These thin-set mortars have all of the same applications as dry-set mortars, plus a few others. They have a higher compressive and bond strength, and greater flexibility. Although latex-portland cement mortars cost a bit more than the dry-set kind, they generally are superior.

Caution: All portland cement materials are caustic and corrosive. Wear suitable rubber gloves and protective clothing.

Organic Mastic Adhesives. Also simply called mastics, organic adhesives are available, ready to use in a premixed paste form. They cure or set by evaporation. Although most of these adhesives do not have the bond strength or leveling properties of thin-sets, they are the easiest to apply. Two drawbacks to using organic mastics are that they can only be applied to relatively smooth, level backings, and most brands cannot be used in wet installations. Suitable backings include drywall, smooth plaster or mortar, plywood, tile backer board, and smooth, dry concrete. Certain brands also can be applied to existing ceramic tile that has been prepared to receive it.

Organic mastics are water-based, and are referred to as Type I and Type II. You will find numerous brands and formulas for mastics, but generally they are specified for use on either floors or walls. Most cannot be used in areas subject to heat, such as fireplace hearths or wood-stove surrounds. Check label instructions for specific applications.

Epoxy-Based Mortars. Epoxies are not used much by do-it-yourselfers because they are more expensive and harder to apply than other adhesives. You must mix the resin and hardener to exact proportions and apply them at the correct temperature to ensure the right setting time and pot life. Use regular-grade epoxy mortars for horizontal sufaces. Because regular-grade will sag on walls, non-sag grades are available, too. You can use non-sag epoxies on horizontal surfaces, but they are harder to work with. However, epoxy mortars, combined with epoxy grouts, provide superior bond strength and excellent resistance to impact and chemicals. Epoxies will adhere to just about any substrate material, including properly prepared existing ceramic tile and metal. They work especially well on plywood. Some are heat resistant, making them a good choice for applications such as range hoods or tiled surrounds for wood stoves or barbecue pits. For most situations, though, resort to an epoxy only when the surface being tiled requires epoxy because of level of service or if other adhesives will not work because of surface conditions.

Epoxies consist of resin and hardener, much like the two-part epoxy glues sold at hardware stores; some include a filler material, such as silica sand. Epoxy mortars are used when a high degree of bond strength is required or when the tiled surface will receive a high degree of physical or chemical wear. For instance, they are an excellent choice for tiling a garage floor or driveway.

After the adhesive is mixed, it is applied by trowel in one thin layer. Pot life, adhesion, water cleanability before cure, and chemical resistance vary with different brands, so you will need to choose formulations carefully to meet your specific requirements. Epoxies are highly water-resistant but not completely waterproof, so, like other adhesives, they should be used in conjunction with a waterproof membrane to protect the substrate in wet conditions.

Similar to epoxy adhesives, furan resin adhesives work as a strong two-part resin and hardener system, and are used in commercial and industrial situations requiring a high degree of chemical resistance. Furan adhesives and grouts very rarely are used for residential applications.

GROUTS

As with adhesives, grouts come in different formulations for various applications. All tile grouts fall into two basic categories: cement-based grout and epoxy grout. Grouts used for tiling should not be confused with caulks, which are elastomeric materials used for filling gaps between various building materials. As mentioned, silicone caulk is used at joints where tile meets other surfaces, but it also is used to grout between tiles in some cases. Pregrouted tile sheets, for instance, have silicone grout joints. They generally come with a tube of matching grout to seal joints where the panels meet. Also, because silicone is highly flexible, it often is used in lieu of grout at tiled corners where movement in the substructure would crack ordinary grout joints. Examples are where a countertop meets a backsplash, or at the junction of two tiled walls or a tiled wall and floor.

Cement-Based Grouts. These grouts have a base of portland cement, but they differ in the types of additives they contain. Coloring pigments are available for many of them, providing a range of color options. A variety of precolored grouts also are available. However, if you use a colored grout, bear in mind that it stains some types of unglazed tiles.

Most cement-based grouts come in powdered form to which water or liquid latex is added. Some grouts are premixed and ready to use, but they usually are the most expensive as well. Cement-based grouts include commercial portland cement, dry-set, and latex-portland cement grouts (see chart next page).

■ *Portland Cement Grout*, a mixture of portland cement and other ingredients, produces a dense, uniformly colored material. Like all cement-based mortars, it is resistant to water but not completely waterproof or stain-proof, so it requires a sealer.

Commercial-portland cement grouts are formulated for use with thick-bed portland cement mortar installations. With these, the installer must soak the tiles in water for 15 to 20 minutes before application. These grouts also require damp curing (keeping the surface moist until the grout cures) to prevent it from shrinking and cracking.

Unsanded grouts are used for joints less than 1/16 inch wide. For joints up to 1/8 inch wide, a mixture of one part cement to one part 30-mesh sand is used; for joints 1/8 to 1/2 inch wide, one part cement to two parts 30-mesh sand is used; for joints over 1/2 inch wide, one part cement to three parts all-purpose sand is used. Consult a tile dealer for the appropriate mixture for your installation.

■ *Dry-Set Grout,* another type of portland cement grout, contains additives that increase water-retentiveness. This allows you to grout tiles without presoaking them and without damp-curing the grout once applied. If you are grouting the tiles on a hot, dry day, the grout might dry out so quickly that it will shrink, requiring you to presoak tiles and damp-cure the grout joints anyway. Damp-curing also can increase grout strength.

■ *Latex-Portland Cement Grout* can be any of the two preceding grout types that has been mixed with liquid latex instead of water, or powdered latex that has had water added to achieve the proper mix. It has the same general characteristics as latex-cement mortar (see page 31) and is the most versatile grout for residential applications.

Epoxy Grout. This grout contains an epoxy resin and hardener, giving it a high degree of chemical resistance, excellent bond strength, and superior impact resistance. It is the most expensive of the grouts, and therefore usually confined to industrial and commercial applications. An epoxy grout would be a good choice where a certain degree of chemical resistance is required.

Epoxy grout is somewhat thick and not easy to apply. If your tiles are more than 1/2 inch thick and the grout joints are less than 1/4 inch wide, the grout will not penetrate.

SEALERS

Clear liquid tile and grout sealers provide protection against stains and, to some extent, against water penetration for unglazed tiles and grout joints. Their application is the final step in tile installation. Although glazed tiles themselves do not require a sealer, their cement-based grouts usually do. Most sealers have a silicone, lacquer, or acrylic base. Different formulations are available for different types of tile and grout in various applications. Special sealers are required for gouged stone tiles. Sealers require reapplication every one to two years to maintain protection.

	GROUP TYPE *See text for complete description*								
	Commercial-Portland Cement		Sand-Portland Cement	Dry-Set	Latex-Portland Cement	Epoxy (1)(6)	Furan (1)(6)	Silicone or Urethane	Modified Epoxy Emulsion
	Wall Use	Floor Use	Wall-Floor Use	Wall-Floor Use	(3)			(2)	(3)(6)
Glazed Wall Tile (More than 7% absorption)	✓			✓	✓			✓	
Ceramic Mosaic Tile	✓	✓	✓	✓	✓	✓		✓	✓
Quarry, Paver & Packing House Tile	✓	✓	✓			✓	✓		✓
Dry or Limited Water Exposure	✓	✓	✓	✓	✓	✓	✓	✓	✓
Wet Areas	✓	✓	✓	✓	✓	✓	✓	✓	✓
Exteriors	✓	✓	✓	✓	✓(4)	✓(4)	✓(4)		✓(4)
Stain Resistance (5)	D	C	E	D	B	A	A	A	B
Crack Resistance (5)	D	D	E	D	C	B	C	A Flexible	C
Colorability (5)	B	B	C	B	B	B	Black Only	Restricted	B

(1) Mainly used for chemical-resistant properties.
(2) Special tools needed for proper application. Silicone, urethane, and modified polyvinylchloride used in pregrouted ceramic tile sheets. Silicone grout should not be used on kitchen countertops or other food-preparation surfaces.
(3) Special cleaning procedures and materials recommended.
(4) Follow manufacturer's directions.
(5) Five performance ratings—Best to Minimal (A B C D E).
(6) Epoxies are recommended for prolonged temperatures up to 140°F, high-temperature-resistant epoxies and furans up to 350°F.

TILING FLOORS

On floors, ceramic tile provides a durable, easy-to-maintain surface that will complement practically any room setting and all furnishings. Bear in mind, though, that tile floors can be noisy, hard, and cold underfoot.

Tiling a floor is an easy do-it-yourself project that does not usually require specialized skills. However, patience is necessary for layout, cutting, and fitting.

Before you decide to lay a ceramic tile floor, the existing floor must meet some basic qualifications. The existing flooring and subflooring beneath must be strong and rigid enough to support the added weight of the tile. The amount of work involved in preparing the floor for tiling may range from simply cleaning the existing surface to completely rebuilding the floor framing itself. Inspect the floor to see how much work is required to prepare it for ceramic tile;

▲ *Use your imagination when creating a floor pattern. Here, wood planks were used as borders for slightly undulated tiles.*

then see page 47. If extensive repairs or major structural alterations are required, you may opt to use a different type of floor covering.

Because ceramic tile and the grout lines between them form a rigid geometric pattern, the room must be reasonably square in order for the installation to work. Few floors, even those that are newly constructed, are perfectly square. Usually minor out-of-square conditions can be corrected by adjusting the tile layout to visually de-emphasize the condition. If the room is too badly out of square, a floor covering with a nondirectional pattern, such as carpeting or resilient sheet flooring, might be a better choice. A floor that is not level does not usually present serious visual problems unless the walls will be tiled as well.

▲ *The deep red of these hexagonal tiles creates an opulent backdrop for a formal living area.*

▶ *For an elegant bathroom without the added expense, use faux marble tiles, like the green ones shown here.*

DESIGN BASICS

The design statement you want your floor to make depends not only on the tile you select but the way that you install it.

Although the subject of design involves numerous considerations—and is largely a matter of personal taste—a few basic principles always apply. When choosing a tile for your floor, there are five elements to consider: size, shape, color, texture, and pattern. All five elements determine the overall visual effect you are trying to achieve. The first four elements apply to the tile selected; the last element—pattern—is dictated by both the tile itself and the way the tiles are arranged on the floor.

SIZE

As a general rule, small tiles make the floor look larger; large tiles tend to decrease the apparent size of the area. However, because small tiles have more grout lines, they produce a busier pattern, especially if you start mixing colors. When used in a small room, such as a bathroom, small patterned tiles will visually break up the space into small segments; for example, a larger solid-color tile with matching grout will give the floor a more open look. Although standard floor-tile sizes range from 6 inches x 6 inches to 12 inches x 12 inches, you do not have to stick with these conventional sizes, or even use tiles of the same size.

▲ *Glazed tiles are baked at high temperatures to produce a decorative, extremely durable surface.*

▼ *The terra cotta floor tiles in this kitchen provide an earthy contrast to the intricately detailed wall and counter tiles.*

▲ *These earthy brown tiles add to the outdoorsy mood of this spacious enclosed porch.*

▼ *For a dramatically modern effect, strong colored tiles are cut into geometric shapes.*

SHAPE

Because most tiles are square, this is the shape we expect to see; when you choose a different shape (hexagonal, octagonal, or ogee, for instance) or combine shapes (e.g., squares and rectangles), you immediately draw attention to the floor.

COLOR

Dark colors tend to make the space look smaller and feel more intimate; light or bright colors provide a more spacious feeling. Warm terra cotta colors suggest a rustic look, whereas black, white, and bold colors can impart a modern, high-tech appearance. Light pastels, such as pink, peach, or light blues and greens can soften a room while lending a light, airy feeling. Sharply contrasting colors and patterns make a bold statement that draws attention to the floor, whereas a single-color or low-contrast color scheme creates a subtle backdrop for furniture or other focal points in the room. Plan color schemes carefully to avoid visual conflicts with other elements in the room.

TEXTURE

The surface texture of a tile often plays a more subtle role than other style elements, yet it is an important link to the overall feeling of a room. For example, handmade Mexican pavers have a rough, uneven texture, which, along with their irregularity in shape and color, impart a distinct rustic effect. On the other hand, machine-made pavers with a uniformly smooth surface texture and even coloring have a crisp, clean look. A highly glazed surface expands apparent space and brightens the room; a matte finish diminishes space and makes a room feel more cozy.

PATTERN

The way you manipulate shape, size, and color determines the overall pattern created. The tile pattern serves not only to add visual interest to the floor, but also can be used to create spatial illusions or to direct the eye. For example, a strong, directional pattern running lengthwise makes a room look longer and narrower; a crosswise pattern makes the room look shorter and wider. A diagonal pattern can increase apparent space while visually separating the floor from other architectural features or floors in adjacent areas.

Manipulating lines of sight also can increase apparent space and create a unifying effect, such as when you continue the same tile pattern out onto an outdoor patio. Conversely, you can use contrasting patterns to define separate areas within a room or space.

Busy patterns decrease apparent floor size while simple patterns enlarge it. Using a contrasting grout color emphasizes the pattern; a matching grout color provides a more subtle effect. Dark grouts hide dirt better than lighter ones (white grout is rarely used on floors for this reason). If you also plan on tiling the wall, usually it is best to use one size of tile on the wall and another on

▲ *An otherwise plain floor design becomes unique with the addition of bright accents.*

the floor, especially if floors and walls are not perfectly level, square, or plumb because grout joints will not align properly. Bear in mind that for trims and borders, special trim tiles or cove tiles applied to the wall at floor level can be used in lieu of a baseboard. Also, you might want to include a strip of border tiles of a contrasting color or pattern around the room perimeter to "frame" a pattern. In either case, be sure to subtract the thickness of the cove or border tiles or width of the border tiles when planning the layout of the field tiles on the floor.

Beyond these basic guidelines are many principles of good design. To work successfully, complex or ambitious designs usually require an expert eye. If you want to experiment with different patterns or designs before purchasing the tile, you can do so by making a scale drawing, (see page 41).

TILE SELECTION

For indoor floors you can use a glazed or unglazed floor tile. Glazed tiles usually are easier to clean and maintain; unglazed tiles require periodic sealing and waxing. If you want to use an unglazed tile indoors, use a vitreous quarry tile, because it will be less likely to absorb stains. In wet areas, such as bathrooms, choose a tile with a slip-resistant surface (avoid slick, highly glazed tiles). Outdoors, unglazed tiles are usually a better choice than glazed ones, because glaze tends to crack and craze because of extremes in temperature and humidity, and will be slick when wet. In mild climates, you can use nonvitreous saltillo tiles or handmade pavers. In cold climates, choose a nonporous vitreous tile—the latter holds up better under continuous freezing and thawing.

▲ *A crisp, black-and-white pattern adds a lively note to this charming country kitchen.*

▶ *This rose-colored ceramic floor is highlighted with floral picture tiles.*

Although many experienced tile-setters simply take measurements of the room, order the correct amount of tile, and compensate for any layout problems during installation. It is best for the novice to first plan the tile layout on paper. A scale drawing will enable you to visualize what the installation will look like before you start, and it will help you estimate the number of tiles you will need. It also will help correct any layout problems in advance, before you establish working lines on the floor itself.

OUT-OF-SQUARE CONDITIONS

You will have to make sure that the walls are straight, and that the floor is level and reasonably square (all walls meet at 90-degree angles).

1. Check Floor for Square

In small rooms, such as a bathroom, you usually can check the squareness of the floor with a framing square positioned at each corner of the room. For larger rooms, you can use the 3-4-5 triangle method: Measure along one wall at floor level a distance of exactly 3 feet; then measure along the other wall exactly 4 feet. Mark these distances; then take a diagonal measurement between the two. If the distance is exactly 5 feet, the two walls are square to each other. Repeat the process at the other inside corners of the room. You also can use the 3-4-5 triangle method to establish square working lines for laying out the tile itself, as described above. In very large rooms, you might want to double the ratio (6-8-10) for greater accuracy. If the floor is less than 1/8 inch out of square in 10 feet, you usually can compensate for the condition by adjusting the working lines according to the pattern in which you will be laying the tile. If it is more than 1/8 inch out of square, the condition will be obvi-

ously visable along at least one wall and you will end up with tapered cuts. If one or more walls are out of square, try to plan the layout so the tapered tiles are positioned along the least noticeable wall in the room.

2. Check Floor for Level

Use a 2-foot level to check the floor along each wall. An out-of-level floor does not present serious problems unless you plan to extend the tile up the wall. If this is the case, consider using a continuous baseboard and a different type of wallcovering.

3. Check for Wavy Walls

Bear in mind that even if the walls are reasonably square to each other, they may be bowed or wavy, which also may be noticeable when the tile is installed. If this condition is not already apparent from inspection of the existing floor covering, you can often detect a bowed or wavy condition by simply sighting down the wall at floor level. Or, snap a chalkline along the floor, parallel to the wall, and take measurements at various points along the wall. In extreme cases, you may want to remove the existing wall material and shim out the studs to correct the condition; then install a new wallcovering.

1. Check Floor for Square

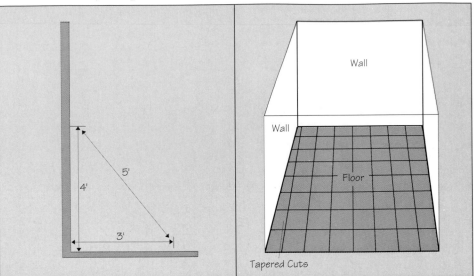

2. Check Floor for Level

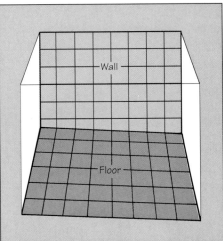

3. Check for Wavy Walls

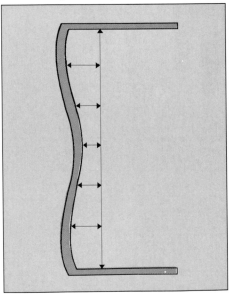

MAKE A SCALE DRAWING

A scale drawing will help you lay out and estimate the tile as well as map out the best way to address the job. Measure the overall dimensions of the floor and make a scale drawing of it on graph paper. Be sure to indicate the locations of entryways and any built-in cabinets or other permanent fixtures. Measure the size of the tile itself and the width of one full grout joint to the length and width of the tile. This dimension will be the basic measuring "unit" that you will use to plan the layout and estimate the amount of tile needed.

If you are using square tiles, plan your drawing so that each square on the graph paper represents one tile and its grout-joint measurement. If your tile is rectangular rather than square, have one square equal the small dimension and use two squares for the long dimension. You also can lay down two or more tiles to create a square dimension.

Odd-Shaped Tiles. Tiles with irregular shapes, such as hexagon, are more difficult to lay. But since they are generally sold by the square foot, it is easy to figure out how many you need. For a more accurate estimate, you can lay out a few tiles with spaced grout joints on the floor to see how many full and partial tiles fill in a square space of arbitrary dimensions. Then, on your scale drawing, divide the room into squares of that dimension, count the number of squares in the room, and multiply by the number of tiles in each square. For estimating purposes, when laying out the octagon and square pattern, treat each square on the graph paper as one octagon tile and one square tile.

Make a Scale Drawing. Standard-shaped tiles are easier to use than irregular-shaped tiles. However, irregular shapes generally are sold by the square foot, so you can make an accurate estimate.

Make a Layout Stick

A layout stick will help estimate the number of tiles needed for a floor, wall, or countertop. It will come in handy when making a scale drawing and when establishing working lines on the floor. It also is good for spacing tiles as you lay them (if spacers are not used). The stick can be a 1x3 piece of lattice, or similar wood, as long as it is perfectly straight and roughly the same thickness as the chosen tile. The length of the stick will depend on the floor size—3 to 4 feet for a small bathroom, and up to 8 feet for a room 10 feet square or larger.

Base the length of the stick on the actual size and number of whole tiles and grout joints between, rather than on an arbitrary number of feet. With a sharp pencil, mark the dimensions of the tile and joints along the length of the stick. (With pregrouted tile sheets, use the size of the sheets instead, leaving spaces for the joints between each sheet.) If the tiles have spacer lugs (for predetermined grout spacing), use them to mark the grout joint spacing on the stick. Otherwise, mark the width of the spacers you are using. If the tiles are irregular in size, as many handmade tiles tend to be, measure a half dozen or so tiles and base the measurement on the average width of tiles and grout joints. Measure the true length of the stick and mark this measurement on the back side for future reference.

To estimate tile amounts, lay the stick along the length of the area to be tiled as if you were measuring it. For example, if there are 34 tiles on the stick, and you lay the stick down twice, then again with half the length of the stick left over, you would need 85 tiles for the length of the area. Then measure the width, and multiply.

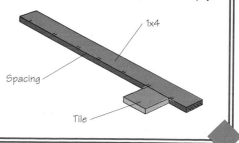

1x4

Spacing

Tile

Base Drawing and Overlays.
Using the tile and grout-joint unit measurement as a guide, make a base-like drawing of the room dimensions (include openings and any built-in fixtures) on graph paper. Then, on a tracing-paper overlay, make a drawing of your tile design to the dimensions. Use as many overlay sheets as you need to come up with a pleasing design. You can use colored pencils to help you visualize what the finished floor will look like.

Adjust the Layout. Use the base drawing to determine where cut tiles will be needed. Because few cases exist where there is no need to cut any tiles at all, you will want to plan the layout so a narrow row of cut tiles does not end up in a visually conspicuous place, such as at a doorway or entry.

The principles of good layout also dictate that any cut pieces should be more than half a tile wide; in most cases, cut tiles at opposite sides of the room should be the same width, to provide a symmetrical look to the installation. If you start by laying a full row of tiles along one wall, you sometimes end up with a narrow row of partial tiles along the opposite wall. In some cases, you may be able to eliminate the narrow row by adjusting the width of all the grout joints. Otherwise, you can do this by shifting the pattern so you end up with wider partial tiles on each opposite wall. Try for a symmetrical layout, where partial (cut) tiles on opposite sides of the room are the same width. Similarly, if you start laying tiles from the exact center of the room out toward each wall, you may end up with narrow

cut tiles at both walls. To correct this, shift the original centerline, or working line, a distance equal to half a tile to the left or right. This will give you wider-cut tiles at both walls. Also try to center the tiles across large openings, such as archways, or beneath focal points, such as picture windows or fireplaces, especially if the tiles are large. If the tiles extend into an adjacent room, lay out both floors so the grout joints line up through entryways.

In short, if you plan the layout carefully in advance on paper, you will not encounter any unpleasant surprises during installation. The drawing can be used as a general guide when you establish the actual working lines on the floor (see page 54).

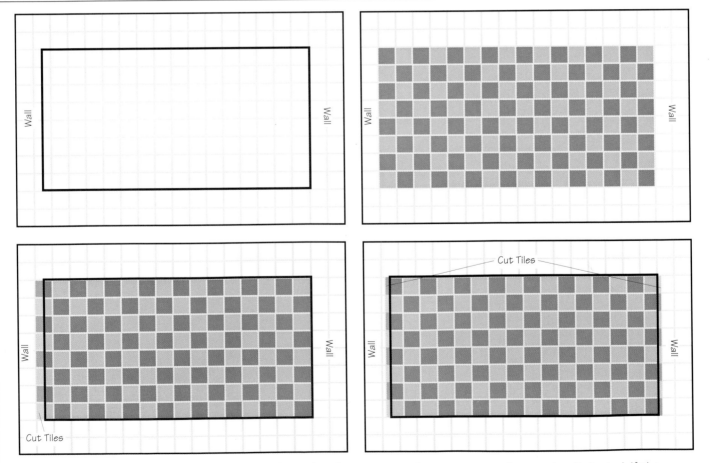

Adjust the Layout. Use your base drawing to adjust the tile pattern so that narrow cut tiles may be eliminated. If they cannot be eliminated, create a symmetrical layout, where cut tiles on opposite sides of the room will be the same width.

ESTIMATE AMOUNTS

Once you have your plan on paper, you can use it to estimate the number of tiles and amount of adhesive and grout that you will need.

Tile. No matter what size or shape, tile often is sold by the square foot. It would be easy enough to simply measure the square footage of the room and make your estimate; then order an additional 10 percent to cover waste due to cut tiles and breakage, and for future repairs. This formula works most of the time, provided you are setting the tiles with grout joints recommended by the tile manufacturer and your installation does not require too many cut tiles. To get a more precise measurement, work from your layout drawing by counting the actual number of whole tiles and partial tiles (counted as whole tiles); than add about 5 percent for breakage, miscuts, and other mistakes. A layout stick (see page 41) will help you quickly estimate the amount of tiles needed.

Adhesive. To estimate the amount of adhesive you will need, simply add up the total number of square feet to be tiled; then check the coverage figures on the label of the adhesive container.

Grout. The amount of grout you will need depends on the size of the tiles and on the width and depth of the grout joints between them. An experienced tile dealer can recommend the amount of grout needed if provided with this information. It is better to end up with some adhesive and grout left over at the end of the job rather than to run out in the middle of the job and have to run back to the tile store for more. Likewise, if you are using a grout sealer, refer to the coverage rate on the container label.

Thresholds

Because tiling a floor generally results in a change of floor level, you must decide how to deal with this change at doorways. Consider how to make the transition where the tile meets different types of floor coverings in adjacent rooms, whether there is a change in level or not. Thresholds (sometimes called saddles or transition strips) made of metal, wood, or marble are used to bridge gaps between different floors. Depending on job requirements, the thresholds can be installed before or after the tile is laid. The threshold is attached to the underlayment, and the tile is then run up to it. A tile dealer can recommend a suitable threshold for your particular installation.

If the room includes an outside entry door, it may be possible to keep the existing threshold in place and to tile up to it. Otherwise, the threshold can be removed, tile installed underneath, and the threshold replaced. Then, trim the door bottom to fit. If either of these options creates a visual problem, replace the old threshold with a new one. Plan for thresholds during the layout stage.

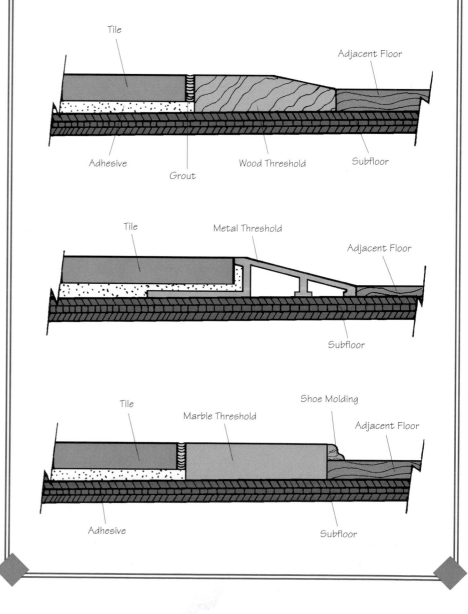

PREPARING THE FLOOR

In most cases, much of the work involved in tiling an existing floor lies not in the actual setting of the tile, but in the preparation of the floor to accept the tile. Ceramic tile may be installed directly over the existing floor covering if the floor covering, underlayment, and subflooring beneath are sound, level, and free from any looseness and buckling; also, the floor framing must be strong enough to support the additional weight of the tile. Most floors need some work. If the existing floor meets these requirements, thoroughly clean the floor and, if necessary, roughen the existing surface with sandpaper to assure a good adhesive bond.

Even if your floor meets the above criteria, the added thickness of the tile will result in a change of floor level, which will have to be dealt with at entryways where the tile meets other floor coverings (door bottoms may have to be trimmed). You also may have to alter base cabinets and plumbing fixtures when they are reinstalled.

Usually the existing floor structure will require some tearout and rebuilding, which can range from removing the existing floor covering (and possibly the underlayment and subflooring) to rebuilding the floor structure itself to support the added weight of the tile.

If you are working with new floor construction, for instance in a new home, plan the job to provide a suitable framing, subfloor, and underlayment. If you have hired a contractor, be sure to inform him or her which areas will be tiled so those places will meet all requirements.

Typical requirements for installing tile over new and existing floors are discussed below. If you have any questions, speak to an architect.

If you are going to tile both the walls and the floor, finish the walls first and then do the floor, so it does not get damaged. Any cove tile is easier to place between the wall and floor if the walls are done first.

Although tile can be laid over many existing floor coverings, it is better to install the tile directly on the subfloor beneath. Doing this will minimize the change in floor level and also will remove any doubts you may have concerning the suitability of that floor covering as an underlayment. If you find that it is too difficult to remove the floor covering, and yet it is in very bad shape, it may be most expedient to properly install a plywood or backer board underlayment over the existing floor before installing the tile. To help make your decision, read further. Then turn to page 47 to determine if additional reinforcement is necessary.

TILE OVER WOOD-STRIP FLOORS

Ceramic tile can be laid over a hardwood strip or plank floor if it is in good repair and firmly nailed to the subfloor beneath (see page 47). Because wood and tile expand and contract at different rates, it is advisable to remove the flooring or to put a membrane, such as polyethelene sheeting or building paper, over the wood floor before tiling.

1. Nail Loose Boards
To prepare the floor, inspect it closely; then nail down any loose boards, using screw-type nails, and replace the damaged ones.

2. Sand Floor Smooth
If the boards are cupped or wavy and the tile-setting adhesive is thin, sand the boards level with a floor sander. Make sure the floor is smooth.

3. Clean the Floor
Clean the floor to remove all dirt, wax, and other contaminants. Depending on the adhesive you are using, you might have to remove the floor finish. Check with your tile dealer for recommended adhesives and surface requirements. If the floor is badly damaged, consider installing an underlayment of 3/8-inch exterior plywood or 5/16-inch cement backer board.

1. Nail Loose Boards

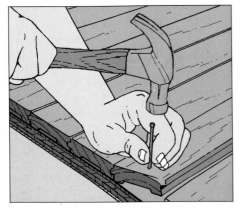

2. Sand Floor Smooth

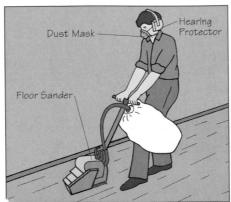

Dust Mask — Hearing Protector

Floor Sander

3. Clean the Floor

TILE OVER RESILIENT FLOORS

You can apply ceramic tile over existing linoleum, vinyl, or asphalt flooring (tiles or sheet goods) if it is in good shape (it should not be cracking or peeling in any places) and securely bonded to the floor. Exceptions include cushioned vinyl or multiple layers of resilient flooring, which can compress under the weight of the tile, causing cracks in tiles and grout joints. It usually is not advisable to lay tile directly over composition flooring in wet areas, such as bathrooms, because these situations usually require a water-resistant underlayment that is sometimes coupled with a waterproofing membrane.

Repair any minor holes, chips, or other defects with a patching material that has been recommended by your tile dealer. Remove any loose tiles, and then scrape off old adhesive from the tile and subfloor. Finally, re-adhere undamaged tiles with fresh adhesive of the same type.

You can repair larger damaged areas of sheet flooring by following these steps:

1. Cut the Area
Cut a scrap piece of flooring that is a little larger than the damaged area. Tape the scrap over the damaged area. With a utility knife, cut a rectangle through both layers of flooring.

2. Remove the Piece
Remove the patch and then use a putty knife to carefully pry out the damaged area.

3. Remove Old Adhesive
Remove any dried adhesive that may be stuck to the subfloor. Then spread new adhesive (of the same type) over the area.

4. Reinsert Cutout
Apply fresh adhesive and insert the patch. Press the patch firmly in place.

1. Cut the Area

2. Remove the Piece
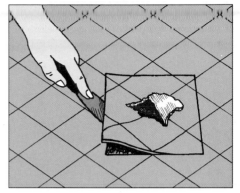

3. Remove Old Adhesive
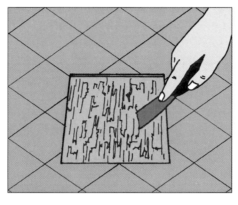

4. Reinsert Cutout
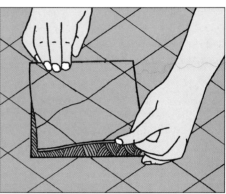

5. Let Adhesive Set

6. Remove Wax

5. Let Adhesive Set
Clean off any excess adhesive around the edges of the piece, then cover the patch with a weight of several heavy books or paint pails until the adhesive sets (see label instructions).

6. Remove Wax
After making any necessary repairs, use a strong household cleaner to remove any dirt and wax buildup, and follow this with a rinse of clear water.

Caution: Some older composition flooring materials contain asbestos and therefore must not be sanded—inhaling the sanding dust puts your health at risk. The clear wear layer on modern vinyl flooring must be roughed up slightly by hand-sanding with 100-grit sandpaper to provide a good adhesive bond. Wear a mask when doing this.

TILE OVER EXISTING CERAMIC TILE

You can lay new ceramic tile over the old one if the existing tile is sound and solidly bonded to the floor. Any obvious cracks in the tile or along grout lines usually indicate a weak subfloor or damaged underlayment. If this is the case, remove the tiles and make any necessary repairs before installing the new tile floor.

1. Re-adhere Loose Tiles

If any tiles are loose, pry them up, butter the tile back with some of the adhesive you will be using to set the new tile, and reset it making sure the reset tile is no higher than the tiles around it. Once the loose tiles are reset, thoroughly clean the floor with a ceramic tile cleaner or household detergent to remove dirt and grease.

2. Level Grout Joints

If the grout joints in the existing tile are recessed below the tile surface, you may want to add more grout to provide a level surface before applying the adhesive. A tile dealer can recommend the appropriate adhesive for your particular installation. If you are using a mortar-based thin-set adhesive, this step probably will not be necessary, because the mortar will fill in the joints.

3. Sand the Surface

Wear a dust mask or respirator when sanding. To assure a good adhesive bond, roughen the tile surface with a portable power sander that is equipped with silicon carbide paper (for small areas, use a carborundum stone). Vacuum up all sanding dust.

4. Apply Primer

With some adhesives, a thin prime coat should be applied beforehand. Use the foam rubber roller to do this. Read instructions on the primer to see if you have to let it dry before applying a second coat.

1. Re-adhere Loose Tiles

2. Level Grout Joints

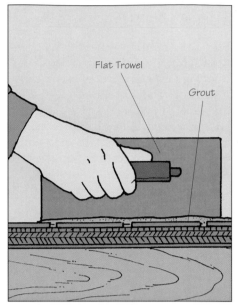

Flat Trowel

Grout

3. Sand the Surface

Belt Sander to Roughen-Up Tile Surface

Tile

Thin-Set Adhesive

Plywood

4. Apply Primer

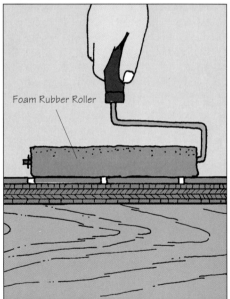

Foam Rubber Roller

Remove Flooring

If the flooring is too damaged to patch easily, either remove it or cover it with an underlayment of 3/8- or 1/2-inch exterior plywood or 5/16-inch tile backer board. If you must remove the existing flooring, see page 44. You can repair surface defects in the underlayment with a floor-patching compound or general-purpose patching compound such as Dowman's Fixall. Check with the tile dealer to make sure that the patching compound will be compatible with the adhesive being used. In most cases, an epoxy adhesive is recommended for adhering tiles to composition flooring materials.

PREPARE WOOD SUBFLOORS

Before laying tile over any existing floor, check to make sure the sub-flooring and framing beneath are structurally sound and rigid. If the floor feels spongy or flexible when you walk over it—or if it squeaks over a large area—it will have to be reinforced. If the floor sags, it will have to be leveled.

1. Reattach Loose Flooring

Start by renailing the subfloor to the floor joists. Use spiral nails and countersink nailheads.

2. Add Shims

If you have a wood-board subfloor, individual loose boards can be shimmed with shingles. Gently tap shims into the space between the joists and the subfloor to prevent movement. Do not drive the shims too forcefully, or they will cause the boards to rise, resulting in a wavy floor. Then, nail down the sub-flooring from the top with 8d nails into the joist.

3. Add Cleat

If several boards are loose, or a sagging joist has created a "springy" spot in a plywood subfloor, nail a 1x4 or 1x6 cleat alongside the joist that supports the loose subflooring. Prop it in place with a piece of 2x4 so it will lie snugly against the joist and the subfloor. Then use 8d nails to nail the cleat to the joists. After installing the cleat, remove the 2x4 prop.

4. Add Bridging

If the entire subfloor is weak, because joists have settled or shifted, the subfloor can be strengthened with wood or metal bridging.

5. Provide a Level Surface

Make sure the existing subfloor or underlayment material itself is in good shape. It should be sound, even, and level (free from buckling). In bathrooms especially, water damage to the underlayment and subfloor might not be apparent until you remove the finish flooring. All rotted or otherwise damaged wood should be replaced. If a wood-board or plywood sub-floor is simply wet but still sound, allow it to dry thoroughly before tiling over it. The problem causing the wetness should be fixed to prevent future problems.

1. Reattach Loose Flooring

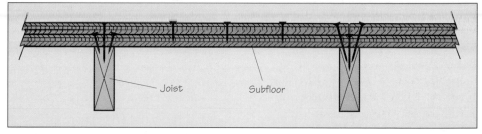

Joist   Subfloor

2. Add Shims

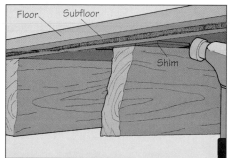

Floor   Subfloor

Shim

3. Add Cleat

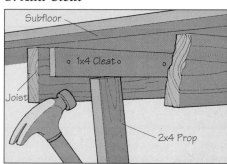

Subfloor

1x4 Cleat

Joist

2x4 Prop

4. Add Bridging

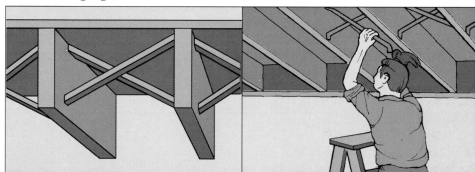

5. Provide a Level Surface

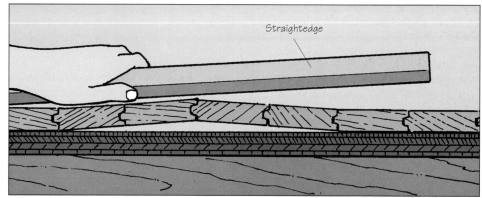

Straightedge

6. *Add to Subfloor*

The subfloor must be rigid enough to support the tile. Typically, the total thickness of the subfloor, underlayment, and existing floor material (if retained) should be at least 1⅛ inches thick. If it is not, build up the subfloor by adding an additional layer of exterior plywood (CDX or better grade) of the appropriate thickness, or better, use cement backer board, which also provides a better base for various types of thin-set adhesives. Since it is unaffected by water, backer board is recommended for wet areas. Do not use interior-grade plywood, particleboard, or hardboard for subflooring or underlayment. None of these materials is water resistant, and none generally provides the rigidity required to support the tile flooring.

You also will need to install an underlayment of plywood or backer board over wood-board subfloors, because flexing between individual boards can crack tile or grout joints. Such underlayment also can be used to provide a smooth, level surface over an uneven subfloor. Both types of underlayment should be at least 3/8 inch thick, no matter what the thickness of the subflooring.

If you plan to install a new subfloor directly over the joists, use two layers, one of at least 5/8-inch exterior plywood, the second of 1/2-inch exterior plywood or backer board. Check local building codes for guidance.

Stagger the joints of the new under-layment so they do not fall directly over those of the subflooring beneath. For plywood, allow an 1/8-inch gap between each sheet and where sheets meet adjoining walls to allow for expansion and contraction. Attach the plywood to the existing subflooring wit con-struction adhesive and 6d ring-shank nails or 1¼-inch galvanized, all-purpose (drywall-type) screws. If you are using backer board,

6. *Add to Subfloor*

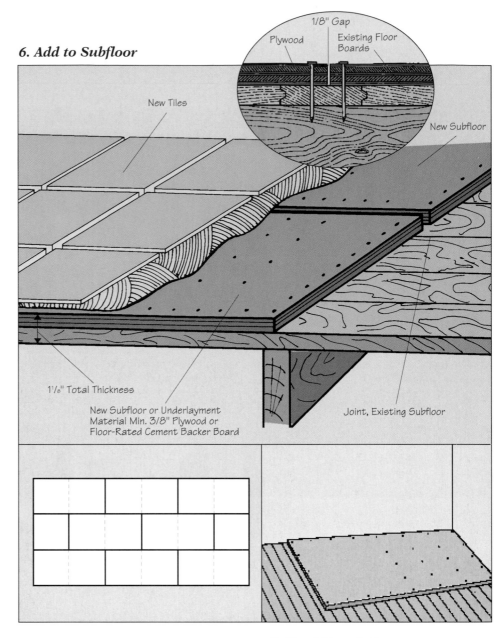

1/8" Gap
Plywood
Existing Floor Boards
New Tiles
New Subfloor
1⅛" Total Thickness
New Subfloor or Underlayment Material Min. 3/8" Plywood or Floor-Rated Cement Backer Board
Joint, Existing Subfloor

consult manufacturer's literature for recommended fasteners and installation methods. Drive nails or screws around the panel perimeter about 1/2 inch in from the edge and 6 inches on center. Then drive fasteners across the face of the panel in rows about 16 inches on center, spacing them 8 to 12 inches apart. Make sure the nail or screw heads are set below the surface to avoid "stress points" that can crack the tile. Joints between backer-board panels are typically filled with tile-setting adhesive and taped with a special fiberglass-mesh tape. Fill the joints between plywood panels with floor patch compound, wood putty, or tile-setting adhesive.

7. *Sand Rough Spots*

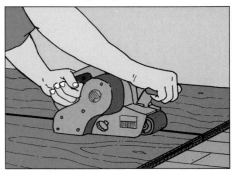

7. *Sand Rough Spots*

After installing the underlayment, sand any rough or splintery sur-faces, and make sure the surface is perfectly clean and free of debris before installing the tile.

CONCRETE FLOORS

Because of its strength and rigidity, concrete provides an excellent structural base for a ceramic tile installation. The only requirements are that the slab is generally in good condition (no major cracks, buckling, or heaving) and that the surface is clean, level, and free of wax, grease, dirt, paint, or other contaminants that would interfere with a good adhesive bond. Use one or more of the following procedures to prepare the concrete floor for tiling:

1. *Check for Moisture*

You cannot lay tile over a damp concrete floor. If the dampness is just surface moisture (caused by leaky plumbing or other damp conditions in the room), simply let the concrete dry out before setting the tile.

The best time to check a concrete floor for moisture is after a heavy rainstorm. Tape squares of kitchen plastic wrap to the floor in various locations. If, after 24 hours, you notice moisture condensation under the pieces of plastic wrap, the floor is too damp to apply tile.

2. *Waterproof Damp Slabs*

If moisture is penetrating the slab from beneath, and is a continuing problem, contact a professional. Minor moisture problems can be cured with a waterproof sealer.

3. *Fill Cracks & Holes*

Hairline cracks do not have to be filled. Larger cracks, holes, or depressions can be filled with a latex/cement-based concrete patching material or a filler (some organic mastics may not adhere to cement-based products).

■ Enlarge the crack with a cold chisel and baby sledgehammer, undercutting the sides so that the patching material will anchor firmly under the beveled edges.

■ Flush out the crack with water to clear out small pieces of debris and to dampen the concrete so the patching compound will adhere to it correctly.

■ With the edge of a trowel, cut the patching material under the beveled edges of the crack, forcing the compound into all the crevices. Finally, smooth the patch and feather the edges to assure an even, level surface.

1. Check for Moisture

2. Waterproof Damp Slabs

3. Fill Cracks & Holes

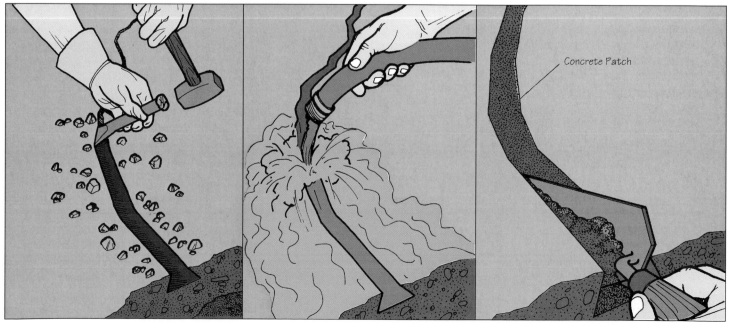

Concrete Patch

4. Remove Irregularities

Chip away minor irregularities, such as concrete splatters, with a wide mason's chisel and hand-held sledgehammer.

5. Level the Surface

You can sometimes grind down high spots in concrete with a coarse-grit abrasive mounted in a belt sander or disc sander (wear a dust mask or respirator).

6. Repair Major Damage

Large holes that need repair require extensive preparation.

■ Break up the cracked concrete with a sledgehammer until the pieces are small enough to remove easily. Angle the edges of the hole toward the center with a chisel and hammer. With a strong wire brush, roughen the edges of the hole and remove any loose particles. Enlarge the hole by digging 4 inches deeper than the concrete slab, and then tamp the dirt on the floor of the hole. Fill the hole with clean 3/4-inch gravel up to the bottom of the concrete slab.

■ Cut a piece of reinforcing wire mesh to fit inside the hole so that the ends of the wire rest against the sloped edges of the hole in the slab. A few bricks placed under the wire will keep it at the right level while the concrete is poured. Add water to the premixed concrete until it is workable. Treat the edges of the hole with an epoxy bonding agent; and, before it dries, pour the concrete into the hole-pushing it forcefully against the sides and under the wire mesh. When the hole is filled, add a few additional shovelfuls of concrete to counter any settling or shrinking.

 Caution: Always wear goggles or safety glasses, gloves, and protective clothing when repairing concrete.

4. Remove Irregularities

5. Level the Surface

6. Repair Major Damage

7. Roughen the Surface

8. Clean the Surface

■ With an assistant, work a 2x4 across the patch, sweeping it back and forth to level the new concrete. Any depressions can be filled and troweled again. When the "bleed water" evaporates and the surface looks dull, use a trowel to smooth the final finish. If you have trouble reaching the center, lay boards across the patch and kneel on them. Let the patch cure for three to seven days. Sprinkle it with water and cover with a sheet of polyethylene to prevent evaporation. Check it every day, adding water if the surface becomes dry.

7. Roughen the Surface

If the concrete floor has been painted or has a slick finish, roughen up the surface to ensure a good adhesive bond. If the floor is larger than a few square feet, use a rented floor sander and coarse-grit abrasive. Vacuum up all dust and debris when finished.

8. Clean the Surface

To clean the surface, use a commercial concrete and driveway cleaner (available at home centers and auto supply stores), followed by a thorough rinse of clean water.

Once you have decided what you need to do to prepare the floor and subfloor for the tile, you can prepare the room for working. Remember that good preparation will help ensure a smooth job.

1. Remove the Doors

First, remove all doors leading to the room and store them in a safe place while you work.

After the tile is installed, you can temporarily rehang the doors, check the clearance at the door bottoms, and trim them, if necessary. (Installing tile almost always raises the level of the floor.)

Generally, you will not need to remove door trims or casings: You can either make cuts in the bottom end and slip the tiles underneath, or cut the tiles to fit around them.

2. Protect the Room

Protect the floors in the rest of the house by laying down drop cloths and hall runners between the room entry you will be using and the location where your materials are stored. If the job calls for any power sanding or other dust-generating procedures, remove heating and cooling registers and cover the openings with cardboard and duct tape. Then, tape temporary "curtains" of polyethylene sheeting over entryways (from which doors were removed) to help prevent airborne sawdust from spreading.

3. Remove Base Molding

If the molding consists of a baseboard with an attached shoe (a thin wood strip along the bottom of the base), and you are tiling the floor only, remove just the shoe. Starting about 1 foot from a corner, insert a chisel or thin prybar between the base and wall at nail locations, and gently pry outward. When removing a quarter-round molding or base shoe, use a second chisel to pry between the base shoe and the floor. Inserting wedges behind the molding will ease removal. Gradually work along the length of the molding until it comes off. If you plan to reinstall the base later, remove the nails from the base, and patch the nail holes with wood putty.

If you cannot remove the base without damaging it, use a hammer and nailset to carefully punch the finish nails completely through. Then, remove the base, pry out the nails in the wall, and patch the nail holes in the base with wood putty.

1. Remove the Doors

2. Protect the Room

3. Remove Base Molding

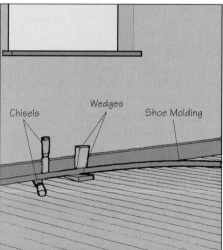

Chisels   Wedges   Shoe Molding

Remove Vinyl Topset Base

A vinyl topset base (used with resilient flooring) can be removed with a wide-blade putty knife. To ease removal, preheat the molding with a hair dryer or heat gun (at low setting) to soften the base adhesive.

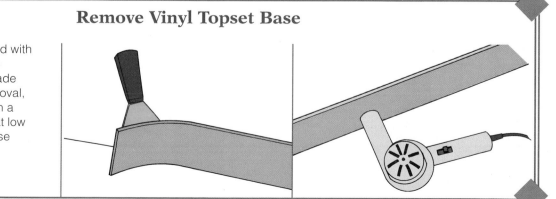

4. Remove Cabinets

Cabinets and vanities usually do not have to be removed unless the subfloor beneath needs to be replaced or repaired, or if the tile installation will create a noticeable change in floor level. Remove any molding at the bottom of the cabinet or vanity, run the tile up to it, and then replace the base moldings. If the cabinet has a toe kick (horizontal strip across the front of the cabinet at floor level), remove this as well; then run the tile a few inches past it, trim the toe kick to fit, and reinstall. If the cabinets include a built-in kitchen appliance, such as a dishwasher, remove it and extend the floor tile into the recess. The tile will raise the height of the appliance, so you may need to raise the countertop slightly or trim the top edge of the opening in the cabinet.

Running the tile underneath a built-in base cabinet or large vanity requires additional work. A change in floor level also means a change in counter height when the fixture is reinstalled, which in turn will affect clearances between the counter and anything above it, such as a wall-mounted faucet. If a sink is involved, you may have to modify plumbing connections to accommodate the increased height.

4. Remove Cabinets

5. Remove Sink

A sink need be removed only if it has a supporting ceramic pedestal or legs. Turn off the water-shutoff valves. Place a bucket below the trap to catch any water. Loosen the slip-joint fitting that attaches the drain and sink (use a wrench if necessary). Disconnect the hot- and cold-water supply pipes. If the sink is attached to the wall, loosen the bolts or clamps that attach it to the wall bracket and lift it off the pedestal. If sink and pedestal are bolted together, detach and remove them separately.

5. Remove Sink
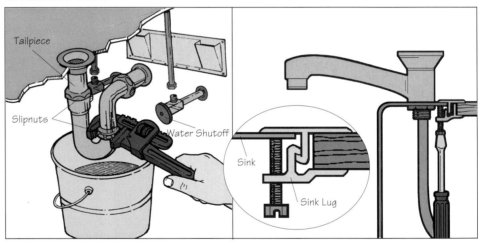

6. Work Around the Toilet

If you are tiling directly over a finish floor (without any changes in subfloor height), the toilet does not have to be removed. Simply cut the tile to fit around it; then finish off the cutline with silicone caulk. However, the finished floor will look nicer if you remove the toilet, extend the tile up to the drain flange, and reset the toilet on top of the tile. Taking this extra step may require minor alterations. For details, see the following page.

6. Work Around the Toilet
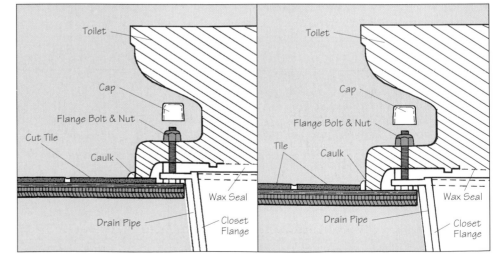

Remove the Toilet

Before removing the toilet, spread a drop cloth around the base of the toilet to soak up excess water that will appear when the toilet is being removed. Decide where the toilet will be set down, and spread out several layers of newspaper in this spot. Then, pour 1 cup of chlorine bleach into the bowl and flush to kill germs.

Types of Toilets. There are three general types of toilets. One type is a floor-mounted toilet with an integral tank close-coupled to the bowl. Another style has a wall-mounted tank connected to the bowl with a short elbow fitting. After the elbow is disconnected from the bowl, the tank can remain mounted on the wall. A third type of toilet (not shown) is a one-piece wall-mounted unit attached to a carrier bracket on the wall. It will not have to be removed.

Shut off the water-supply valve to the tank. Remove the tank lid and set it aside. Flush the toilet to empty the water in the tank and bowl. Use a cup to bail out remaining water in the bowl and tank; then sponge dry.

Lift Toilet off Flange. Disconnect the water-supply valve to the tank, and remove the caps that cover the flange bolts and front-base screws, if any. Remove the bolt nuts and screws. Use a putty knife to break the caulk seal between toilet base and floor. Lift the toilet off the flange.

Clean the Flange. Set the toilet on its side. Use a putty knife to clean any wax off the closet flange. Spray the flange with a disinfectant; then stuff a rag into the drain hole to prevent

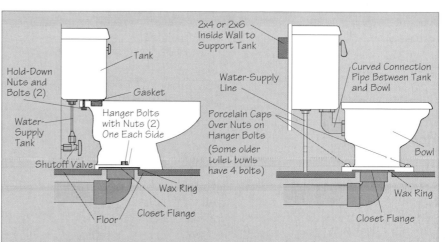

Types of Toilets. *A floor-mounted toilet and integral tank are connected by bolts found on either side of the gasket (left). A wall-hung tank need not be removed, but it must be disconnected from the bowl (right).*

sewer gasses from escaping. Duck-walk the toilet out of the bathroom.

Cut Tile to Fit. Lay all full tiles as close to the flange as possible. Use tile nippers to cut partial tiles to fit roughly around the flange. The cut edges need not be perfect since the toilet will cover them.

Install Wax Ring. Before resetting the toilet, install new bolts on the closet flange. Turn the toilet over so it is balanced on the tank top and bowl rim. Clean off any wax or plumber's putty around the discharge horn, and any caulk stuck to the base. Install the new wax ring to the discharge horn of the bowl, making sure it sticks tightly. If the closet flange is recessed below the newly tiled surface, the wax ring between the flange and toilet base might not be thick enough to seal it properly. Two wax rings can

be sandwiched together to compensate for the change in height. Run a bead of silicone caulk around the perimeter or the base. Tilt the toilet onto the front edge of the bowl; then flip it to an upright position—do not let the base of the bowl touch the floor. Place the toilet base over the flange, aligning the holes in the base with the flange bolts. The bolts and screws that fasten the toilet to the closet flange may need to be replaced with ones that are long enough to allow for the additonal thickness of the tile. Press the toilet into place, making sure the wax ring seats firmly. Then, tighten down the nuts on the bolts. Do not overtighten the bolts or the toilet base and tiles beneath may crack. Replace the tank, if you removed it; then reconnect the supply lines.

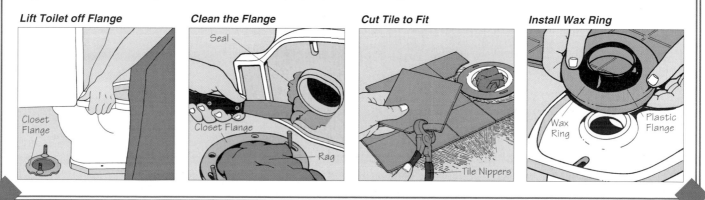

Lift Toilet off Flange | *Clean the Flange* | *Cut Tile to Fit* | *Install Wax Ring*

Once the pattern has been established and the tile selected, and a suitable surface upon which to lay the tile has been provided, the working lines used to guide the tile installation can be snapped.

Lines for Square Rooms.

If the room is relatively square, snap a chalkline along the length of the area down the center of the room. Then, snap a second chalkline across the width of the room so that each chalkline crosses in the approximate center of the room. Check the cross with a framing square to make sure the intersection forms an exact 90-degree angle. These will be your working lines, or layout lines, used to position the tiles.

Starting at the intersection, either dry-lay a row of tiles along each working line, or use a layout stick to determine where cut tiles are needed and what size they will be. Be sure to include the width of grout joints when setting down the tiles. If a row of partial tiles along one wall is less than half a tile wide, reposition the tiles so that the cut row is half a tile or wider.

If the layout results in a narrow row of cut tiles, the grout joints can be made a bit wider to eliminate that row. Otherwise, the layout lines will have to be repositioned (see page 40). Similarly, if the last tile against the wall is almost the width of a full tile, all the grout joints can be made a bit narrower to fit a full row of tiles in that space. Using this layout method, start laying out the tile from the center of the room, filling in one quadrant at a time.

Lines for Out-of-Square Rooms.

If the room is out-of-square, tiles must be aligned square to at least one wall. To do this, establish a set of square working lines and begin laying out the tiles from one corner of the room. Typically, the lines will be projected from the "most square" corner of the room.

To determine which corner is most square, place a tile tightly against the walls in each corner of the room. Project chalk lines from the outside corner of each tile in both directions; then check the intersections of the chalk lines at each

corner for square. Choose the one that is closest to 90 degrees. From this corner, measure out the width of two grout joints and snap a second pair of chalk lines. These will be the working lines. If they are not perfectly square, select the longest wall, or the wall that will be most visible in the room. Then adjust the working line along the adjacent wall until the two working lines form an exact right angle. With the above method, the tiles are laid out from the square corner along the working lines, which, if the two walls are square, will result in whole tiles along the two adjacent walls and cut tiles on the walls opposite them. As with the center-cross layout lines discussed, dry-lay the tiles along the two working lines to determine the size of the cut tiles on the opposite walls. If cut pieces will be less than half a tile wide and will detract from the installation, adjust the width of the grout joints, or reposition the working lines to compensate. Bear in mind that repositioning either of the working lines will mean resulting partial tiles on the wall next to the line that has been moved.

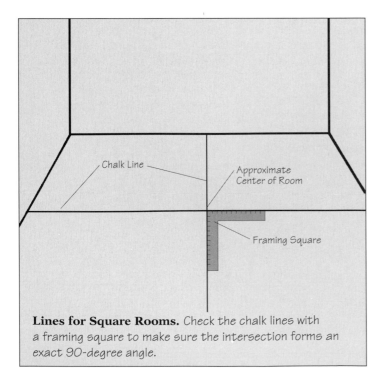

Lines for Square Rooms. Check the chalk lines with a framing square to make sure the intersection forms an exact 90-degree angle.

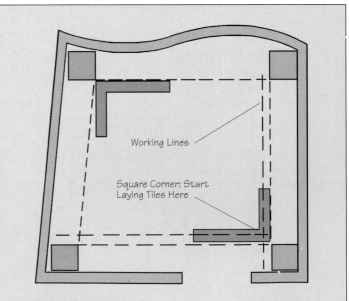

Lines for Out-of-Square Rooms. Place a tile tightly against the walls in each corner of the room; then project chalk lines from the outside corner of each tile.

Lines for L-Shaped Rooms.

Divide the room into two sections, and snap layout lines. Adjust the lines so that all intersections are at 90 degrees. Adjust lines as necessary so that cut tiles around the room perimeter will be larger than half a tile.

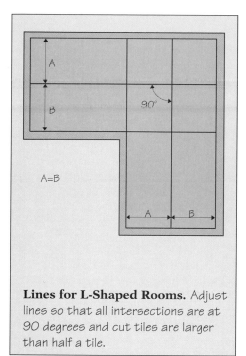

Lines for L-Shaped Rooms. Adjust lines so that all intersections are at 90 degrees and cut tiles are larger than half a tile.

Lines for Adjoining Rooms.

When extending the tile into an adjoining room, make sure the grout joints line up between the two rooms. If the entrance is wide, try to center the tiles so that cut tiles on each side are of the same width.

Lines for Large Tiles.
Large, irregular-size quarry tiles and pavers generally require additional working lines to ensure that the grout joints align properly and are of approximately the same width. Typically, extra chalk lines are added to form a grid. Each square in the grid can contain four, six, or nine tiles; the lines represent the middle of the grout joints between the tiles. When setting the tile, fill in one block at a time, adjusting the tiles until all of the grout joints are evenly spaced.

Lines for Diagonal Layouts.
When laying tiles diagonally, a second set of working lines will be required. From the intersection of the original working lines, measure out an equal distance along any

three of the lines, and drive a nail at these points (A, B, and C on the drawing). Hook the end of a tape measure to one of the nails, and hold a pencil against the tape measure at a distance equal to that between the nails and centerpoint. Use the tape measure and pencil as a compass to scribe two sets of arcs on the floor.

Snap two diagonal chalk lines: one between the center intersection and point D on the drawing, and one between the center intersection and point E. Extend these lines in each direction to the four walls. Erase or cross out the original working lines, and lay the tile to the diagonal ones. Use your layout stick or rows of actual tiles to determine the size of the cut tiles at the walls. Adjust the working lines, if necessary, to achieve the best pattern of partial tiles at all four walls. When setting the tiles, fill in one quadrant at a time, using the sequence shown below. In a diagonal layout, the cut tiles will always end up against the walls. Ideally, these will be full diagonal half tiles.

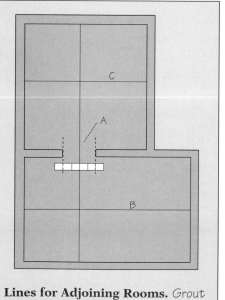

Lines for Adjoining Rooms. Grout joints should line up between two adjoining rooms.

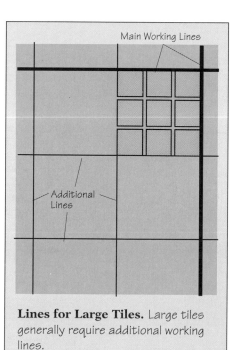

Lines for Large Tiles. Large tiles generally require additional working lines.

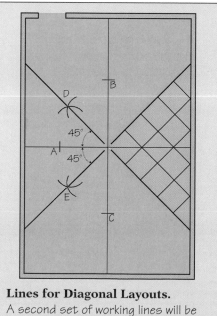

Lines for Diagonal Layouts. A second set of working lines will be needed when tiles are layed diagonally.

When it comes to installing tiles, there are many sequences in which to lay them.

JACK-ON-JACK

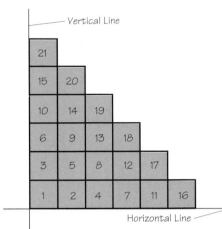

The easiest way to install a jack-on-jack layout is to fill in one row of tiles all the way from the vertical line to the corner; then continue the courses toward the walls. Once one half of the floor has been completed, fill in the other half. Check the straightness of your tile and grout lines often, using a carpenter's square.

DIAGONAL JACK-ON-JACK

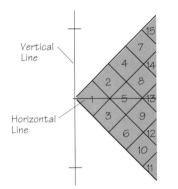

In a diagonal jack-on-jack layout, you always will end up with cut tiles against the walls. Ideally, these would be full-diagonal half tiles; but if you extend the diagonal tiles all the way to the walls, you are more likely to end up with small, partial-diagonal tiles around the perimeter of the room. Diagonal layouts generally look best when framed with a border of square tiles.

HORIZONTAL RUNNING BOND

Lay down the tiles according to the sequence shown in the drawing; you will fill half of the floor at a time. In every other course, the working line will run through the center of the tile.

Begin at the vertical working line, with the vertical line running through the center of the first tile that is laid. Install the horizontal baseline course for the entire floor. You may now complete one row at a time, starting at the vertical working line and staggering the tiles by one half at the beginning of each course.

PYRAMID RUNNING BOND

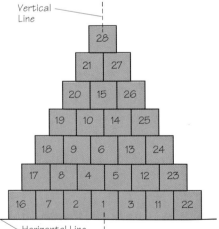

As an alternative method of laying running bond, a stair-step pyramid may be created. However, this pyramid will stair-step up on two sides, instead of one, and will cover the entire wall in one continuous process. Begin row 1 on the horizontal working line. Take six tiles. Lay tile 1 so that the

Mosaic Tiles

If you are using ceramic mosaic tiles, dry-lay the sheets from the centerpoint of the floor out to all walls. Adjust slightly for the minimum number of cut tiles and, as always, avoid excessively small-cut tiles. Although the tiles can easily be separated from the backing sheets with a utility knife, cutting the small, individual tiles can be tricky as well as time-consuming.

To cut small mosaic tiles, score the face of the tile with a glass cutter and straight-edge; then flip the tile upside down and support two opposite edges (parallel to the cutline) with small finish nails. Center a wood chisel over the cutline; then strike it with a hammer. Make sure the chisel comes in full contact with the tile surface when you do this. (Do not use your best chisel for this because its edge can quickly dull or chip.)

vertical working line runs through the center of the tile. Set tiles 2 and 3 on either side of the vertical working line. The grout lines between tiles 1 and 2 and between tiles 1 and 3 will fall in the centers of tiles 4 and 5. Cap the pyramid with a single tile (tile 6), which is cut in half by the vertical working line.

Once the basic pyramid shape is established, add a set of tiles to each side of each course until the pyramid shape is completed again. Always begin laying the tile at the horizontal base line, and progressively work up the side and over to the vertical line.

Once the working lines are established, collect all of the tools and materials needed to lay the tile and grout the joints (see Chapter 2). Stack the tiles in a convenient location near the work area. Be sure to order extra tiles for mistakes and trim pieces.

1. Install Battens
The appearance of the finished job depends on how accurately the first few tiles are set and aligned. To keep the first rows straight, nail 1x2 or 1x3 battens along the working lines at the chosen starting point. (If the floor is concrete, glue down the battens with some of the tile adhesive.) Be sure the battens form a perfect right angle.

2. Spread Adhesive
Do not apply more adhesive than can be covered with tile before the adhesive skins over or sets up. The area that can be covered depends both on the working time or "open" time of the adhesive, as well as the speed at which tiles are laid. Start by covering a small area (1 square yard); then work up to larger areas.

Use the method and notched-trowel size recommended by the tile dealer. Some adhesives are spread at an angle to the tile; others are spread in overlapping arcs. Be careful not to cover the working lines with adhesive—and spread only a little bit of adhesive near the wood batten guides (if they have been installed). For extra-thick tile or tile that has a deep-ridged back pattern, both the back side should be "back-buttered" as well as the floor upon which it is to be laid.

3. Place & Set Whole Tiles
After spreading the adhesive, press each tile into place, twisting it slightly to bed it firmly. Do not slide the tiles against each other, since excess adhesive will build up in the grout joints. Frequently check for alignment with a straightedge and framing square. Do not panic if they are a bit out of line; simply wiggle them on the setting bed until they are true. If you must walk over tiles already set, lay a sheet of plywood or particleboard over them to distribute your weight.

Caution: When working with an organic adhesive or other volatile or toxic material, provide plenty of ventilation and wear a respirator and safety gloves.

Before spreading the adhesive, it is a good idea to lay out tiles or sheets of tile in a dry run. If the room is large, lay a single row of tiles along each of the working lines to the wall. Use a layout stick or the chosen spacers to include the width of the grout joints. The dry run is a means of double-checking the accuracy of the layout lines, to make sure all the tiles will be positioned properly and all cut tiles at walls are half a tile wide or wider (see pages 54-55). If the room is small, you might want to dry-lay all the tiles to see how they fit; then make any necessary cuts in advance. If you choose to do this, be sure to key the tiles to their locations by marking corresponding numbers on the back of each tile and on the floor. Advance layout of the tiles permits proper blending of possibly varying shades of the tiles if more than one manufacturing lot is used.

1. Install Battens

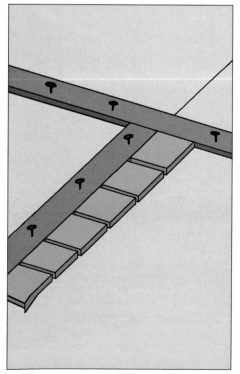

2. Spread Adhesive

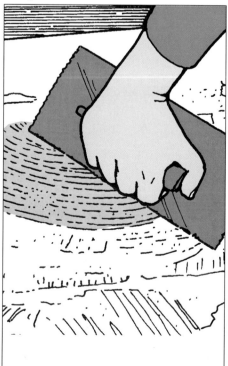

3. Place & Set Whole Tiles

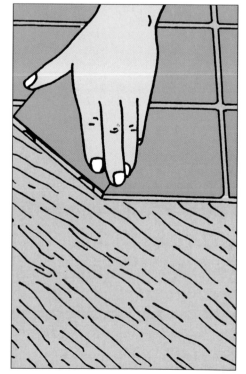

4. *Embed Tiles*

Use a bedding block to ensure that the tiles are flat and firmly embedded in the adhesive. Slide the block across the tiled surface while tapping it lightly with a hammer or rubber mallet. Check tiles frequently with a straight-edge to make sure they are level with each other. If a tile "sinks" below the surface of surrounding tiles, remove it, add more adhesive, and then reset it.

5. Cut Partial Tiles

When all of the full tiles are down, cut and place all the partial tiles around the room perimeter. Unless cove or trim tiles will be installed, the cut field tiles butt directly against the wall (with a slight gap between tile and wall, for expansion). Install any trim tiles first; then cut a piece of filed tile to fit between the trim and last row of full tiles.

To cut partial field tiles, take two loose tiles (tiles A and B) and a pencil. Place tile A directly on top of the full-size tile next to the space to be filled. Place tile B on top of tile A; then move tile B up against the wall. Using the edge of tile B as a guide, draw a line on the surface of tile A. The exposed portion of tile A will be used. From the initial mark that was made, measure back a distance equal to two grout joints. Mark a second, parallel line. This will be the cutline.

This procedure can be used for cutting L-shaped tiles at outside corners, and for fitting partial tiles between full tiles and cove or trim strips.

4. *Embed Tiles*

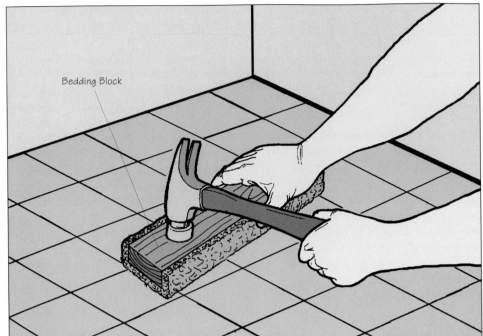

Bedding Block

5. *Cut Partial Tiles*

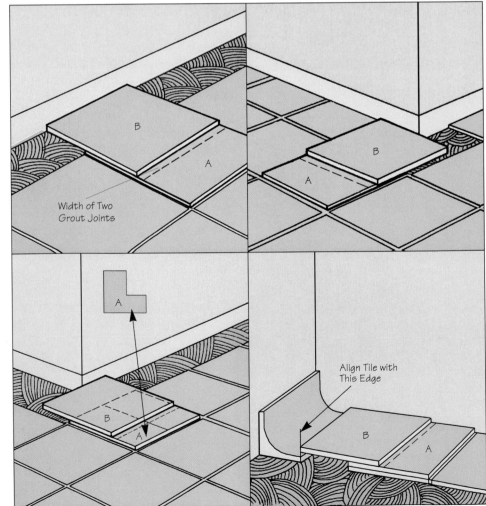

B
A
Width of Two Grout Joints

A
B

A

B
A

A

Align Tile with This Edge

B
A

6. *Apply the Grout*

Before grouting, allow the adhesive to cure for at least 24 hours (preferably 48 hours) or the time specified by the adhesive manufacturer. Clean any debris from the joints, and, if necessary, remove spacers.

■ To prevent the grout from staining the tile surface, protect the tile with a removable sealer. Make sure the sealer has cured fully before applying the grout. Do not use grout to fill the joint between the last row of floor tiles and the wall. Instead, use a flexible silicone caulk to allow for expansion and contraction between the two.

Mix the grout according to manufacturer's instructions.

■ Use a rubber float or squeegee to spread the grout diagonally across the joints between the tile, packing the grout firmly into every joint.

■ As soon as the grout becomes firm, use a wet sponge to wipe off excess grout from the tile surface.

7. *Tool the Joints*

Shape the grout joints with a striking tool (such as a toothbrush handle, spoon, or shaped stick). Clean off the tiles again and smooth the joints with a damp sponge. Allow a dry haze to form on the tile surface; then polish the tiles with a clean, damp cloth. In most cases, the grout will take several days to a week or more to cure completely; read labels.

8. *Seal Tile & Grout*

If the tile or grout joints require a finish sealer (see page 33) apply it according to label directions. Usually it takes at least two weeks for the grout to fully cure before a sealer can be applied. Make sure the floor is clean and completely dry. Starting in the corner farthest away from the door, apply a thin, even coat of sealer with a foam-rubber paint roller or sponge. Wipe off any excess to prevent discoloration of the tile.

6. *Apply the Grout*

7. *Tool the Joints*

8. *Seal Tile & Grout*

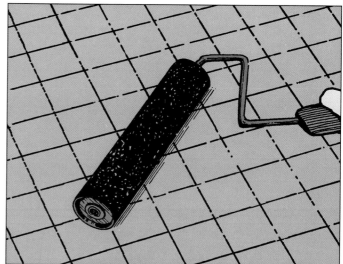

4

TILING WALLS

More than any other surface, walls provide a perfect opportunity for the tiler to show off his or her creative talents. You will find more choices in wall tiles than in any other kind—even the most conservative of designs often include a simple line of border tiles in a contrasting color, or decorative accent tiles spotted into the tile field for visual interest. At the other end of the spectrum, a wall can serve as a blank canvas for unique hand-painted tile murals or bold graphic designs. On a wall, tile makes a design statement—subtle or bold, simple or elegant—setting the overall mood of a room.

Because tile resists heat, water, and a variety of stains, it is well suited to kitchen and bathroom walls. In kitchens, most often you will see wall tile bridging the gap between countertops and upper cabinets or the ceiling. You also may find it on walls behind sinks and stoves. Consider unifying a combination kitchen and dining room by running a tile wainscoting into the dining area.

In the bathroom, tile need not be restricted to shower stalls, vanities, and tub surrounds. You can give a bathroom a more open, unified feeling by extending the tile to one or more adjacent walls. Behind a vanity, a tile backsplash can be extended up the wall to frame a mirror; likewise, wall tiles and trim strips can be used to frame windows or doors in any room of the house.

To find out how much work will be involved in tiling a wall—or if the job can be done at all—you will first need to check for plumb, level, and square. Then you will have to decide whether tile can be put directly over the existing wall surface. You may need to remove the tile and provide a suitable backing.

◄ *The intricate trim partnered with an otherwise plain tile adds interest to the plate rail.*

▶ *Etched tile and colorful trim pieces create a seaside look in this bathroom.*

DESIGN & LAYOUT

The same basic design considerations that apply to floors—color, size, shape, texture, and pattern—also apply to walls (see pages 36-38).

However, when planning your layout, bear in mind that most wall applications incorporate a design that uses tiles of contrasting colors. This not only makes estimating the number of tiles a bit more difficult, but requires a more precise layout. Also, walls typically involve various-shape trim tiles for inside and outside corners, caps, borders, and so on, which also must be figured into the layout scheme (see the section on trim tiles on page 22). If you plan to tile both the walls and the floor, first install the row of cove or other finishing tiles at the floor level, and then do the walls; finally, tile the floor. You do not want to damage the new floor or mess it up with adhesive and grout as you work on the wall above. Preparation for all surfaces (walls, floors, countertops, etc.) should be completed before tiling.

▶ *This bathroom simulates a tropical paradise with aquamarine "glass" ceramic tiles and highlights in white.*

▼ *Decorative tiles bring international style to this kitchen, proving that time-honored artistry transcends decorating trends.*

▶ *Even a small cooking area can have a big personality with specialty wall tiles like the ones used here.*

MAKE A SCALE DRAWING

If you are incorporating a design onto the wall, a scale drawing will help you visualize the finished result. It also will come in handy for estimating and layout purposes.

1. Measure the Wall

First, measure the overall dimensions of the wall to be tiled. Then make a scale drawing of these dimensions on graph paper; be sure to indicate the location of doors, windows, and any built-in cabinets or other permanent fixtures.

2. Measure the Tile

Measure the size of the tile itself plus the width of one grout joint. This dimension will be the basic measuring "unit" that you will use to plan the layout and estimate the number of tiles needed.

3. Divide into Squares

If you are using square tiles, plan your drawing so that each square on the graph paper represents one tile and its grout-joint measurement. If your tile is rectangular rather than square, have one square equal the small dimension and use two squares for the long dimension; or figure how many tiles are necessary to make a square shape. Tiles with irregular shapes are more difficult to lay out, but are generally sold by the square foot, so it is easier to figure out how many you need. For a more accurate estimate, you can lay out a few tiles to see how many full and partial tiles fill in a square space (see page 41). Then, on your scale drawing, divide the wall space into squares of that dimension, count the number of squares, and multiply by the number of tiles in each square.

4. Make a Drawing

Using the tile and grout-joint measurement unit as a guide, make a base drawing of the wall on the graph paper. Then, on a tracing-paper overlay, make a scale drawing of your tile design to the same dimensions. If you want to experiment with different tile patterns, use colored pencils to help visualize what the finished installation will look like. Use as many overlay sheets as you need to come up with a design that pleases you. Be sure to include the size and location of all trim and border tiles.

1. Measure the Wall

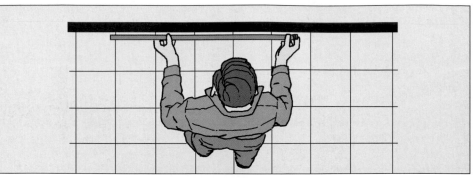

2. Measure the Tile

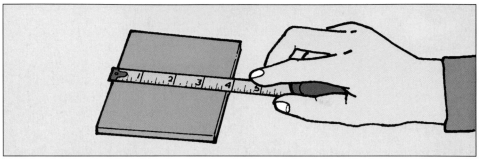

3. Divide into Squares

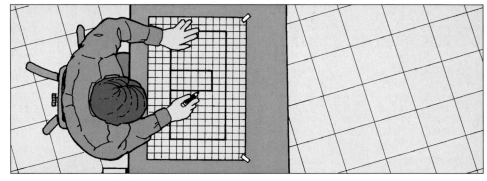

4. Make a Drawing

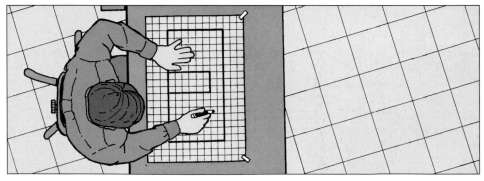

OUT-OF-SQUARE CONDITIONS

Check Walls for Square. As with floors, an out-of-square wall will result in a row of tapered cuts along one or more sides of the tile installation. If one or more adjacent walls are not plumb vertically, a row of tapered-cut tiles will be required at the intersection of the two walls. The problem will be compounded if you extend the tile to the adjoining wall and both walls are out of plumb. You will end up with tapered cuts on both walls. If a floor or countertop is not level, the bottom row of tiles along the wall will be tapered. The same holds true for the top row of wall tiles when they meet an out-of-level ceiling or soffit.

Check Walls for Plumb. Use a 2-foot (or longer) spirit level to check for out-of-plumb or out-of-level conditions. To check the extent of these conditions on adjoining walls, you can use a plumb bob suspended from the ceiling at each end of the tile wall, and, with a chalk line, snap a vertical line a few inches away from the adjacent wall; then take measurements. Similarly, to check the extent of an out-of-level floor, use a level and chalk line or a long, straight board to establish a level line a few inches above the floor; then take measurements between the line and floor at various points.

Typically, if a wall is no more than 1/8 inch out of plumb in 8 feet, or if the floor is no more than 1/8 inch out of level in 10 feet, you will not need to taper-cut the tiles because the bottom grout joint will hide any discrepancies. More serious out-of-square conditions will require tapered tiles, unless you decide to make structural alterations to the wall itself. For example, if the wall is out of plumb, you can remove the existing wallboard or plaster, place shims

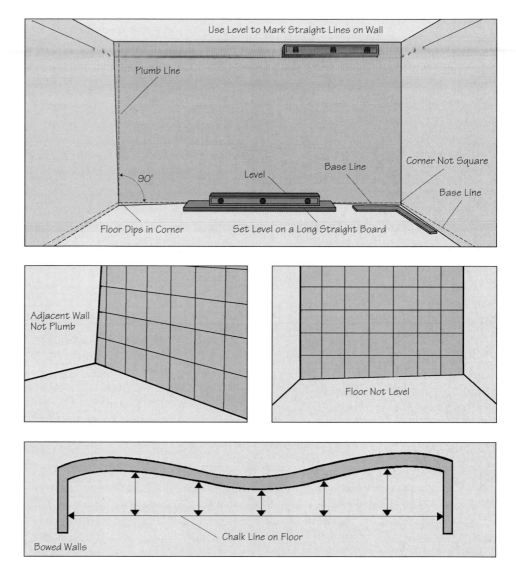

between the studs, and install a new backing. You also can apply new backing over the existing walls, and place shims between the two. You can "build out" masonry walls by floating a thick, tapered mortar bed over it (a job best left to a professional). Another option is to attach furring strips to the wall, add shims, and attach backer board or wallboard.

Check for Level Floors.
Although countertops and attached cabinets are relatively easy to level, an out-of-level floor is much harder to correct, so you will usually have to live with it. One way to visually minimize the effect (and eliminate tapered-cut tiles) is to install a continuous wooden base molding

6 inches or wider along the floor, with the top edge set level and the bottom edge taper-cut or planed to follow the floor angle or contour. The wider the base molding, the less noticeable the out-of-level condition will be after the tile has been installed.

Check for Wavy Walls. Slightly wavy walls usually do not present a problem unless you are tiling the floor (see page 40) or extending the tile to an adjoining wall or onto the ceiling. You can snap a chalkline along the floor and take measurements at various points along the wall to determine if the surface you are tiling should be relatively flat and smooth (see page 72).

TILES WITH AN UNUSUAL DESIGN

If you are creating your own design, the amount of detail you can include will be determined in part by three elements: the size of the wall, the size of the design, and the size of the tiles themselves. Because tiles are rigid geometric units, you will be confined largely to geometric patterns (for example, a downward curve will proceed in stair-step fashion). Smoother, more-flowing patterns, such as free-form tub surrounds and adjoining walls, will require many precisely cut tiles. Such designs require an accurate, detailed drawing and possibly a full-scale "map" sketched onto a grid pattern drawn directly on the wall itself.

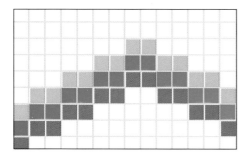

Hand-Painted Tile Murals.

Hand-painted tile murals come in "sets" of individual tiles—from as few as four to well over 50—with each tile representing a "piece" of the picture, like a puzzle. Take the overall dimensions of the mural (including grout joints) and draw it on the overlay sheet. By shifting the overlay on the base drawing, you can determine the best placement of the mural on the wall, much as you would if you were deciding where to hang a large painting.

Cut Tiles.
A good layout plan will help determine in advance where cut tiles will be needed. Because few cases exist where you will not have to cut any tiles at all, plan the layout so you do not end up with a narrow row of cut tiles in a conspicuous place, such as at an outside corner, around a window or door, or above a countertop.

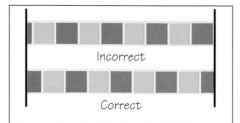

Any cut tiles should be more than half a tile wide, and, in most cases, cut tiles at opposite sides of the wall should be of equal width, to provide symmetry. You may be able to eliminate cut tiles by adjusting the width of all the grout joints. Otherwise, shift the pattern so you end up with wider cut tiles on each opposite wall.

Also be aware of where cut tiles will be needed around doorways, windows, cabinets, and countertops. For example, cut tiles on either side of a window or door opening should be the same width, so the opening appears "centered." When planning the vertical layout, it is best to start with a row of full tiles at floor level and above countertops. However, if you have to cut a course of tile, cut the first row of tiles above the base tiles.

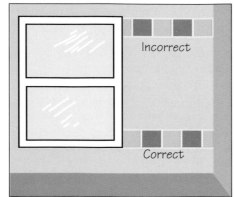

Tile across Adjoining Walls.
If you are extending the tile to one or more adjoining walls, or across a "break" in the wall, such as a doorway, you will want to align the horizontal grout joints to form a continuous line across all the areas to be tiled. The same applies if you are extending the tile onto a horizontal surface, such as a floor or countertop, or onto the ceiling.

Finding the Best Compromise

As you might have guessed by now, if you lay out the tile to meet one of the above requirements, the layout may fail to meet another requirement. For example, if you center the tile layout around a window, you might end up with cut tiles of two different widths at opposite ends of the wall. Similarly, starting with a full row of tiles along the floor might necessitate a row of narrow-cut tiles above a countertop or beneath a window opening. In short, a layout generally involves compromises; but if you plan it out in advance on paper, you will be able to anticipate any problems and come up with the best possible solution—before you start laying the tile.

ESTIMATE AMOUNTS

Once you have your plan on paper, use it to estimate the amount of tiles, adhesive, and grout that is needed for the job.

Tile. Tile usually is sold by the square foot. If you are not working to a drawing and the layout is relatively simple, you need only measure the square footage of the wall space to be tiled. Make your estimate; then order an additional 5 to 10 percent to cover waste due to cut tiles and breakage.

If the wall has a small window or opening, figure the job the same way you would if the wall were solid. If the wall has a large window, several windows, or other obstructions, such as built-in sinks or cabinets, divide the exposed wall space into square or rectangular sections, figure the square footage of each section; then add these figures together to get the total square footage, again adding 5 to 10 percent for waste.

If your installation includes a design incorporating different-color tiles, use your drawing to count the actual number of tiles of each color, adding 5 to 10 percent to the figure for miscuts and breakage. If the layout includes cut tiles, count each partial tile as a full tile.

If you are not working to a scale drawing, a layout stick will help you estimate the number of tiles needed. The stick also is handy for spacing the tiles as they are laid (see page 41).

It is better to overestimate rather than to underestimate the number of tiles needed. Tile dealers usually will let you return any unused tiles, but always keep a few extras for future repairs. This is especially important if you have ordered custom tiles, which may vary in color from batch to batch, and may not be available several years down the road.

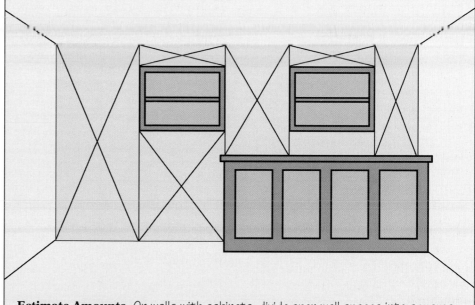

Estimate Amounts. On walls with cabinets, divide open wall spaces into squares; then figure the number of tiles required to fill each square. Add these together to get the total number of tiles needed. Then add 10 percent for cuts and mistakes.

▲ *An otherwise ordinary bathroom becomes extraordinary with the a red border and red floor accents.*

Adhesive. To estimate the amount of adhesive needed, add up the total number of square feet to be tiled; then check the coverage figures on the label of the adhesive container.

Grout. The amount of grout needed will depend on the size of the tiles and on the width and depth of the grout joints between them.

Grout joints for glazed wall tiles typically are 1/8 inch to 3/16 inch wide. Inform your tile dealer of the size of the tiles, the number of square feet to be covered, and the grout-joint width that will be used so he or she can provide you with the correct amounts of grout and adhesive. It is better to have more than you need rather than risk running out in the middle of a job.

The first step in any remodeling job, including tiling, is to make general room preparations to prevent damage to surrounding surfaces and fixtures.

Although you may not need to remove all the furniture in the room, especially when tiling just one wall, remove enough to allow plenty of working space. Protect any remaining furniture with clean, heavy drop cloths.

1. Remove Fixtures

First, remove all wall hangings and permanent wall-mounted fixtures, including drapery and curtain rods, electrical switch and outlet covers, wall-mounted light fixtures, towel racks, and the like. Store these in a safe place and patch any screw or nail holes they have left. Wall-mounted faucets and supply valves for sinks and toilets need not be removed. Usually there is a chrome-plated escutcheon ring around the supply pipe to cover the hole where it goes through the wall. Simply pry the escutcheon away from the wall, cut the tile to fit around the pipe, and then slide the escutcheon back into place.

2. Protect the Floor

Protect the floor in the room that is to be tiled, as well as floors in other rooms or hallways that will be used during the job—it is easy to pick up spilled tile adhesive or grout on the soles of your shoes and track it throughout the house. To protect

floors in the general area, lay down a layer of waterproof kraft paper, followed by heavy painter's drop cloths. For additional protection from accidentally dropped tools or tiles, lay down sheets of thin plywood or particleboard on the floor directly beneath the walls you are tiling. Use the same method to protect countertops and other horizontal surfaces in the immediate work area.

If the job calls for any power sanding or other dust-generating procedures, remove heating and cooling registers and cover the openings with cardboard duct tape. If you have removed any doors, tape temporary "curtains" of polyethylene sheeting over the open entries to help protect airborne sawdust from spreading to other rooms of the house.

3. Remove Trim & Moldings

The procedure for removing base moldings, door trim, cabinet moldings, and other wood moldings is the same. Starting about 1 foot from a corner, insert a chisel or thin prybar between the base and wall at nail locations and gently pry outward. Gradually work along the length of the molding until it comes off. If you plan to reinstall the moldings, remove the nails, patch tile nail holes with wood putty, and store the moldings in a safe place. If the moldings do not come off easily without damage by the method just described, use a

hammer and nailset to carefully punch the finished nails completely through the base. Then remove the base, pry out the nails that are now in the wall, and patch the nail holes with wood putty.

Vinyl Topset Base

Vinyl topset base (used with resilient flooring) can be removed with a wide-blade putty knife. To ease removal, you can preheat the molding with a hair dryer or heat gun (at low setting) to soften the base adhesive.

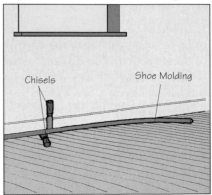

1. Remove Fixtures

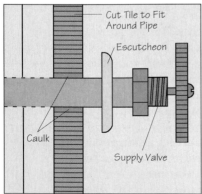

2. Protect the Floor

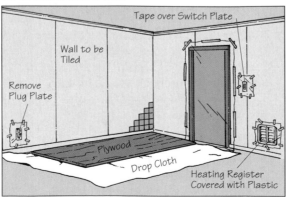

3. Remove Trim & Moldings

You will not have to remove cabinets or vanities unless they will be replaced with new ones, or if for some reason you want to tile behind them. More often, you will simply leave them in place and tile up to the edges. However, you might need to remove cabinets to plumb and level them and avoid having to taper-cut tiles along the sides, top, or bottom of the cabinet.

COUNTERTOP CABINETS

1. Remove Drawers, Trim & Nails

To level a base cabinet or vanity with a solid countertop (wood, marble, Corian, plastic laminate, or similar), start by removing all shelves and drawers. Remove any trim or molding between the cabinet and wall; then pull out any nails or screws holding the cabinet to the wall and floor.

2. Remove the Countertop

Next, use a utility knife or broad chisel to cut the caulk bead between the countertop and wall, if any, and remove the countertop (most countertops are attached by screws driven through corner-blocks or braces in the cabinet from underneath). If the counter-top contains a sink, you may be able to lift off the whole thing with the sink in place, if you are careful. Make sure you disconnect the trap and supply lines first. Remove large or heavy sinks before attempting to lift them off the countertop.

3. Remove Screws

If a series of small individual cabinets have been screwed together through their face frames to form a continuous run, remove the screws and level each cabinet separately, beginning with the corner cabinet.

4. Establish a Level Line

To level the cabinet or cabinets, use a level and chalk line to establish a reference line on the wall along the top back edge of the cabinet (the line will be flush with the cabinet top at the "high" end and slightly above at the "low" end).

1. Remove Drawers, Trim & Nails

2. Remove the Countertop

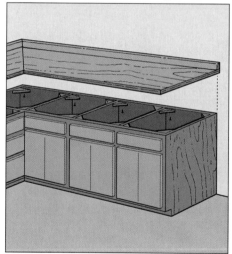

Tiled Countertops

Cabinets with tiled countertops are considerably more difficult to level. If the cabinet is small, you may be able to leave the countertop in place; all you need to do is to remove any backsplash tiles adhered to the wall; then follow the same steps (without countertop removal). In most cases, though, you will need to tear out the old countertop and replace it with a new one (see Chapter 5).

3. Remove Screws

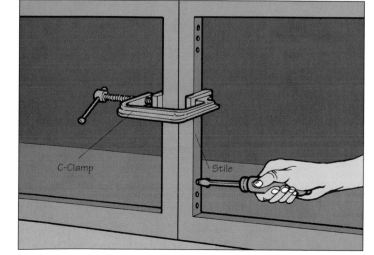

C-Clamp

Stile

4. Establish a Level Line

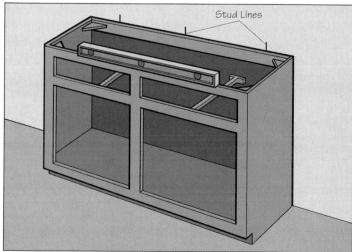

Stud Lines

5. *Align Edge of Cabinet*

Remove the toe kick at the front of the cabinet. Wedge wooden shim shingles between the floor and cabinet base until the back edge of the cabinet or cabinets align with the reference line marked on the wall.

Check the cabinets with a level to make sure they are level.

6. *Reinstall Cabinet*

Once the cabinets are level, trim the shims flush to the front edge of the cabinet and replace the toe

kick. If the cabinet was screwed or nailed to the wall, replace the nails or screws.

Installing a countertop is the reverse process of removing it.

5. Align Edge of Cabinet

6. Reinstall Cabinet

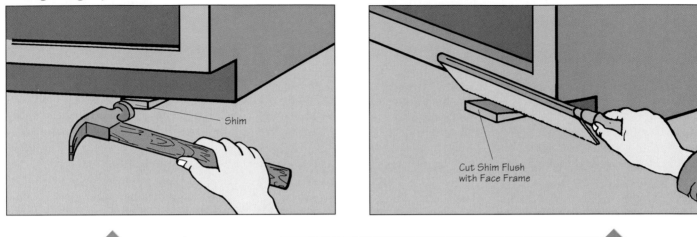

Shim

Cut Shim Flush with Face Frame

WALL-HUNG CABINETS

Wall-hung cabinets must be detached from the wall in order to be leveled, so it is best to have a helper on hand. Also, tack a 2x4 cleat to the wall 1/2 inch below the edge of the cabinet for support.

1. *Remove Trim & Nails*

Remove trim and moldings where the cabinet meets the wall and ceiling. Remove all nails, patch the holes with wood putty, and put aside. Once the cabinet is leveled, you may need to reattach the moldings in a slightly different

position to cover any gaps. This can be done before or after the wall is tiled. It is neater to run the tile up to the sides and bottom of the cabinet, and then to reinstall the moldings to cover cut edges.

2. *Level the Cabinet*

Prop the cabinet from beneath, and have a helper steady it while you remove the screws or nails that attach it to the wall. Holding a level vertically on one side, shift it slightly until it is plumb; then drive several nails through the back of the cabinet, partway into the studs, to hold it temporarily in place.

Check all surfaces for level. If the cabinet was built out-of-square, it may be plumb but not level. You may need to shift it to visually minimize an out-of-square condition.

3. *Fasten Cabinet*

Attach the cabinet permanently to the wall with screws or nails about 1/2 inch longer than the ones you removed.

Caution: Wall-hung cabinets must be attached firmly to studs behind the wall; the wall surface itself cannot sustain the nails or screws.

1. Remove Trim & Nails

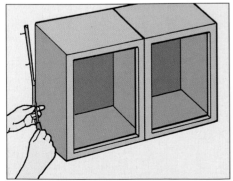

2. Level the Cabinet

3. Fasten Cabinet

REMOVE A WALL-HUNG SINK

For wall-hung sinks (with or without a pedestal), there are two options: You can tile around them, which involves making many curved tile cuts; or you can remove the sink, tile behind it, and reattach it to the wall. The latter procedure usually makes for a neater installation (and fewer cut tiles), but you will have to shim out the mounting bracket a distance equal to the thickness of the tile in order to rehang the sink. One way to do this is to use a plywood shim equal in thickness to the tile, cut to the width and length of the bracket.

1. Remove the Sink

After shutting off the supply valves to the sink, disconnect the trap and supply lines, remove the sink's front legs, if any, and lift the sink off the bracket.

2. Outline Bracket

Next, remove the bracket, trace its outline on the plywood, and cut out the shim.

3. Fasten Bracket

Nail the shim to the wall at the bracket location; then reattach the bracket with screws that are long enough to go through the bracket, shim, existing wallcovering, and well into the bracing behind the wall.

Some brackets can be attached directly to a tiled wall; but this requires drilling holes in the tile for the bracket screws, and the pressure exerted on the bracket by the sink may crack the tiles behind it.

If the sink is recessed into a countertop, you need not remove it unless you are removing or retiling the countertop itself (see page 69).

Freestanding pedestal sinks need not be removed if there is enough clearance between the sink and wall to work comfortably.

1. Remove the Sink

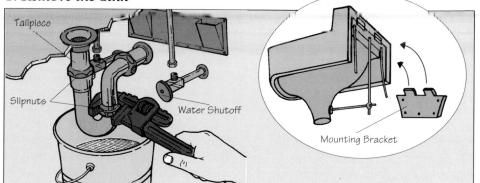

Tailpiece

Slipnuts

Water Shutoff

Mounting Bracket

2. Outline Bracket

3. Fasten Bracket

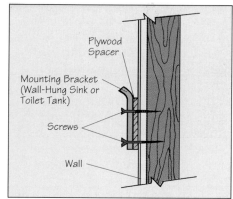

Plywood Spacer

Mounting Bracket (Wall-Hung Sink or Toilet Tank)

Screws

Wall

REMOVE A TOILET

Wall-Mounted Toilets. One-piece, wall-mounted toilets are attached to a sturdy carrier, which contains both the drain system and supply lines, and is built directly into the wall framing. Actual attachment methods vary. If you are uncomfortable with the idea of removing the toilet, leave it in place and cut the tiles to fit around it.

Wall-Mounted Tanks. With these units (see page 53), often the tank can be removed, leaving the bowl in place. Shut off the supply valve and disconnect the line to the tank; then bail out the water and disconnect the elbow fitting that attached the tank to the bowl. Lift the tank off its mounting bracket. The mounting bracket may need to be shimmed out to compensate for the tile thickness (see page 52).

Floor-Mounted Toilets. On close-coupled floor-mounted toilets the tank is not attached to the wall, but there is usually not enough clearance to install tiles easily. To remove the tank, shut off the supply valve, disconnect the supply line, bail out the tank, and remove the two bolts connecting the tank to the bowl. Then, lift the tank off the bowl and store in a safe place (see page 53).

Wall-Mounted Toilet

Most interior walls in residential construction are surfaced with wallboard (also called gypsum board or drywall). In many older homes, the walls are plastered. Both surfaces generally make a good backing for ceramic tile, provided the surface is smooth, flat, and solid. Other walls and surfaces suitable for tiling (provided they are in good shape) include plywood (1/2 inch thick minimum), masonry (concrete, cement block, brick), and existing ceramic tile.

Wood-board paneling and wainscoting generally cannot make a good backing for ceramic tile because the individual boards tend to expand and contract with changes in temperature and humidity. This movement can cause grout joints to crack. Likewise, thin veneered plywood and composition paneling (hard-board, plastic laminated panels and "tileboard") are too thin and flexible to support ceramic tile, unless they are firmly adhered to a wallboard or plaster backing. Also, the surfaces of some of these materials may not provide a good bond for some adhesives. (In all cases, plastic laminates or other slick surfaces need to be roughened with sandpaper to assure a good adhesive bond.) However, wood-board paneling and composition panels usually are easy to remove, and it would be worthwhile to do so to remove any doubt.

Tiling over wallpaper is not recommended because the weight of the tile will cause the paper to loosen and peel off. To remove wallpaper; use a liquid wallpaper remover (available at paint dealers and hardware stores); or, in tough cases, rent a steamer from a tool-rental company. After removing the wall-paper, scrape off any remaining adhesive and rough up the surface with sandpaper.

Similarly, tile should not be laid over loose or peeling paint. Scrape away any loose paint and rough up any glossy surfaces with sandpaper.

No matter what surface you are tiling over, the wall itself also must be square (see page 65). Any out-of-square conditions should be corrected during the wall-preparation stage. If you are tiling a wall that is subject to moisture or water, such as behind a kitchen sink or in a bathroom or laundry room, you will need to install some type of waterproofing membrane, water-resistant backing, or both. If you have any doubts as to the suitability of the wall surface, consult a tile dealer.

PREPARE WALLBOARD

You can tile over existing wallboard if the panels are generally in good condition, firmly attached to the studs, and rigid enough to support the weight of the tile. Any flexing in the wall will cause tiles and grout joints to crack. Re-adhere loose panels with drywall screws, spaced 8 inches to 10 inches apart, along all framing members. (You can locate studs and other framing behind the wall with an inexpensive magnetic "stud finder" purchased at a local hardware store.) If the panels are too thin or weak to support the tile, add a second layer of 1/2-inch wallboard or cement backer board over the existing panels to provide extra rigidity. When covering existing panels with new ones, make sure joints between the new panels do not fall directly over those in the existing ones.

Generally, a wall is considered too weak for tile if you can cause it to flex by pressing the heel of your hand against the panel midway between two studs. Putting a new backing over the old is a good way to cover major surface defects. If the extra thickness becomes a problem, remove the wallboard panels altogether and replace them with a suitable backing material. If necessary, reinforce the wall framing with blocking or additional studs to provide adequate support for the backing and tile. In general, studs should have a maximum spacing of 16 inches on center, and wallboard or other backing materials should be a minimum of 1/2 inch thick. Additional support may be required for large, or weighty tiles.

In wet areas, replace conventional wallboard with cement backer board, the latter being more durable. Depending on the extent of moisture exposure, a waterproof membrane (usually tar paper or 4-mil polyethylene sheets stapled to studs) also may be required to protect the framing behind the backer board. Check local building codes for recommended water-proofing materials and building practices in your area.

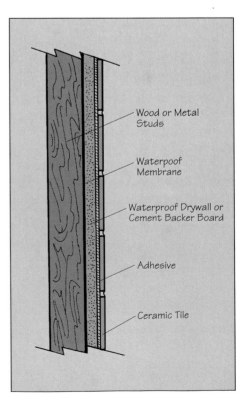

Wood or Metal Studs

Waterpoof Membrane

Waterproof Drywall or Cement Backer Board

Adhesive

Ceramic Tile

Patch Wallboard. Minor imperfections such as dents, scratches, and hairline cracks need not be patched because they will be filled by the adhesive when you tile. Loose or "popped" nails should be removed. First drive a drywall screw above and below the popped nail to re-adhere the panel; then pull out the popped nail.

Along joints, check for splits or bubbles in the drywall tape. Carefully slice the damaged tape from the wall with a razor blade or utility knife. Replace it with fiber-glass-mesh drywall tape, bedded in the tile adhesive you will be using.

Large holes or dents (such as those caused by doorknobs) will require patching. Large dents should be treated the same way, because even if the paper covering on the wall-board is still intact, the gypsum core will probably be cracked.

Using a carpenter's square, draw a rectangle around the damaged section. Drill starter holes inside opposite corners, cut the piece with a keyhole saw, and pull it out. If the damaged area is large, cut back to the nearest studs on each side.

Cut two pieces of 1x3, each about 6 inches longer than the vertical sides of the hole, as braces for the patch. Insert a brace in the opening and hold it vertically against one edge, centered, so that half the width of the brace is behind the wall and half is showing through the opening. Attach above and below with wallboard screws. Repeat with the second brace on the other side of the opening. Then, cut a patch the size of the hole, fit it in place, and attach with screws through the patch into the braces.

Finish the seams around the patch with tape and joint compound. Feathering (applying successively wider layers of compound on each side of the tape) helps blend the seam into bare wallboard.

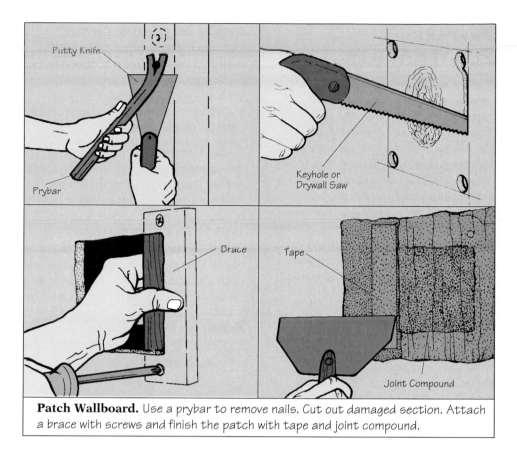

Patch Wallboard. Use a prybar to remove nails. Cut out damaged section. Attach a brace with screws and finish the patch with tape and joint compound.

Replace Entire Panel. In some cases, damage to the drywall will be so severe that you will save more time by replacing the entire panel rather than trying to repair individual defects. In water-damaged areas especially, the drywall core may be soft and crumbly, even if the painted surface remains intact. In some instances, the paper coating will have separated from the core, caus-ing "bubbles" in the surface. Although it may be tempting to simply cut out the bubbles and apply the tile directly over the exposed gypsum core, do not do it. Once the core is exposed, it will deteriorate quickly and will not hold the tile. The same applies if you have accidentally torn off the paper surface while removing any wallcovering.

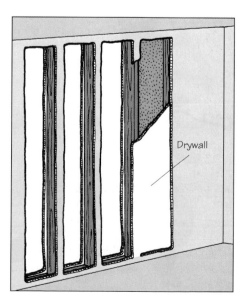

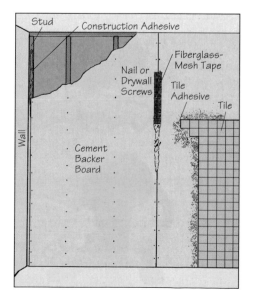

PREPARE PLASTER WALLS

Plaster walls consist of solid layers of plaster built up over wood or metal lath attached to the studs. These walls make a good surface for tiling, provided the surface is relatively flat, sound, and free from major cracks or crumbling plaster. If the plaster wall is sound, wash it thoroughly with a general-purpose cleaner to remove any dirt or grease; then rinse thoroughly. A glossy painted surface will require sanding to ensure a good adhesive bond.

Extensive cracking in a plaster wall indicates seasonal soil movement or shifting of the house. Such cracks eventually will travel to the tile. In this case, you will need to remove the plaster, fix the problem, and install a cement backer board. Some plaster mixtures are too soft to tile over. If the plaster cracks or crumbles when you poke it with a screwdriver, it should be removed.

Patch Holes. Small holes or depressions can be filled with patching plaster. Clean and moisten the area to be patched, and remove any loose plaster. Apply patching plaster with a wide putty knife. After the patch shrinks, repeat the process and let it dry; then sand the patch flush to the wall.

Repair an Outside Corner.
Outside corners often take a beating over the years. If the damage is minor, usually it can be repaired with drywall joint compound and a wide drywall knife. Use a straight-edge to shape the corner.

If the damage is extensive, clear damaged plaster from the edges and follow the procedures shown for patching holes. Tack a batten lightly to one side of the corner with its straight edge flush to the wall surface. Use the batten as a guide for filling one side of the damaged area with an undercoat of patching plaster to within 1/8 inch of the sur-

rounding surface. Move the guide and repeat on the other side. When the plaster is dry, fill the patch flush to the surrounding wall with more plaster. Then, sand smooth.

Replace Entire Wall. Use a hammer and chisel to chip away a hole in the plaster wall. Then wedge a crowbar between the plaster and wood lath and pry slabs of plaster away from the lath. Wear safety goggles to project yourself from flying plasters chips and a mask or respirator to protect you from plaster dust. Remove the wood lath with the crowbar. Replace plaster with wallboard.

Repair an Outside Corner

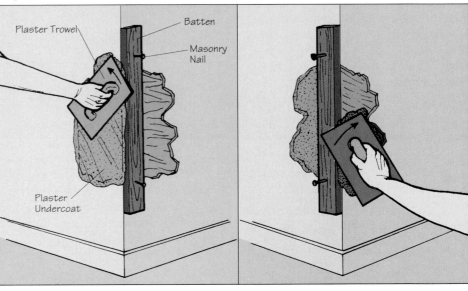

Patch Holes

Replace Entire Wall

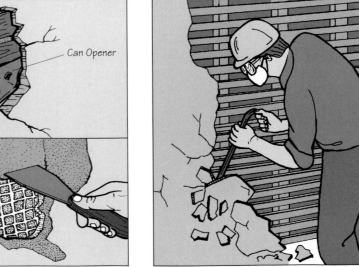

PREPARE PANELING & PLYWOOD

As mentioned, most wood and composition paneling is too weak to support ceramic tile. However, if you have determined that the surface will make a suitable substrate, first clean the surface thoroughly to remove any wax, grease, oil, or dirt; and rinse thoroughly with a general-purpose household cleaner. Roughen the surface with sandpaper to provide a good adhesive bond. Fill any holes, cracks, or dents with wood filler or some of the adhesive you will be using to set the tile. Slick composition surfaces, such as plastic laminates or tileboard, also must be roughened with sandpaper.

Prepare Paneling & Plywood

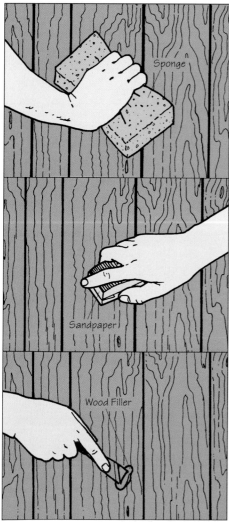

PREPARE CONCRETE & MASONRY SURFACES

New concrete walls should be allowed to cure for at least one month before the tile is applied.

1. Check for Water Beads

If a form-release agent or acceleration compound was used on the wall, it will interfere with a good

1. Check for Water Beads

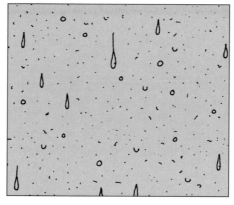

2. Remove Dirt

3. Fill Holes

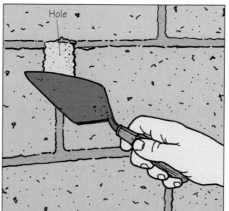

adhesive bond. Use this test: If water beads up on the surface rather than getting absorbed, chemicals have been used. If so, you will have to install a suitable backing over the wall.

2. Remove Dirt

For old concrete or masonry block walls, remove any dirt or residue with a mild detergent. Avoid using harsh chemical cleaners such as concrete and driveway cleaners, which may leave a residue that interferes with the adhesive bond.

3. Fill Holes

Fill any holes with mortar.

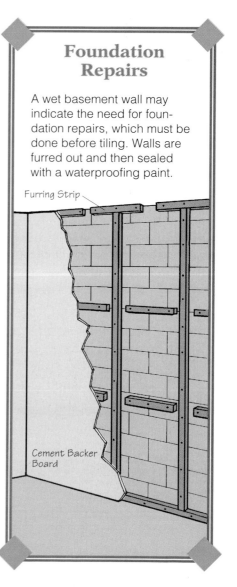

Foundation Repairs

A wet basement wall may indicate the need for foundation repairs, which must be done before tiling. Walls are furred out and then sealed with a waterproofing paint.

PREPARE CERAMIC TILE

An existing ceramic tile surface makes a good base for new ceramic tile if the surface tile is fastened securely to the wall. One or two loose tiles usually present no problem; simply re-adhere them with the appropriate adhesive. Many loose tiles may indicate problems with the substrate; remove these and check the backing for water damage. Because you cannot lay new tile over a weak surface, remove all the old tile and the damaged backing. If water damage is apparent inside the wall, leave the area open to dry for a few days to make sure the framing is perfectly dry before reinstalling a water-resistant backing. If the damage is caused by leaky plumbing, repair the problem so it does not happen again.

If the backing is sound and loose tiles are simply a result of a poor adhesive bond, remove all the loose tiles, scrape off all the old adhesive from the backing, and re-adhere the tiles with new adhesive. If a majority of tiles are loose, remove all of them, scrape off the old adhesive, make any necessary repairs to the backing, and adhere the new tiles directly to the backing.

If the existing tile is sound, first use a tile cleaner to clean any wax, grease, or soap scum off the surface. Using a carborundum stone or an abrasive disc in an electric grinder, roughen the surface to provide "tooth" for the new adhesive. Then, rinse off the sanding dust.

If you are tiling over a wainscoted wall (that is, the tile does not extend all the way to the ceiling), use one of the methods shown to deal with the change in wall thickness above the tile wainscoting.

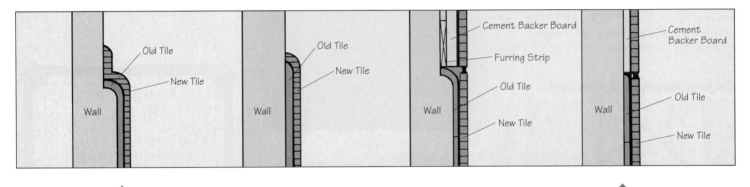

PRIME THE SURFACE

Once you have prepared the wall for tiling, you will have to prime the surface to seal out moisture and provide a stronger bond between the adhesive and the backing. This often is called a bond coat. In most cases, the bond coat will be a skim coat of the adhesive you are using, or a primer recommended by the adhesive manufacturer. You apply the bond coat of adhesive with the flat side of your trowel, let it dry, and then sand it smooth. Be sure to pack adhesive around pipes and

Caution: Some primers are flammable, so be sure to extinguish any open flames, and provide plenty of ventilation. Wear a respirator with the appropriate filter cartridge. Follow all label instructions.

other wall openings. Primers are applied with a brush or rolled according to label instructions.

In moist areas, a bond coat of water-resistant adhesive usually provides a sufficient barrier against moisture penetration between the tile and backing. Check with your tile dealer for specific recommendations.

Installing wall tile follows the same general procedures as installing floor tile, with one major difference: Because you are tiling a vertical surface, gravity works against you. Always start laying the tiles from the lowest point up, so that the tiles and spacers (if used) that have just been laid support the next course above them. Tiles set over openings, such as windows, will need to be supported by battens tacked to the wall.

Most adhesives used for wall tile are formulated to hold the tiles in place while still wet. Tile-setters refer to this ability as "hang." The ability of an adhesive to hold the tile once dry is called "grip." Adhesives with high hang properties include thin-set latex-portland cement and organic mastic adhesives.

Also, wall installations usually require more trim tiles than floor installations do. As mentioned, these must be carefully planned into the layout and are usually installed before filling in the field tiles. Plastic and metal trim strips also are available for ceramic wall tiles. Install these before setting the last row of tiles.

ESTABLISH WORKING LINES

On simple wall installations, you will establish a vertical working line near the floor, and next a horizontal baseline at or near the centerpoint of the wall. Then you will start laying the tiles at the intersection of the two lines, either in pyramid (or running-bond) fashion or in a jack-on-jack arrangement (see page 56). Additional layout lines will be helpful if the wall is large or contains openings, counters, cabinets, or other built-in fixtures. It also is a good idea to add lines that show the location of any trim and border tiles. Additional working lines will speed up the actual process of laying the tile and result in neater installations.

Draw a Working Line. Once you have worked everything out on paper, you can use your drawing as a general guide to establish the actual working lines on the wall. These will be the guidelines to which you set the tile. They will help to avoid errors in layout and will make the drawing easier to read, especially if your installation includes a complex pattern or multicolored tiles. Bear in mind, though, that the drawing, no matter how accurate, will be a general guide only. You will need to take accurate measurements when you establish the working lines on the wall, and you will probably have to make minor adjustments to the working lines themselves to make the layout work. To become familiar with the procedure, see page 54. Then, indicate the locations of the working lines on your drawing.

1. Establish Vertical Line

In most cases, you will establish a vertical working line at or near the center of the wall. If the wall has a large window or other opening, you may want to adjust the vertical line so that the opening is centered between vertical grout joints. (Tiles on both sides of the opening will be of equal width.)

In many cases, though, you will want cut tiles at both ends of the installation to be of the same width.

To establish the vertical line, first measure the width of the tiled area (from corner to corner if you are tiling across the entire wall); then find and mark the centerpoint. Use your layout stick (or a single row of spaced tiles placed on the floor) to mark off tile and grout-joint widths to either side of this point. If the last tile at each end is going to be

1. Establish Vertical Line

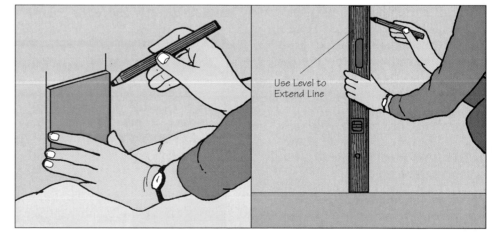

Use Level to Extend Line

more than half a tile wide, you can use the centerpoint to establish the vertical guideline. If the end tiles are going to be less than half a tile wide, move the vertical guideline a distance of half a tile to the right or left of the centerline. This will result in wider-cut tiles at each end.

Or, if your layout requires a row of full tiles at one end or the other, mark the tile and grout-joint widths starting from that end until you reach the approximate center of the wall. Use a carpenter's level to project the vertical guideline at the proper point on the wall.

2. Establish the Horizontal Baseline

Because ceramic wall tiles are installed from the bottom row up, the first step is to establish a level horizontal baseline to ensure that the first row—and all rows above it—will be perfectly level. First find the lowest point on the floor where the floor meets the wall edge. With a level and chalk line or long straightedge, establish a level line across the wall, several inches above the floor. If more than one wall will be tiled, continue this line through all of the wall space you want to tile. Find the spot where the distance between the line and the floor is greatest: This will be the lowest spot on the floor. Use the same procedure for tiling above a countertop, vanity, or tub.

If the floor or counter is less than 1/8 inch out of level along the length of the wall or walls to be tiled, establish the height of your baseline from the highest point; if it is more than 1/8 inch out of level, establish the baseline from the lowest point. Place a full tile (or a trim tile plus one full tile, if you are using base trim) against the wall at the spot you have chosen (high end or low end). Holding the tile or tiles at the proper grout spacing, or butted on spacer lugs if the tile has these, mark the wall at a point one grout space above the tile. Then, with your level and straightedge or chalk line, project a level line across the wall at this height. Continue the line to all wall surfaces to be tiled.

If the wall includes a countertop, vanity, or tub and you are tiling the wall from floor level, you may have to adjust the baseline at the floor. Usually, it is best to have a row of full tiles above these features, even if it means having a row of cut tiles at floor level. Similarly, if the wall includes a window or other opening, plan the layout so there is a full row of tiles directly beneath the sill.

2. Establish the Horizontal Baseline

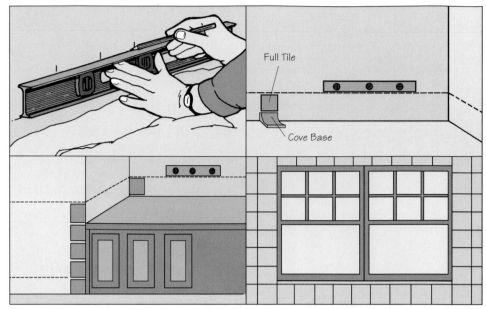

Full Tile

Cove Base

Establish the first horizontal guideline above the countertop or tub, then extend this line across all wall surfaces to be tiled. Use your layout stick to measure down to the floor, or to the top edge of the trim or cove tiles, if you are using these. The row of cut tiles, if needed, will be the first course of field tiles above the trim or cove tiles (which should not be cut). Establish the floor-level horizontal baseline directly above the course of cut tiles. If the course of cut tiles will be less than half a tile wide, it is best to install two rows of wider-cut tiles to fill the space, rather than one very narrow row and one full one. In this case, both courses of cut tiles fall directly beneath the horizontal baseline.

If you are tiling only partway up the wall, establish another horizontal guideline above the baseline to indicate where to stop tiling.

Mark for Ceramic Accessories

If you are installing a ceramic soap dish, towel bar, grab bar, or other ceramic accessory that will sit flush to the wall, you will want to position these to line up with the horizontal

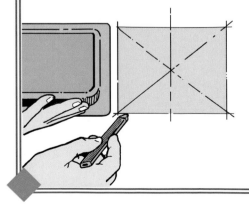

and vertical grout lines of surrounding field tiles. Many wall tiles come with matching accessories sized in multiples of the tile size. Some pieces have flanges that overlap surrounding tiles. Mark off the dimension of the part that will sit flush to the wall. Although such accessories will be the last pieces you will install, you should plan their exact location at the layout stage. Holes and any required framing for recessed soap dishes and similar fixtures also should be made at this time. If framing is required, install according to manufacturer's instructions.

3. Establish the Tiling Sequence

Typically, you will start by installing all the trim tiles at floor level and then fill in with field tiles. Trim pieces for inside and outside corners are installed just ahead of the whole field tiles, and cut pieces are filled in as needed. In all cases, you will be building up the tile from the bottom so that each new course is supported by the course beneath it.

First, install the row of cove or other trim tiles at floor level. Lay the first tile against the vertical working line where it meets the floor. Work over to one corner, then to the other, allowing for grout lines between each tile. If you have to cut tiles at either corner, cut the one preceding the corner piece.

Next, install the inside and outside cove pieces partially up the wall, if you are using these. If the first course (or two) of field tiles above the base cove are cut tiles, you will need to cut the first cove tile to the same size.

It is best not to install the cove tiles all the way up the wall at this time. Instead, run them about 3 feet up the wall and fill in the field tiles up to that point; then install the remaining cove tiles in short sections, always keeping a little ahead of the field tiles. This will enable you to adjust grout lines between the field tiles and cove tiles while the adhesive is still wet.

There are two basic ways to lay field tile on a wall: (1) Build the tiles up from center of the wall in a pyramid, running bond shape; or (2) start by laying the length of the bottom row; then work from one corner at the bottom diagonally up the wall, filling in one half of the wall at a time in a jack-on-jack pattern. This is an easier method to use if the adjoining walls are not absolutely plumb.

3. Establish the Tiling Sequence

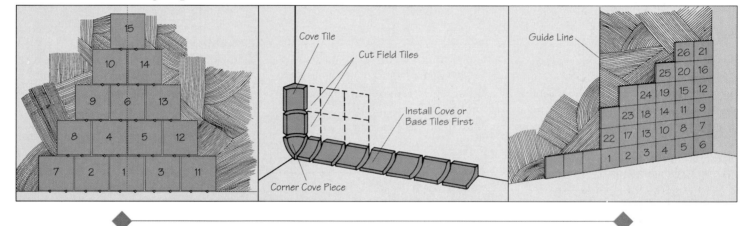

4. Cut Tiles

There are two cutting techniques that you will need to learn: one for straight cuts, one for odd shapes.

Straight Cuts. Use a tile cutter to make straight cuts. It holds the tile in place while the surface is scored by a wheel. Run the cutting wheel back and forth, applying some pressure; then tip the handle back to break the tile along the score line. Tiles that have ridges on the back should be cut in the same direction the ridges run. The cut is likely to have some rough edges that should be squared off with a small piece of metal plaster lath.

Odd Shapes. To fit tile around a shower head or pipe, you must cut it bit by bit with tile nippers. This work requires a strong wrist and a lot of patience. Most pipe areas and holes that are cut around later will be covered by an escutcheon or flange, so the ragged edge will be concealed. To fit around pipes, cut the tile into two sections and nip out a semicircle, the size of the pipe, on both meeting edges. If you need a precise circular cut, drill it with a carbide-tipped hole saw, cutting from the back of the tile.

4. Cut Tiles

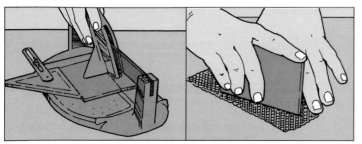
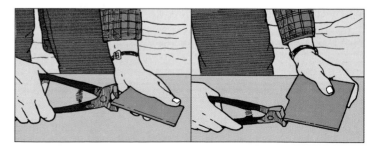

5. *Apply Adhesive*

Do not apply more adhesive than you can cover with tile before the adhesive skins over or sets up. The area you can cover depends on both the working time or "open" time of the adhesive and the speed at which you lay the tiles. If you are working on a small wall, usually you can cover the entire surface with adhesive and lay the tiles before the adhesive sets or loses its tack. On larger walls, start by working in small sections (for example, 4 feet by 4 feet); then work up to larger areas when you get a better feeling for the working time.

Spread the adhesive using the method and notched-trowel size

5. Apply Adhesive

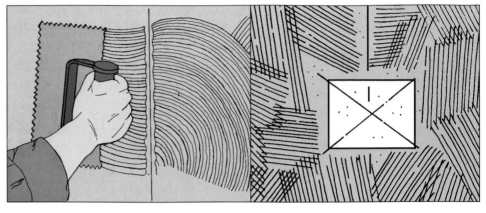

recommended by the manufacturer. Some adhesives are spread at an angle to the tile; others are spread in overlapping arcs. Be careful not to cover your working lines with adhesive. If your tile is

extra thick or has a deep-ridged back pattern, butter the backside of the tile with adhesive. Keep the appropriate solvent on hand to clean off your trowel and wipe up spills as you work.

6. *Lay the Tile*

After spreading the adhesive, press each full tile into place, using a slight twisting motion to bed it firmly into the adhesive. Do not slide the tiles against each other, or you will end up with excess adhesive in the grout joints. If adhesive does bulk up, clean it out before it hardens.

As you lay the tiles, frequently check their alignment with a level and make sure you maintain uniform grout spacing. After laying a section of tiles, use a beating block to ensure tiles are flat and firmly embedded in the adhesive. The block should be large enough to cover several tiles at a time. Slide it across the tiled surface while tapping the block lightly with a rubber mallet. Check tiles frequently with a straightedge to make sure they are level. If a tile "sinks" below the surface of surrounding tiles, pry it out, butter the back with adhesive, and then reset it.

When the installation requires a row of cut tiles, cut either horizontally or vertically and do not presume that all the cut tiles will be the same width. Each must be cut individually to fit its space.

6. Lay the Tile

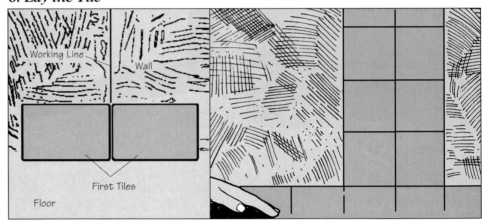

Working Line

Wall

First Tiles

Floor

Tile Sheets & Mosaic Tile

If you are using sheet-mounted tiles or ceramic mosaic tiles with perforated mountings, use the adhesive and mounting methods recommended by the manufacturer. Pregrouted tile panels usually come in a kit, which includes step-by-step instructions for installation.

Because you will be applying sheet tiles to a vertical surface, the sheets will have to be light

enough to lift into place and adjust once they are set into the adhesive. Tile sheets that are 2 feet square or smaller are easily managed by one person. Have a helper handy for installing larger sheets or cut them into manageable sections. The tiles can easily be separated from the backing sheets with a utility knife (see page 12).

7. *Mount Accessories*

Although you want to plan the location of ceramic accessories during the layout stage, these are the last items you should install. Soap dishes, towel racks, and similar accessories often are subject to unusual stress, and may require a special adhesive or epoxy putty to be mounted. Make sure that the mounting surface is clean, dry, and free of any tile adhesive. After you press the fixture into place, secure it to the wall with strips of tape until the adhesive dries.

Other fixtures that require screws or similar mechanical fasteners should be installed after the tile installation is complete and the grout has fully cured. To mount these, you will need to drill holes

7. *Mount Accessories*

Epoxy Putty

through the tile at screw-hole locations with a carbide-tipped masonry bit. Heavy fixtures, or those subject to stress, such as grab bars or towel racks, should be (if possible) fastened to the studs behind the tile and backing

material. Lightweight fixtures can be attached between the studs with toggle bolts or screws and plastic or metal screw anchors inserted into the hole. Be careful not to overtighten the latter, as they may crack the tile.

8. *Apply the Grout*

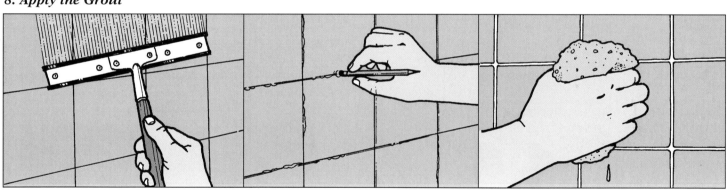

8. *Apply the Grout*

Before grouting, allow the adhesive to cure for at least 24 hours. Then, clean any dried adhesive or other debris from the joints. If you have unglazed tiles, they should be sealed before grouting. Make sure the sealer has fully cured before applying the grout. Reseal after grouting.

Do not use grout to fill the joint between the last row of wall tiles and any adjoining surfaces. Instead, use a flexible silicone caulk to allow for expansion and contraction.

Spread the Grout. Mix the grout and apply it with a squeegee,

spreading it diagonally across the joints between the tile. Be sure to pack the grout firmly into every joint, eliminating any air bubbles.

Shape the Joints. As soon as the grout becomes firm, use a wet sponge to wipe off any excess from the tile surface. Shape the grout joints with a striking tool.

Clean the Tiles. Clean off the tiles again and smooth the joints with a damp sponge. Allow a dry haze to form on the tile surface; then polish the tiles with a clean, damp cloth. In most cases, the grout will take several days to harden completely.

Seal the Tile

If the tile and grout joints require a sealer, apply it according to label directions. Usually, you must wait at least two weeks for the grout to fully cure before applying a sealer.

Make sure the tiled surface is clean and completely dry. Apply a thin, even coat of sealer with a foam-rubber paint roller or sponge; then wipe off any excess with a clean rag (see page 33).

5

TILING COUNTERTOPS

If you have never tiled before, a kitchen or bathroom countertop is a good first-time project. Generally, you will be covering a relatively small area, and most or all of the tiles will be laid on a flat, horizontal surface. Layout procedures are similar to those used for floors. To set the tiles, you will use a thin-set adhesive or mortar—either an organic mastic or epoxy adhesive (for plywood tops) or a latex-portland cement mortar (for backer-board tops).

The procedures outlined in this chapter for kitchen and bathroom counters also can be applied to wet bars, pass-throughs, serving counters, open shelving, and tiled tabletops.

Glazed ceramic tile makes an excellent countertop material because it resists heat, moisture, and stains. Although you can use thinner 1/4-inch glazed wall tiles for countertops in light-duty areas, such as a bathroom vanity, they are usually too thin to withstand hard knocks. Tiles made especially for countertop use are between 3/8 inch and 1/2 inch thick (to resist impact), with a durable glaze to resist abrasion and moisture penetration. They also come with the appropriate trim strips to finish off the front edge.

Tiles with a matte finish are generally preferable to those with highly glazed surfaces. The surface texture should be relatively smooth to facilitate cleaning, but not slick.

Thicker floor tiles are sometimes used on countertops, but they are harder to cut, and unglazed quarry or paver tiles must be sealed to prevent moisture and stain penetration.

Caution: Some tile and grout sealers remain toxic after they have dried, and should not be used in food-preparation areas. The same holds true for grouts and pregrouted tile panels treated with a mildewcide or fungicide. Silicone-based grouts should not be used for countertops, although silicone sealers may be used where dissimilar materials meet, or to set a sink or lavatory. Consult your tile dealer for appropriate tiles and related products.

◄ *Trim strips provide rounded edges and a neat border around the tiled countertop.*

► *For a uniform look in the kitchen, use the same tiles on the countertop and walls.*

In most cases, you will not need to make a scale drawing of the tile layout, as is often done with walls and floors. Usually, the tile can be dry-laid on the top, and arranged for the least number of cuts. Before you build the rough countertop for the tiles, though, decide in advance how the edges will be finished.

OVERHANG

First, determine how much overhang you want and what type of edge trim you will be using. Make sure the edge treatment you have chosen provides enough clearance for opening the top drawers in the cabinets (avoid finger-pinching situations) and for the installation of under-counter appliances, such as a dishwasher or trash compactor. If you run into clearance problems, choose a more narrow trim treatment, or build up the countertop thickness to accommodate the trim you have chosen (see pages 22-23).

Additional Bracing. Counters with large overhangs, such as pass-through counters, serving counters, or bars, will require some type of bracing to support the overhang.

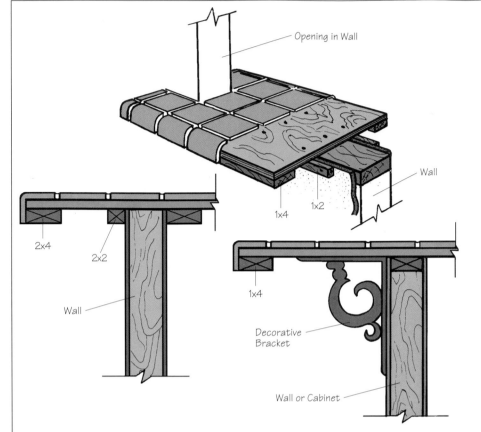

Additional Bracing. If your counter will have a large overhang, for a breakfast bar for instance, it will require bracing of some sort.

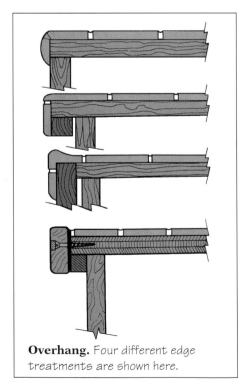

Overhang. Four different edge treatments are shown here.

▲ *A breakfast bar is a handy addition that frees up the adjacent countertop.*

As with walls and floors, the existing countertop surface must be clean, rigid, smooth, and level.

TILING OVER EXISTING MATERIAL

Ceramic Tile or Plastic Laminate. In most cases, you can lay the tile over an existing ceramic tile or plastic laminate countertop, provided the tile or laminate is firmly bonded to the substrate and is generally in good condition. Re-adhere any loose tiles to the counter with some of the adhesive you are using to set the new ones. Often you can re-adhere loose or bubbled sections of plastic laminate by carefully heating the loose section with a heat gun or iron to soften the adhesive beneath, and then re-adhering the laminate by rolling it with a rubber J-roller or tapping it with hammer and beating block. Before applying new tile, roughen the surface with silicon carbide sandpaper or a carborundum stone.

Wood. Wood butcher-block countertops make a good surface for setting tile, provided the counter is not cracked or warped. Before tiling, sand the surface smooth and flat with a belt sander. Consult your tile dealer for the appropriate sealer and adhesive. In wet areas you may need to install a waterproof membrane between the wood and new tile. A 4-mil polyethylene sheeting followed by cement backer board works well.

In all cases, tiling over an existing countertop will mean a change in counter height and thickness. This may create visual problems at edges (special trim tiles must be used) or interfere with the reinstallation of sinks or other countertop appliances. In many cases, it is easier in the long run to remove the old top and replace it with a plywood countertop (see next page).

▲ *A stark black-and-white countertop is brought to life with red accents and decorative tile strips.*

Estimate Amounts

Because ceramic tiles come in a variety of sizes, you will want to choose a size that will fit the space without too many awkward cuts. It is worth buying just a few tiles first so you can experiment. Most suppliers will sell single tiles. Alternatively, you can use cardboard cutouts, cut to the size of the tile plus half the width of the grout joint on all sides. Use the individual tiles or cutouts to estimate the amount of tile needed and the cuts that will be necessary. As always, count cut tiles as whole tiles and allow about 10 percent extra for mistakes.

When choosing underlayment materials for a rough countertop upon which tiles will be laid, there are two choices: plywood or a combination of plywood and cement backer board. The latter is preferable in wet locations, such as around sinks. In both cases, use 3/4-inch exterior plywood (minimum B-D). Do not use interior plywood or particleboard.

PLYWOOD COUNTERTOPS

Because tile is heavy and inflexible, the plywood top must be rigid. Bracing beneath the top may or may not be required. Typically, the cabinets or counter-base framing should include crossbraces spaced 36 inches apart (or less) for countertops up to 24 inches wide, and 18 to 24 inches apart for wider tops. You can use 1x2s on edge or 2x4s laid flat for the crossbraces. If the top is to be made up of two or more pieces, install additional braces to support the pieces where they join. Make sure the braces will not interfere with the sink or other drop-in fixtures. If you need a thicker rough top (to accommodate wide trim tiles, for instance), a second layer of plywood need not be added over the first. Instead, cut and attach 3- to 4-inch-wide plywood trim strips to the underside of the top, around the perimeter, and across the top where it will be attached to the cabinet or counter base with crossbraces. If the top is made from more than one piece, reinforce the joints from underneath with plywood strips.

Measure, cut, and fit the plywood to provide the appropriate overhang on all open edges. If the top is to butt against a wavy wall, cut it to the finish width plus about 1/8 inch more than the maximum depth of the wall irregularities. Then, use a compass to scribe the top pieces, and cut to fit.

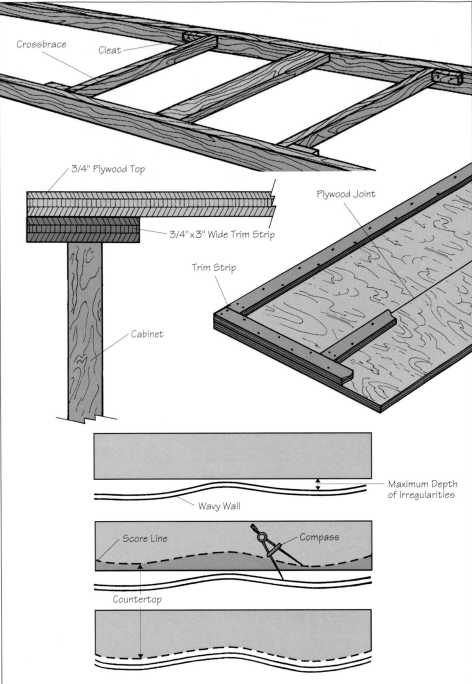

Plywood Countertops. In some cases, crossbraces are necessary. Add trim strips for smooth edges and reinforcing strips where panels join. If the top is to butt against a wavy wall, special measures are necessary.

Place the rough countertop on the cabinets or counter base and check for level in both directions. The counter should not be more than 1/8 inch out of level in 10 feet. If necessary, add shims to level it.

Working from underneath, drill two evenly spaced pilot holes into each brace. Place the plywood top on the cabinets or base, and screw the top to the base, through the braces. Attach filler strips to the front and side edges to support the trim tiles. After the top is attached, check it to make sure it is flat and level. If not, back off the screws and add shims.

PLYWOOD & BACKER BOARD COUNTERTOP

1. Install Plywood

Install a 3/4-inch plywood top (see previous page). If the countertop is to be subjected to water, staple a layer of 4-mil polyethylene film or 15-pound building felt over the entire surface. Or you can use a trowel-applied membrane.

2. Cut Backer Board

Cut 1/2-inch backer board pieces to size, using a circular saw equipped with a carborundum blade.

3. Attach Backer Board

Nail or screw the pieces to the top, using 1¼-inch galvanized roofing nails or galvanized drywall screws. Space nails or screws 6 to 8 inches apart along edges and across the counter surface.

4. Seal Joints

Where backer board sheets abut, allow a 3/16-inch gap to be filled in with mortar. Joints between backer board sheets and all exposed edges should be taped with fiberglass-mesh tape and adhesive. When tiling over backer board, use an appropriate latex-cement mortar.

1. Install Plywood

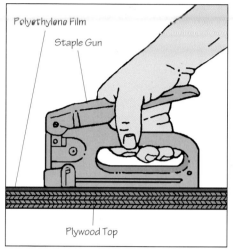

2. Cut Backer Board

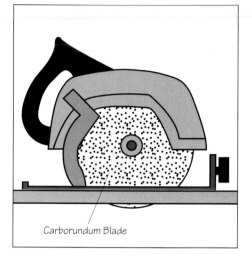

3. Attach Backer Board

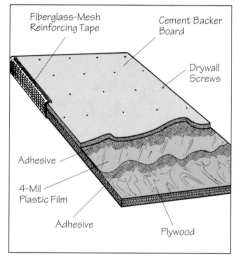

4. Seal Joints

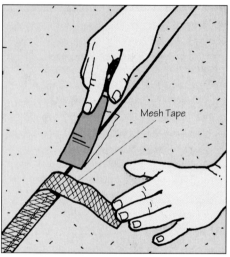

▼ *Ceramic tile is a smart, water-resistant choice for the bathroom counter.*

CUTOUTS FOR SINKS

If the countertop is to include a sink, you will need to decide if you want to install it before or after you lay the tile. This will, in part, determine the size of the cutout. Also, depending on the type of sink you are installing, you may have no choice.

If you choose to tile over the rim with bullnose tiles, you will need to cut a rabbet (notch) into the rough top around the sink opening, so that the rim sits flush with the surface. A deeper rabbet will enable you to use quarter-round trim. No matter which way you go, you will need to make the cutout before laying the tile. Also, it often is easier to measure and mark the cutout, and then remove the top for cutting.

1. Position Sink

Typically, the sink rim should be set back a minimum of 2 inches from the front edge of the counter and centered between the front and back. Also make sure that there are no braces or other obstructions underneath the countertop that interfere with the sink basin. If you have problems centering the cutout, measure to find its center underneath the countertop; then drive a nail up through the top and take

▲ *No matter what the shape or style, tile can be cut to fit around any sink.*

▶ *An elaborate island like this one benefits by tile's easy-to-clean quality.*

measurements from the nail on the top side.

2. Trace the Outline

Most new sinks come with templates for the cutout. If no template is available, position the sink upside down on the countertop and trace its outline.

3. Make the Cutout

Offset the cut lines by the width of the sink rim (typically 1/2 inch). For square cutouts, drill at each corner a hole that matches the radius of the sink corners; then

make straight cuts with a handsaw or portable circular saw. Use a jigsaw for round cutouts.

4. Install the Sink

Install the sink according to manufacturer's instructions. Use silicone caulk to seal joints between the sink and countertop and, again, between the sink and tile.

1. Position Sink

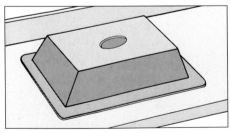

3. Make the Cutout

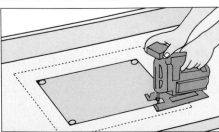

2. Trace the Outline

4. Install the Sink

Cutouts for Burner Tops

Cutouts for these are made the same way for sinks. For new drop-in appliances, the rough opening size is usually specified in the installation manual. If you are reinstalling an existing one, simply use the cutout in the old countertop as a guide. In practically all cases, the lip of a burner top rests on top of the tiled surface.

Do not caulk or grout the joint between the burner top and tile: You will want to remove the top occasionally for cleaning. Also, when you cut the tiles around the burner top, do not fit them too tightly; allow space for expansion and contraction as temperatures change.

ESTABLISH WORKING LINES

After you have prepared the countertop for tiling, loose-lay all the tiles (including trim tiles, if any) on the countertop to determine the best layout. If you are using square-edged tiles without spacer lugs, fit plastic tile spacers between the tiles to allow for grout joints.

Ideally, your layout should be arranged for the least number of cuts. Be sure to take into account the width of trim tiles when laying the whole tiles. If you plan to have a wood edging, butt the whole tiles up to the front edge of the surface. If the tiles have spacer lugs, there will be a grout joint between the tile and wood molding; if not, the tiled edge will be flush against it. Always work from front to back so that any cut tiles will fall at the back.

Rectangular Countertop.
If you are tiling a rectangular countertop, find and mark the center of the front edge of the countertop.

(If there is a sink, use the center-point of the sink as your starting point.) Then, match the center of a tile to this mark and lay a row of loose tiles on each side along the front edge. If the countertop is open at both ends, adjust the tiles so that any cut tiles at each end are equal in width. If the cut tiles are much less than half a tile wide, shift the row of tiles by half a tile width or adjust the grout joint width to avoid this situation. If the counter is open at only one end, lay out the tiles with fill tiles along the open end and cut tiles along the wall at the opposite end. If the

counter is freestanding, plan the layout in such a way that border tiles are equal all the way around.

L-Shaped Countertop.
For an L-shaped countertop, position a tile at the inside corner of the L and pencil around the edges to mark the starting point. Because this point cannot be adjusted, you may have to cut tiles to fit exposed edges. L-shaped countertops with corner sinks usually involve odd cuts of tile. In such cases, it is best to start with full tiles at the ends of each leg of the top and work toward the sink opening.

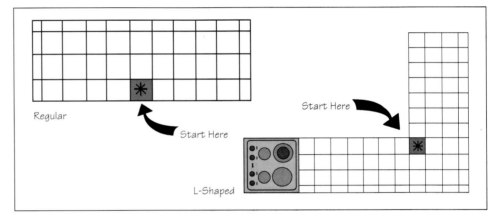

Regular

Start Here

Start Here

L-Shaped

Plan the Backsplash

If the counter will include a backsplash, make it a part of the layout.

The backsplash can be built out by a 3/4-inch plywood strip attached to the back edge of the rough counter-top before it is installed; but the simplest method is to adhere one or more courses of tile directly to the wall behind the countertop.

The last row of countertop tiles will determine the tiling sequence. If cut tiles are used for the last row on the countertop, butt these tiles against the wall; then place the backsplash tiles on top to hide the cut edges. If full tiles are used for the last row, leave space to fit the backsplash tiles behind them, if possible. In all cases,

position backsplash tiles to align with countertop tiles, and use full tiles for the first course on the backsplash. The top course can be finished off with bullnose tiles or quarter-round trim tiles, or the backsplash can be extended up to the bottom edge of an upper cabinet.

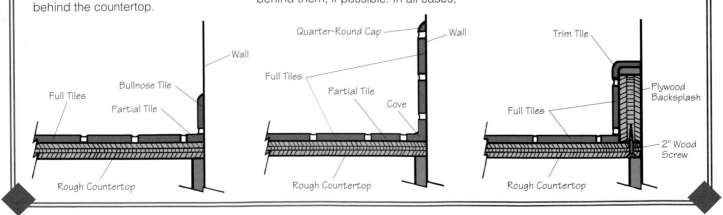

LAY THE FIELD TILE

Once you have determined the best layout, remove all the dry-laid tiles from the countertop.

1. Prepare Straight Edge

Tack a straight 1x2 guide strip along the front of the countertop for positioning the first row of tiles in a straight line.

If you are using sink caps or similar trim tiles along exposed edges, mark a line along the edges on the rough countertop to allow for the width of the trim tiles. Then, align the guide strip with the pencil line and use it as the edge for laying the first row of full tiles. Using this method, you will lay the trim tiles after all the field tiles are in place. If you are finishing the edge with bullnose tiles, set them before you fill in the field tiles.

Use a wood edging or bullnose tile edging so that it projects above surface the thickness of one tile. Mark the centerline (starting point from your layout) for the first tile on the guide strip. Extend the line to the back of the countertop to aid in aligning tile courses.

2. Lay First Course

With your starting point in mind, apply enough adhesive with a notched spreader to lay four or five tiles along the front edge. Lay the key tile first, butting it against the wood guide strip. Press it gently but firmly in place. Continue filling in tiles on either side of the key tile, using spacers, if necessary, until you cannot fit any more whole tiles. As you work, check tile alignment frequently with a straightedge or framing square; if the layout starts going askew and is not corrected at this point, the error will get progressively worse.

3. Lay Remaining Courses

Spread more adhesive and continue laying rows of full tiles, working back to the wall as far as you can go without cutting any tiles. Check alignment frequently with a straightedge or framing square as you work. Leave cut, partial tiles and trim tiles until last, but scrape off any adhesive before it dries in the area where these will be placed. Once the full tiles are set, use a hammer and bedding block to bed them firmly in the adhesive. (See page 27.) Then check the surface with a straightedge or square to make sure it is level. If any tiles have "sunk" below surrounding ones, gently pry them out, apply more adhesive, and reset them.

1. Prepare Straight Edge

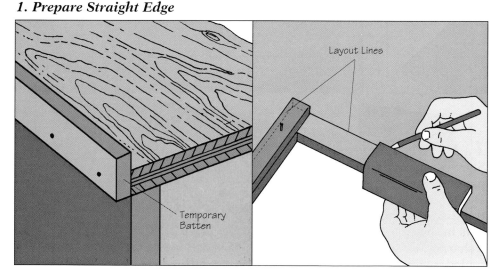

Layout Lines

Temporary Batten

2. Lay First Course

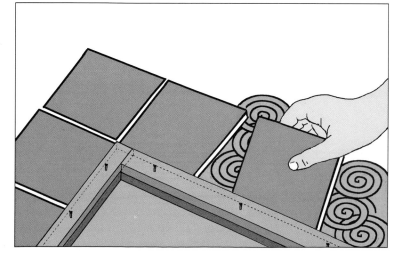

3. Lay Remaining Courses

INSTALL BACKSPLASH

Backsplash tiles are set so that they align with the countertop tiles. Use full tiles for the first course. The simplest method is to adhere one or more courses of tile directly to the wall behind the countertop. The top course can be finished with bullnose tiles or quarter-round trim tiles, or the backsplash can be extended all the way up to the bottom edge of an upper cabinet. If cut tiles are used for the last row on the countertop, butt these tiles against the wall; then place the backsplash tiles on top to hide the cut edges. If full tiles are used for the last row, fit the backsplash tiles behind them, if possible. Another way to build a backsplash is to attach a 3/4-inch plywood strip to the back edge of the rough countertop before it is installed.

If you are tiling around electrical outlets, turn off the power source before applying adhesive. If the outlet falls in the center of a tile, split the tile in two; then nibble out the opening in each half.

▼ *This custom-designed mural takes advantage of the long, uninterrupted backsplash found in this unique kitchen.*

SEAL, GROUT & CAULK

1. Prepare for Grouting

Allow the adhesive to set for an hour or two; then remove tile spacers (if used). Use a damp cloth to clean any adhesive off the tile surface; then use a screwdriver or other pointed object to remove any excess adhesive in the joints between the tiles. Allow the adhesive to cure for at least 24 hours before grouting. If you have used unglazed tiles on the countertop, seal them before grouting. Use the sealant recommended by the tile manufacturer. Make sure the sealer has cured fully before applying the grout.

2. Apply the Grout

Mix the grout according to the manufacturer's instructions, and apply with a rubber float or squeegee, spreading the grout diagonally across the joints between the tiles. Pack the grout firmly into every joint, carefully eliminating any air bubbles.

When the grout becomes firm, use a damp sponge or rag to wipe off any excess from the tile surface. Then, shape the grout joints using a striking tool (toothbrush handle, spoon, shaped stick, etc). Clean off the tiles again and smooth the joints with a damp sponge. Allow a dry haze to form on the tile surface; then polish the tile with a clean, damp cloth. In most cases, the grout will take several days to harden completely.

3. Install Sink & Drop-Ins

After the grout is dry, seal it with a finish sealer, and then install the sink and any other drop-in appliances. Installation methods vary for different types, so follow the maker's instructions carefully.

4. Caulk All Joints

Use a flexible silicone caulk to seal the joints where tiles meet with a sink or basin, and to fill the gap between the countertop (or backsplash) and the wall. As mentioned, do not use caulk or sealant around burner tops, as you will want to lift off the top occasionally for cleaning.

1. Prepare for Grouting

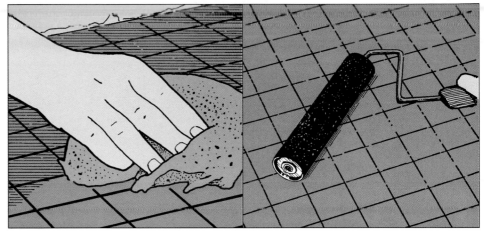

2. Apply the Grout

3. Install Sink & Drop-Ins

4. Caulk All Joints

6

TILING SHOWERS & TUB ENCLOSURES

F ew materials are as suitable—or as common— in showers and tub surrounds as glazed ceramic tile. Smooth, highly glazed tiles are easy to keep clean. The glazed surface should be durable enough to stand up to abrasive and chemical cleaners. If you are tiling the shower pan, select a vitreous or impervious glazed tile with a slip-resistant surface.

Layout and installation techniques for shower and tub surrounds are essentially the same as those for walls, so read "Tiling Walls" (pages 60-81) to become familiar with the procedures.

More than any other tiled surface in the house, a tub surround or shower enclosure will be subjected to water and steam, so the tile installation and backing must be perfectly watertight. For maximum protection against water penetration between the tiles, you will need a water-resistant adhesive and grout (latex thin-sets are usually used). Some grouts also contain additives that help prevent the growth of mildew, a continuing problem in poorly ventilated bathrooms.

Perhaps the easiest way to tile a shower enclosure or tub surround is with pregrouted ceramic tile panels (see page 12). As mentioned, the panels come in a variety of sizes, although color options are limited. If you are tiling a shower, you will be working in tight quarters, so it is usually preferable to work with smaller sheets: 12-inch x 12-inch panels containing nine 4-inch x 4-inch tiles are easily manageable. Larger panels are generally preferred for tub surrounds because there are fewer panel joints to seal, lessening the chance of leaks through grout joints. Sheet-mounted tile (without grout) and ceramic mosaic tiles are two other alternatives to setting tiles individually.

◀ *This whirlpool becomes a haven when tucked neatly into a bathroom corner, decorated with slightly undulating tiles and a diamond border.*

▶ *The same tile used in the bathroom area is extended to the shower enclosure, creating a greater sense of space.*

▲ *A shell border complements the vine and stripe pattern in this quaintly decorated tub enclosure.*

Often, do-it-yourselfers are faced with the decision of whether or not to tile over existing tile. As long as the tile is in good shape, firmly bonded to the wall, and there is no water damage behind the wall, it can be tiled over (make sure the added thickness of the new tile will not interfere with plumbing fixtures). In all cases, clean the surface thoroughly and roughen it with a carborundum stone or silicon carbide sandpaper to assure an adhesive bond. (See pages 22-23 for trim treatments.)

A molded fiberglass enclosure is too thin and flexible to tile over, so remove the unit and install an appropriate substrate.

TILE OVER EXISTING TILE

If you are tiling over existing tile, clean the surface to remove any dirt, soap scum, or other contaminants.

Roughen the surface with sandpaper or a carborundum stone, and rinse the surface with clean water to remove any sanding dust. Reglue loose tiles and refill holes with an all-purpose patching compound.

 **Caution:** Wear a mask when sanding a tile surface.

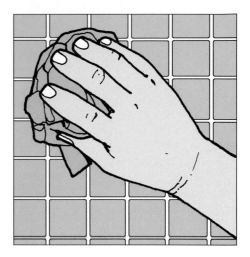

Investigate Water Damage

Loose tiles or any flexing in the wall may be an indication of water damage. Missing or cracked grout also should be investigated. Water damage to the wall is not always apparent from the tile surface, especially if caused by leaky plumbing. If you can access the area from underneath the house, look for water stains in the subflooring. In some houses, there is an access panel to water-supply lines on the other side of the wall. If no such panel exists, remove several tiles around the faucets, tub spout, and shower head and inspect the substrate. If it is damp or crumbly, you will need to remove all the tiles and damaged sections, fix the leak, and install new backing. Also remove a couple of tiles along the joints where the tile meets the tub or shower pan. Because water damage is often a slow process, any installation over 20 years old should be closely examined.

REMOVE EXISTING TILE

If you are removing the existing tile, be prepared for a messy and potentially dangerous job.

1. Protect Surrounding Surfaces

First, cut a piece of 1/4-inch plywood or particleboard to fit over the tub or shower pan. This will protect the surface from falling tiles and mortar. Then lay a heavy canvas tarp over the plywood and another one on the floor.

2. Remove Tiles

Use a hammer and wide-blade mason's chisel to remove the tiles, starting from the top course and working downward toward the tub or pan. You may want to place a large bucket directly beneath the tiles you are removing so tiles drop directly into the bucket as you knock them off the wall. This makes cleanup easier.

3. Remove Mortar Bed

To remove a mortar bed, use the hammer and chisel to cut the dry mortar into manageable sections. Then, starting at the top, use a prybar to pry the sections away from the wall. If the mortar has been reinforced with wire mesh, cut through the mesh with wire clippers to release the sections of mortar from the wall. Work slowly and carefully and try to avoid letting large chunks of mortar fall onto the tub or pan beneath.

4. Remove Barrier & Nails

When you have removed all the mortar, tear off any tar paper or other moisture barrier and remove any projecting nails from the studs.

5. Repair Substrate

When you remove tiles or other adhesive-applied materials from wallboard, some of the paper facing usually tears off, exposing the gypsum core. Once this happens,

1. Protect Surrounding Surfaces

3. Remove Mortar Bed

5. Repair Substrate

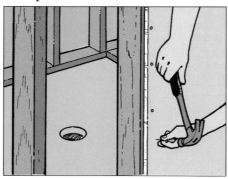

the wallboard cannot be satisfactorily waterproofed, so you will either need to remove it or install another layer of suitable backing material over it. Also, if plaster or conventional wallboard has been used for the walls around the tub or shower, cover it or replace it with a suitable backing.

6. Install Plumbing

Faucet valves and shower fittings should be installed before you tile so you can pack the openings around them with adhesive. Do not attach the shower head, faucet handles, or escutcheons at this time, as they will just get in the

2. Remove Tiles

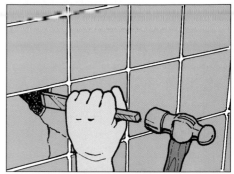

4. Remove Barrier & Nails

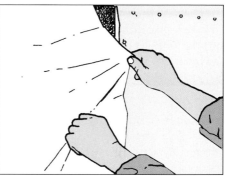

6. Install Plumbing

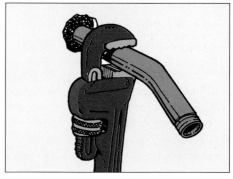

way of tiling. This also eliminates the possibility of accidentally knocking the handles to the "on" position and getting a bath or shower while you are working.

Caution: To protect yourself from falling tiles and sharp edges, wear a hard hat, safety goggles, heavy canvas gloves, and a heavy, long-sleeved shirt. Also wear a dust mask. If you are removing a mortar bed in a shower stall, wear heavy boots. Large chunks of mortar are heavy and can fall off the wall unexpectedly, and broken ceramic tiles can cut a person as easily as broken shards of glass.

WALLBOARD & BACKER BOARD

For thin-set installations, you can use one of two materials: water-resistant (green) wallboard, or, better, cement backer board.

Install Panels. Both materials require a special joint tape and mastic to make the panel joints and exposed edges water-resistant. When you install green wallboard, leave a 1/4-inch gap between the bottom of the panel and the lip of the tub; install cement backer board all the way to the lip. Follow the manufacturer's instructions for specific installation techniques.

Waterproof Membranes. Cement backer board will not be affected by water, but water may eventually penetrate through the backer board, especially in the hot, humid environment of a tub or shower enclosure. For this reason, building codes in most areas now require that a waterproof membrane—either 15-pound building felt (tar paper) or 4-mil polyethylene sheeting—be installed between the studs and backing material. Because building codes and practices vary in different communities, check with your local building department for specific requirements.

Wallboard Walls

Even with water-resistant tiles, adhesives, and grouts, some moisture eventually will penetrate, so the backing must be water-resistant as well. Plastered walls or walls covered with conventional wallboard will eventually deteriorate when subjected to moisture, so they do not make suitable substrates. Remove these and replace them with a suitable water-resistant backing, such as green wallboard or cement backer board.

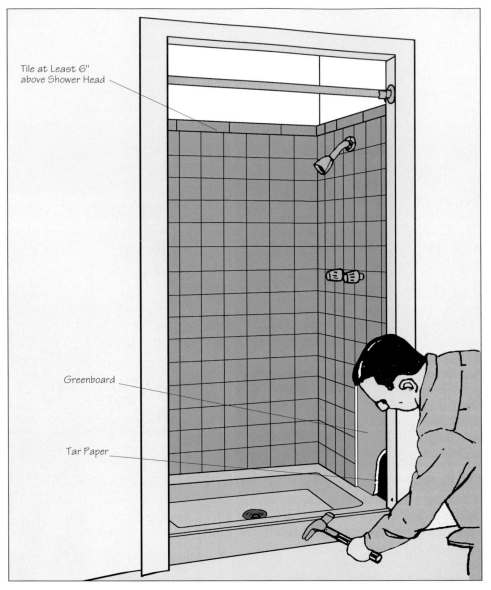

Tile at Least 6" above Shower Head

Greenboard

Tar Paper

▼ *A tiled wainscoting decorates this secluded tub alcove.*

Laying out tiles for a tub surround or shower enclosure is basically the same as for walls. If you also are tiling the shower floor, see pages 40-42 for basic layout and estimating considerations. If you are incorporating a design into the walls, a scale drawing will help you visualize the finished installation and serve as a guide for estimating the number of tiles.

Because you will be working in a confined area, tile the back wall first; then fill in the sidewalls, and, finally, stub walls and threshold (if any). If you proceed in this way, you are less likely to disturb tiles that have already been set.

ESTABLISH WORKING LINES

The back wall of the shower or tub surround is the one that will be the most visible, so establish your vertical and horizontal working lines on this wall first. Then, project the horizontal lines to the adjoining walls and center vertical working lines on each wall to be tiled.

Ideally, you want a course of full tiles around the tub rim or shower pan. When you establish the horizontal line, allow for a 1/8-inch gap between the tub or shower pan and the first course of tiles surrounding it. The gap will be filled with a mildew-resistant silicone or acrylic or latex tub-and-tile caulk to allow for expansion and contraction between the two dissimilar materials.

1. Draw the Horizontal Line

If the tub or shower pan is level to within 1/8 inch, locate the horizontal line from the high point of the rim, measuring 1/8 inch plus the width of one whole tile (or tile trim strip if you are using trims) plus one grout joint. The slight variation in the gap between the rim and first course of tiles will not be noticeable after it is caulked. If the

▲ *The same tile that is used on the floor can be run up the side of the tub. Garden windows allow an exceptional amount of light to enter.*

tub or pan is more than 1/8 inch out of level, strike the horizontal line from the low end (again, measuring 1/8 inch plus one tile and one grout joint). The first tile in the bottom course will be a whole tile; the rest will need to be taper-cut to maintain the required 1/8-inch gap.

2. Install Battens

As mentioned, the second course above the rim is set first, supported by a batten attached to the working

line. The batten helps maintain alignment and prevents the tiles from slipping until the adhesive sets. Once the tiles are set, remove the batten and set the first course of tiles. Wood spacers or matchsticks can be used to maintain the gap between the rim and first course. Then fill in the rest of the tiles, using one of the methods described on page 56.

1. Draw the Horizontal Line

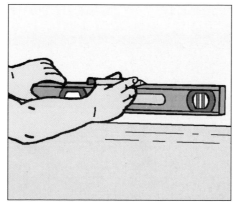

2. Install Battens

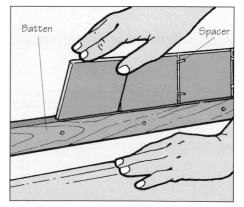

Batten

Spacer

3. *Establish Vertical Line*

Center the vertical working line on the back wall; then adjust it so any cut tiles at each end will be more than half a tile wide and equal in width. Now establish the vertical lines on the side walls. The installation will look best if cut tiles on the inside corners of the end walls are equal in width to those on the back wall. Also take into consideration the location of plumbing fittings when planning the layout.

If you are using trim tiles at inside and outside corners, figure their width into the layout and adjust the working lines accordingly.

4. *Establish Additional Working Lines*

Establishing additional working lines for trim pieces will facilitate the tile-setting process. If you are tiling a shower enclosure with stub walls on either side of the opening, plan on cutting tiles to fit around the threshold to maintain continuous grout lines. If possible, adjust layout lines to avoid extremely narrow-cut tiles around the opening.

5. *Apply the Adhesive*

Spread adhesive only along the surface you are going to tile at the moment. Lay the first tile against the vertical working line where it meets the batten; then work outward to each corner, allowing for grout lines between each tile. If you must cut tiles at either corner, cut the one preceding the vertical trim tiles (if used).

When applying the adhesive and setting the tile, complete one full wall before starting on the next. If you apply adhesive to more than one wall before setting the tiles, the job will become very messy—very quickly.

Do not spread more adhesive than you can cover with tile before the adhesive sets up or skins over (see adhesive label for open times). If you are covering a small area of the wall, often it is possible to cover the entire surface with adhesive and lay the tiles before the adhesive sets up or loses its tack. On larger surfaces, fill in small sections at a time. Pack plenty of adhesive into all openings around plumbing fittings to help waterproof the installation. After the tiles are installed around the fittings, fill the space with caulk. For more on adhesive application, bedding the tiles, grouting, and sealing the joints, see pages 57-58.

6. *Apply Grout*

For information on grouting and sealing the joints, see page 59.

3. Establish the Vertical Line

Plumb Line

4. Establish Additional Working Lines

5. Apply the Adhesive

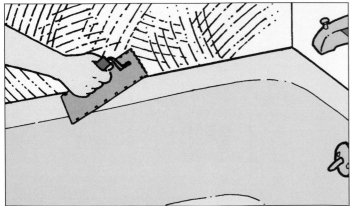

6. Apply Grout

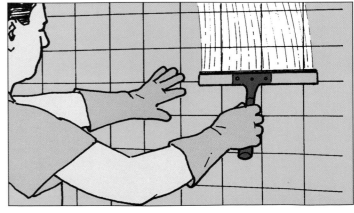

In conventional tub and shower surrounds, the tile usually extends from the top edges of the tub to about 6 to 8 inches above the shower head, or all the way to the ceiling. Tubs without shower heads can be fitted with a tiled backsplash extending 1 to 3 feet above the tub, depending on how much splashing the bathers like to do. In situations where the walls extend beyond the sides of the

tub but you do not want to tile the entire wall, it looks neater if the surround is extended by the width of one tile beyond the front edge of the tub and down to floor level. This also makes for a more water-proof installation. Typically, the last vertical row of field tiles is set flush to the front edge of the tub, and bullnose tiles or trim tiles are used to finish off the edges of the surround.

The ceiling above the tub or shower enclosure also may be tiled, but the practice usually is not recommended, especially for beginners, because the tiles are difficult to set. (You need to use a fast-setting adhesive as well as a plywood sheet supported by long wooden props to keep the tiles in place until the adhesive sets up.) Also, incorrectly installed tiles may fall off—a potential hazard to bathers.

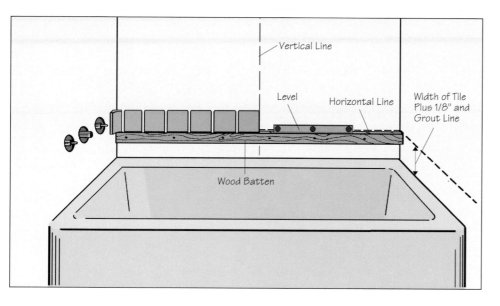

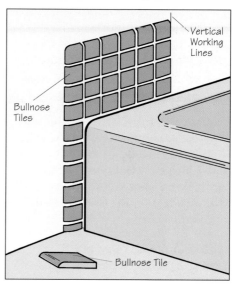

Soap Dishes & Grab Bars

If you are installing a ceramic soap dish, position it to the horizontal and vertical grout lines of surrounding field tiles; then mark its location on the wall. Many wall tiles come with matching accessories sized in multiples of the tile size. Some pieces have flanges that overlap surrounding tiles. Mark off the dimension of

the part that will sit flush to the wall. If the soap dish is to be recessed, cut any holes and install any required framing before you tile. Soap dishes attached directly to the wall require a stronger adhesive than the tile, so do not apply tile adhesive within this area. The soap dish itself will be mounted

after you tile the wall around its marked location.

Conversely, you should install fittings for grab bars before you tile. Typically, each end of the bar is mounted into studs behind the wallcovering or backing; then the tiles are cut to fit around them.

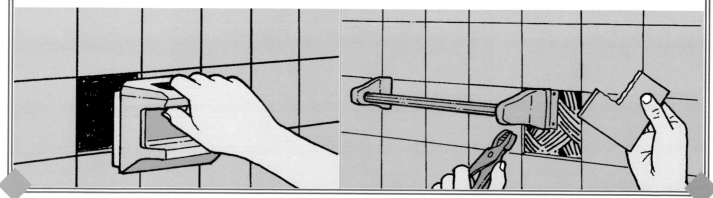

If you are building a shower stall from scratch, the easiest way is to install a prefabricated fiberglass shower pan, and then tile the walls above it. The pans themselves are easy to install; follow manufacturer's instructions.

TILE THE SHOWER PAN

If you want a tiled shower floor, the most common practice is to build a custom-made pan of reinforced concrete or mortar. Such pans are installed when a fiberglass pan will not fit the exact space of the shower stall, or if you simply prefer the look of a tiled shower floor to the look of a fiberglass pan.

As with tiled tubs, the pan must be watertight, adequately reinforced, and slightly sloped toward the drain. Mortar-bed pans typically are installed over wood subfloors, whereas reinforced concrete pans are installed directly on grade (usually in houses with concrete slab floors). As with concrete tubs, building a watertight shower pan requires experience, so we recommend that you have a qualified contractor install the pan, and then you can tile it along with the rest of the enclosure.

CLOSE OFF THE SHOWER

The first decision you must make is whether you want to install a glass shower door or simply hang a shower curtain across the opening. The second is whether or not you want to build stub walls on either side of the opening. Stub walls are framed in before the tile and backing are installed. The walls form a rough opening sized to accommodate the width and height of the shower door (the finished opening dimensions include the thickness of the backing and tile placed over the framing). The stub wall also will include a threshold. If a reinforced concrete or mortar pan will be installed, the threshold forms the front edge. If a fiberglass pan will be installed, the pan flange is attached

▲ *The checked tile pattern found in the shower enclosure mimics the bigger checks on the floor.*

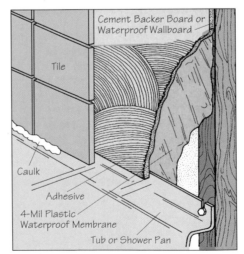

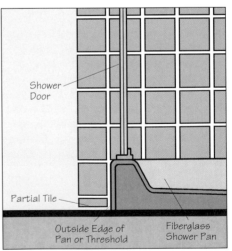

to the sole plate of the threshold. Waterproofing requirements for stub walls are the same as for the other walls of the enclosure.

If you decide not to use stub walls, the front edge of the fiberglass pan

serves as a threshold. On concrete or mortar pans, the threshold is framed in when the pan is built. On such installations, it usually is best to extend the tiled enclosure past the front edge of the pan, as you would for a tub.

The easiest method for making a raised enclosure is to buy a drop-in tub and frame the platform around it.

1. Design the Platform

The platform must be sturdy enough to support the weight of the tub and tile. In addition, the surfaces on which you lay the tile must be waterproof. Use basic wood framing construction. Then, cover the entire surface with a layer of 3/4-inch plywood topped with a layer of 1/2-inch cement backer board. The tiles themselves should be slip-resistant. The platform must meet the same installation requirements as a countertop with a drop-in sink. (Refer to page 88.) The basic framing in the drawing can be modified to fit your tub and bathroom. Also, the installation will look better if you purchase the tiles first, and then design the platform size in multiples of full tiles so that no tiles have to be cut.

After you have designed the platform, but before you build it, you will need to determine the exact location of water-supply lines and rough drain plumbing beneath and install them. Because this may require an extensive reworking of the existing plumbing, you may want to have a plumber do the work.

Plan the building sequence so that you can make the connections to the tub before the platform is completely enclosed, or cut a hole through the wall at the head of the tub so that you can access the connections from an adjoining room. To facilitate any future repairs, it is best to cover the hole with a removable access panel.

2. Frame the Platform

Use pressure-treated lumber and galvanized nails or screws for all framing components. If the platform abuts one or more walls, remove the wallboard up to the height of the platform and fasten the platform directly to the wall

▲ *With its mosaic tiled steps, this raised tub becomes a central focal point in the bathroom.*

framing. If the wallcovering is conventional plaster or wallboard, replace it with water-resistant wallboard or cement backer board (see page 72). While building the platform, check frequently to make sure it is level. If the floor beneath the platform is not level, use shims to correct this condition. The steps should have a very slight downward slope, from back to front, so water will not collect on them.

1. Design the Platform

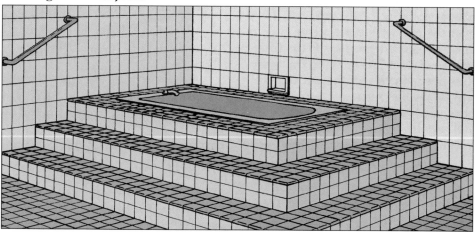

2. Frame the Platform

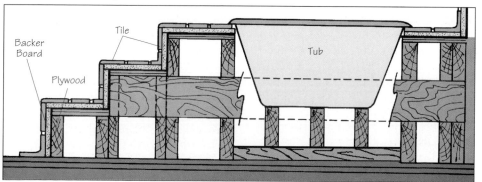
Backer Board — Tile — Plywood — Tub

3. Insert the Tub

There are two basic options for inserting a tub in the platform. The first calls for laying the tiles up to the edge of the tub cutout in the platform, and then setting the tub in place over the tiles.

In the second, the tub is set into the cutout, then the top of the rim is tiled over, either with bullnose tiles or quarter-round tile trim. The method you choose will determine the exact dimensions of the tub cutout in the platform.

Each method has its advantages and disadvantages, and the tub you buy may, in part, determine which you choose. In the first method, the weight of the tub (including water and occupant) may crack the tiles. However, this method provides a much neater finished appearance because the cut edges of the tile will be hidden by the tub rim. For the second method, you will need to rout a rabbet around the edges of the tub cutout so the rim sits flush with the rough platform surface. You then tile over the rim with bullnose or quarter-round trim tiles. If the first course of field tiles around the trim tiles needs to be cut, the cut edges will be visible. Also, oval tubs or ones with large radiused corners will require complicated cuts and irregularly shaped grout joints.

In both cases, all edges of the tub cutout must be firmly supported by the framing members beneath. Also, the tub rim should be well caulked to prevent water from running back under the lip and eventually rotting out the wood platform.

4. Tile the Platform

The layout for a tile platform combines the basic principles used for tiling walls and countertops (see Chapters 4 and 5). Any cut tiles should be more than a half tile wide, if possible. Be sure to include the width of grout joints when you

3. Insert the Tub

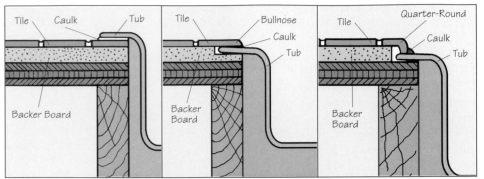

4. Tile the Platform

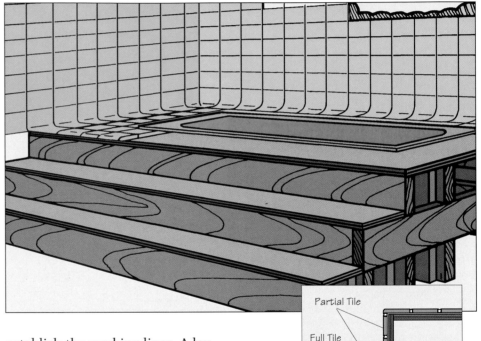

establish the working lines. A lay-out stick will help you determine exact locations for the tiles. (See page 41 for instructions on making a layout stick.)

Once you have planned the layout for the best tile arrangement and established your working lines, tile the surfaces in the following order: step risers, step treads, platform surface, platform sides, and walls surrounding platform. Bear in mind that if the tub is dropped in first, you will need to rout a rabbet around the edges of the tub cutout so the rim sits flush with the rough platform surface. Then tile over the rim with bullnose or quarter-round trim tiles. If the first course of field tiles around the trim tiles needs to be cut, the cut edges will be visible.

Also, oval tubs and those with large radiused corners will require complicated cuts and irregularly shaped grout joints.

If you are using cove trims where the platform meets the walls, install these pieces before you set the full tiles on either surface. The front edge of the step treads typically is finished off with bullnose tiles. You also can use special stair-nosing tiles for this purpose, if they are available. Do not use sink caps or other trim pieces that will trap water on the step treads.

Create your own custom-tiled tub, either sunken flush to the floor, or raised above floor level (your only alternative if the tub is on a second story). Tiled tubs can be virtually any shape or size you want. Curved or free-form tubs are generally covered with small ceramic mosaic tiles. Building such a tub requires hard, back-breaking work, as well as considerable experience in plumbing and concrete work.

The actual techniques involved are beyond the scope of this book. Hire professionals to build the concrete-mortar bed, install the plumbing, and prepare the surface to accept the tile. Then you can opt to do the easier job of tiling.

POUR A REINFORCED CONCRETE TUB

The preferred method for building a tiled tub is to pour a reinforced concrete shell. A waterproof membrane is applied over the concrete shell, followed by a thick-set mortar bed. Such a concrete "tank" requires a strong concrete footing set directly into the ground. It also must be waterproof, and the floor should slope slightly toward the drain.

BUILD A WOOD FORM

A second option requires building a wood form and applying a reinforced mortar bed over it. But

▲ *A tiled tub can be built to virtually any size or shape. This one uses two sizes of tile for a more intricate pattern.*

such installations must be well reinforced, or movement in the wood substructure will crack the mortar bed and tile, causing leaks. For this reason, the concrete tank is usually a better way to go.

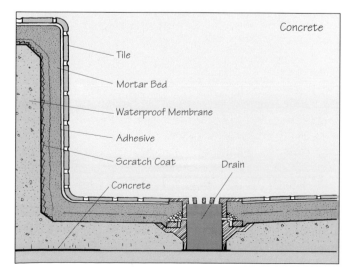

Concrete

Tile
Mortar Bed
Waterproof Membrane
Adhesive
Scratch Coat
Concrete
Drain

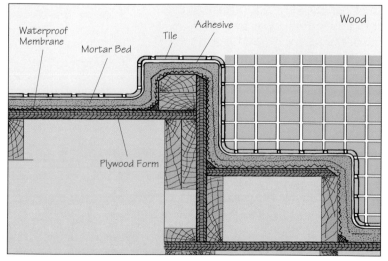

Wood

Waterproof Membrane
Mortar Bed
Tile
Adhesive
Plywood Form

7

OTHER INDOOR TILE PROJECTS

U p to this point, the most common indoor applications for ceramic tile—floors, walls, countertops, and tub or shower surrounds—have been covered. In this chapter, you will find four other popular tile projects: fireplace hearths and facings, wood-stove surrounds, tiled range hoods, and tiled stairs or steps. Because of its beauty and distinctive style, tile is a unique addition to all areas of the home; and once you begin working, you will realize that the creative possibilities are endless.

Each of these projects employs the basic layout principles and tiling techniques discussed in earlier chapters. As you become more accustomed to working with tile, you will probably come up with other projects of your own design.

▼ *As a practical, fireproof covering for a fireplace opening, tile also provides a multitude of decorating options.*

Whether you are building a new fireplace or simply want to change the face of an existing one, ceramic tile makes an elegant, fireproof covering for a hearth or fireplace face—either by itself or in conjunction with other materials. You can choose to tile the hearth only, the hearth and firebox surround, or even just a single row of tiles around the fireplace opening as an accent.

SELECT TILE & ADHESIVES

The tile that is selected for the hearth should be resistant to heat and heavy impact (such as a dropped log). Heavy-duty quarry tiles, pavers, or glazed floor tiles are good choices. Check with a tile dealer for recommendations.

If you are tiling over concrete, brick, or another masonry surface, use nonflammable heat-resistant mortar, such as a dry-set cement or latex-portland cement mortar. If you are tiling over a plywood subfloor, use a heat-resistant epoxy. Special cement-based and epoxy mortars that resist temperatures up to 360°F are available.

Whether the hearth is flush or raised, provide a 1/8-inch gap between the tiled hearth and surrounding floor, and fill it with silicone caulk, to allow for seasonal movement between the dissimilar materials. Use a heat-resistant dry-set or latex-cement grout to finish off the installation.

FIREPLACE HEARTH

The term "hearth" applies to the horizontal surface immediately in front of the fireplace opening that protects the floor against heat, sparks, and burning embers. In masonry fireplaces, the floor of the firebox itself is sometimes referred to as the inner hearth, and is constructed of dense, heat-resistant fire bricks, along with the rest of the fireplace interior.

The outer hearth in front of the fireplace may be brick, tile, stone, or other masonry material. A tiled hearth can be flush to the surrounding floor or raised above it. In new fireplace construction, you can extend the hearth any distance to either side of the fireplace itself, providing space for fireplace tools and equipment, wood, and fireside seating.

If you are installing a new fireplace, the hearth foundation on which you lay the tiles also must be made of noncombustible materials in strict accordance with local building codes. As a general rule, the foundation consists of a brick or poured concrete slab at least 4 inches thick, which extends at least 16 inches out and 8 inches to either side of the fireplace opening. If the opening is larger than 6 feet wide, the last two dimensions increase to 20 inches and 12 inches. If the existing hearth is not up to code, it is a good idea to bring it up to code before tiling it. Metal fireplace inserts and heat-recirculating fireplaces have their own set of requirements. Check local building codes for specifics.

FIREPLACE FACE

Ceramic tile can add new life to an outdated fireplace surround, covering up chipped bricks or damaged surfaces. Cover the entire face or use tiles in conjunction with other materials. The tiles used for the fireplace face need not be as thick or durable as those used for the hearth. In new fireplace construction, the builder will provide the appropriate backing—usually a smooth coat of mortar or plaster—for the tile. Then, the tiles are set directly into the wet mortar or plaster. Or, when the mortar dries, you can set the tiles over it with a latex-cement mortar. Metal fireplace surrounds may be made of tile backer board, wallboard, or similar material, depending on requirements. On existing surrounds, use a heat-resistant epoxy mortar to apply tile to wood, metal, or existing ceramic tile. Use heat-resistant cement mortars on masonry surfaces.

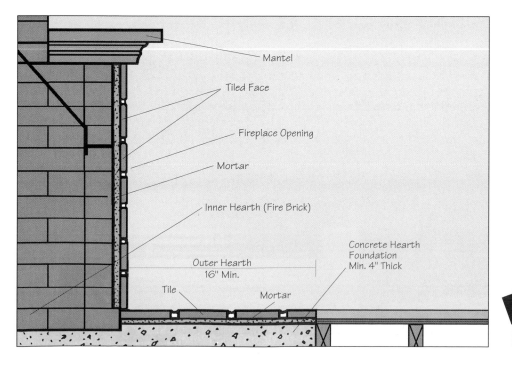

Mantel

Tiled Face

Fireplace Opening

Mortar

Inner Hearth (Fire Brick)

Concrete Hearth Foundation Min. 4" Thick

Outer Hearth 16" Min.

Tile

Mortar

Caution: Under no circumstances should you use organic adhesives. They are flammable.

TILE THE HEARTH

You can set ceramic tile over an existing hearth of brick, concrete, or old tile, provided the surface is relatively flat. Rigidity usually is not a problem with masonry, although a flush hearth set directly on weak wood may be too flexible to tile over (see pages 47-48).

If you are dealing with a brick or other rough surface, a thick bond coat of mortar will fill in the mortar joints and provide a smooth surface for the tile.

1. Level & Clean
Grind down any high spots; then clean the surface thoroughly to remove any soot or dirt.

2. Apply Bond Coat
Apply a smooth bond coat of mortar or underlayment, filling in any irregularities.

3. Set the Tiles
When the bond coat dries, apply a second coat of mortar to set the tiles according to the manufacturer's instructions. For more on tiling over existing tile, see page 46.

If you are tiling a flush hearth, use the same tiling sequence used for a countertop (see pages 90-95). Any cut tiles should be placed at the back where the hearth meets the firebox.

To tile a raised hearth, start by tiling the front, and then the sides, using the same layout procedure that is used for walls (see pages 77-81). If you are using trim tiles on the top edges of the hearth, install these before you lay the field tiles across the top. Again, place any cut tiles at the back of the hearth, and at floor level.

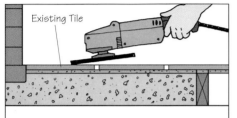

1. Level & Clean

Existing Tile

2. Apply Bond Coat

3. Set the Tiles

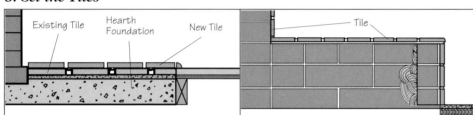

Existing Tile   Hearth Foundation   New Tile

Tile

ENLARGE AN EXISTING HEARTH

You may want to extend a hearth to provide additional protection or to change its appearance. If the hearth is covered with tile already, you may have a tough time finding matching tiles. If so, use a contrasting tile border to complement the old tile.

Whether you are extending a floor-level hearth or a raised hearth, you will need to provide a suitable backing for the extension. Most "floor-level" hearths actually are 1/4 to 1/2 inch higher than the floor.

Wood strip, plank, or particleboard underlayment (usually found under carpeted floors) do not make suitable substrates for ceramic tile. Remove these materials down to the plywood subfloor. Depending on the thickness of the new and existing tile, filler strips of 1/4- to 1/2-inch cement backer board may have to be added to the extension area. Laminate the strips to the existing plywood subfloor with latex mortar and ring-shank nails. Leave a 1/8-inch gap between the old hearth and the extension to provide for expansion. It will be filled in with tile adhesive later.

Tiling a hearth is similar to tiling a countertop or raised tub platform. If the existing hearth is 1 to 2 inches higher than the floor, use layers of 1/2-inch tile backer board to raise the extension flush with the existing hearth. Use latex mortar to laminate each layer, combined with nails long enough to reach into the subfloor. If the hearth is 2 to 4 inches high, you can build a framework of 2x4s, either laid flat or on edge to build up the extension. Use wider two-by lumber for higher hearths. Plan the hearth dimensions in multiples of full tiles to avoid cut tiles.

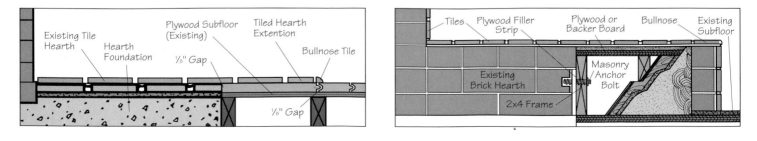

Existing Tile Hearth   Hearth Foundation   Plywood Subfloor (Existing)   ⅛" Gap   Tiled Hearth Extension   Bullnose Tile   ⅛" Gap

Tiles   Plywood Filler Strip   Plywood or Backer Board   Bullnose   Existing Subfloor   Existing Brick Hearth   Masonry Anchor Bolt   2x4 Frame

TILE THE FACE

Because fireplaces come in many different designs and materials, we cannot give specific tiling instructions for every situation. On existing surrounds, use a heat-resistant epoxy to apply tile to wood, metal, wallboard, or existing ceramic tile. Use heat-resistant cement mortars on masonry surfaces or cement backer board. Ask a tile dealer which is best for you.

A common tiling project consists of a single row of decorative tiles around a prefabricated fireplace insert, with a wood mantel designed around it. In this case, the tiles are adhered directly to the existing wall around the fireplace opening; the wood mantel components are added after the tiles have been set. Adapt these tile-setting techniques to your specific project.

1. Set Horizontal Row

Tack a 1x2 batten across the top of the the fireplace opening to support the horizontal row of tiles. Spread adhesive only on the wall area to be tiled. Set the horizontal row of tiles, spacing them so the end tiles align with the sides of the fireplace opening.

2. Remove Batten

When the adhesive has set (about 2 hours), remove the batten and set the tiles on both sides of the opening.

3. Apply Grout

Using a rubber float or squeegee, apply grout to the tile joints. If you used spacers, remove them. Strike the grout joints.

4. Install Mantel or Trim

Add wood mantel pieces, if used. Quarter-round tile trim pieces also can be used.

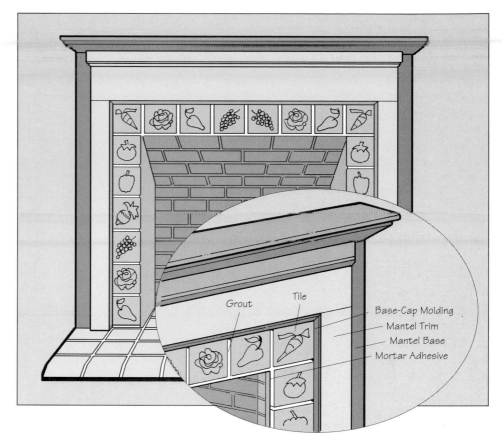

Grout · Tile · Base-Cap Molding · Mantel Trim · Mantel Base · Mortar Adhesive

1. Set Horizontal Row

1x2 Batten

2. Remove Batten

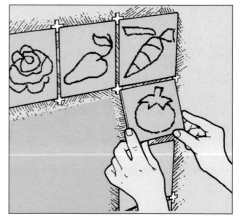

3. Apply Grout

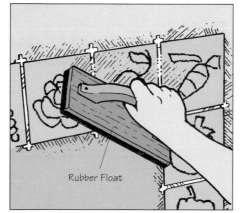

Rubber Float

4. Install Mantel or Trim

Ceramic tile is a good choice for hearths around wood stoves and freestanding fireplaces. The hearth can be flush or raised, round or square. If you place the unit close to one or more walls, these also should be fireproofed.

PRECAUTIONS

Building and Fire Codes. Local codes will dictate the size of the hearth, clearances, and the type of protective backing required. In most communities, the codes are quite specific and may require building permits.

Insurance Policies. Your homeowner's insurance rates may be affected by the installation, so be sure to inform your insurance company. After the stove is installed, have a building inspector and your insurance representative inspect the stove. Their written approval is necessary to ensure that your policy will cover any damages resulting from a stove-caused fire.

CLEARANCES

Typically, the codes require minimum clearances between the stove and any combustible surfaces (any surface that contains any flammable material). For example, wood-frame walls and floors covered with a noncombustible surface, such as wallboard or tile, still are considered combustible. Solid masonry walls (brick, stone, or concrete) are considered noncombustible, unless covered with a combustible material, such as paint, wallpaper, wood, or carpeting.

The clearances between the stove (front, sides, and rear) and combustible surfaces vary with the type of stove. Radiant stoves are those that enclose the fire with a single layer of metal, a Franklin fireplace for example. Minimum clearances are recommended by the National Fire Protection Association.

▲ *Pay close attention to building and fire codes when tiling the hearth around a wood stove.*

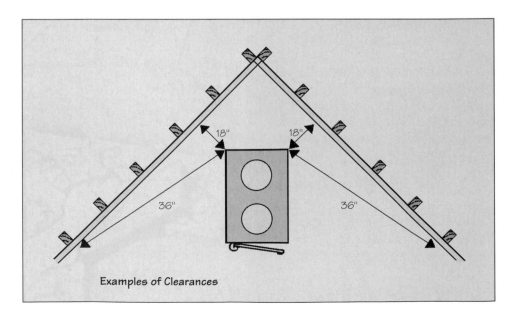

18"   18"

36"   36"

Examples of Clearances

When it comes to reducing clearances between combustible materials and the stove or fireplace, you have several options.

In most cases, the tile alone will not provide sufficient protection. Typically, a panel of 1/2-inch noncombustible insulation board or 24-gauge sheet metal spaced 1 inch away from the wall (with noncombustible spacers) is installed. Then the tile is set over it. Some places allow the use of cement backer board in lieu of insulation board. Check local codes.

LAY THE TILES

If you are building a hearth that will extend up one or more walls behind the stove or fireplace, position any cut tiles at the floor of the hearth in the back corners. If you need to cut tiles at the sides of the hearth floor or wall, arrange for cuts wider than half a tile and of equal width on both sides. The type of trim tiles used will depend on the height of the hearth's floor and the thickness of any protective backing applied to the walls behind the tile. Use a heat-resistant epoxy or cement-based mortar and grout. See pages 77-81 for specific tile-setting techniques.

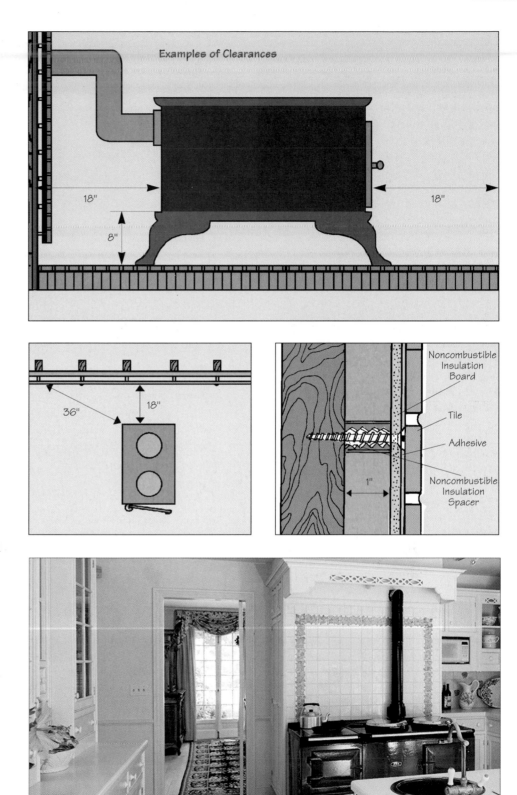

▲ *As a backdrop to an old-fashioned wood stove, these floral tiles create a decorative frame.*

"Zero-Clearance" Stoves

Many modern wood stoves and freestanding fireplaces are of the "zero-clearance" variety, which means they require little or no clearance between the firebox and combustible surfaces. However, these too should at least have a floor hearth to protect the floor in front of the firebox opening from errant sparks and embers.

SELECT TILE & ADHESIVES

As with tiled hearths for fireplaces and other heat-generating appliances, you will need to use a noncombustible adhesive and grout. Depending on the range hood design and distance from the burner tops, you also should use a heat-resistant adhesive, although most hoods remain cool enough that one is not necessary. If in doubt, consult an architect.

The tile itself need not be impact-resistant as it does for the floor of a hearth, however. In fact, thin, glazed ceramic wall tiles are preferable to thicker floor tiles or counter-top tile because they are lightweight and easy to keep clean. If the hood is curved, ceramic mosaic sheets would be a good choice.

BUILD THE HOOD

There are several approaches to building a hood upon which tiles will be applied. However, actual construction will be dictated by local building codes.

Hood Dimensions. Although the hood will be constructed primarily to fit its designated space, try to base the hood on dimensions that avoid (as much as possible) the use of narrow or odd-shaped cut tiles. You can design the hood apron, for instance, to be one tile (plus one grout joint) wide for the width of one tile plus any trim strips. Because most range hoods slope inward from bottom to top, some wedge-shaped tiles on the sides of the hood will be inevitable. If you plan the tile layout carefully, these tiles can be cut beforehand and quickly set after the other tiles are applied.

Sheet-Metal Hood. A sheet-metal company can fabricate a heavy-gauge steel hood. (Do not use aluminum or copper because most tile adhesives will not bond to these.)

▲ *When designing the range hood, try to avoid dimensions that will create odd-shaped tiles.*

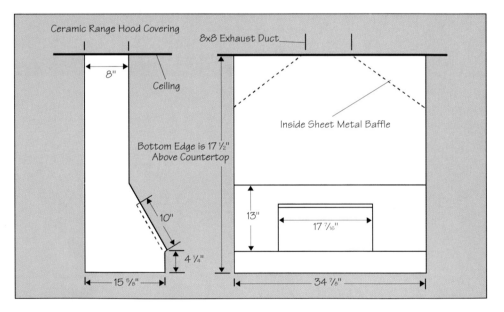

Ceramic Range Hood Covering

8x8 Exhaust Duct

8"

Ceiling

Inside Sheet Metal Baffle

Bottom Edge is 17 ½" Above Countertop

10"

13"

17 ⁷⁄₁₆"

4 ¼"

15 ⁵⁄₈"

34 ⁷⁄₈"

The hood must be designed to provide rigid support for the tiles. After roughening the steel surface with sandpaper, set the tiles with an epoxy adhesive or with a latex-cement thin-set mortar with additives that bond to steel. One brand is Laticrete 4237, combined with Laticrete 211 Crete powder. This adhesive resists temperatures up to 360°F, although the surface of most properly installed range hoods never reaches this temperature.

Wooden Hood. You can build a plywood-covered wood frame and install drywall or tile backer board over the frame. Then set tiles with a noncombustible thin-set mortar. Check local codes for details.

Prefabricated Hoods. Do not attempt to tile over these hoods. The thin sheet metal used for these hoods is too flexible to support the weight of the tile, and their size and shape often require too many odd cuts.

TILE THE HOOD

Because ceramic tile is heavy, it is best to install the hood before tiling it. Once the hood is in place, shut off the circuit to the fan (and light, if any); then roughen the entire surface thoroughly with 80-grit sandpaper.

1. Establish Working Lines

Lay out the working lines on the hood so that any cut tiles in the layout fall near the high edges of the hood. (If you will be tiling the sides of the hood, place cut tiles at the back edge.)

Treat each side of the hood as if you were laying out a wall (see pages 62-67). Establish vertical working lines so that cut tiles at either end of the hood are larger than half a tile and equal in width. The bottom edge of the hood will serve as the horizontal baseline. You also may want to tile the inside of the hood or at least the visible portions of it. If you do, extend the working lines into this area. You can finish the edges of the hood with one of several types of trim tiles. Bullnose tiles such as those used for tub surrounds (see pages 22-23) are a good choice. Additional working lines that indicate the location of trim pieces will speed up the tile-setting process and help ensure straight joints.

2. Apply the Adhesive

Using the appropriately sized notched trowel, apply the adhesive according to the manufacturer's instructions. Do not apply more adhesive than you can cover with tile in about 20 minutes or the open time listed on the label.

Caution: If you are using an epoxy adhesive, provide plenty of room ventilation and wear a respirator designed to filter out epoxy fumes.

1. Establish Working Lines

2. Apply the Adhesive

3. Tile Inside & Outside

4. Grout

3. Tile Inside & Outside

Apply the tile to the inside before covering the outside. That way, the hardest part is finished first.

On outside surfaces, start tiling at the intersection of the vertical and horizontal lines, setting the first course of trim tiles along the bottom edge. Depending on the dry-time of the adhesive, you may need to support the first row of tiles with a batten or by temporarily attaching these tiles to the hood with tape. Even with epoxy, you will need to hold the tiles in place as you go. Build up successive courses so that each course supports the one above it.

4. Grout

After you have tiled the entire hood, let the adhesive cure for at least 10 hours before grouting the tiles. Apply grout and grout sealer according to manufacturer's instructions. Let the grout cure for 10 to 12 hours (or overnight) before making electrical connections and putting the hood in service.

DESIGN & TILE OPTIONS

Indoors or outdoors, tiled stairs or steps naturally call attention to themselves. A variety of tile treatments are possible. With floors, long flights of stairs connecting one story to another often use a combination of wood and tile, typically hardwood treads and tiled risers. Because the risers are not stepped on, you can cover them with thin, decorative glazed wall tiles.

Another option is to cover both steps and risers with tile. If you are tiling just a few steps, such as a front entry or where floors of different levels meet, the front edge of the treads can be finished off with bullnose tiles. The procedure is the same for a raised tub platform (see page 106).

Large (8- or 12-inch-square) unglazed quarry or paver tiles often are used for the treads on outdoor steps; 6- or 12-inch-square glazed floor tiles are used for treads on interior steps. Tiles for stair treads should be slip-resistant, whether glazed or not, and durable enough to withstand heavy foot traffic. They should be at least l/2 inch thick. Typically, any cut tiles are placed along the back edge of the tread and top edge of the riser.

Use a single course of special "stair-tread" tiles for long flights of stairs. These have a rounded nosing that projects slightly past the front edge of the riser, which typically enables you to build a steeper flight of stairs without reducing the tread width. Several manufacturers offer unglazed stair-tread tiles with shaped nosings.

▲ *Be sure to choose non-skid tiles when tiling stair treads.*

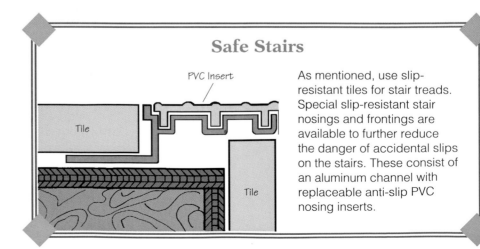

Safe Stairs

PVC Insert

Tile

Tile

As mentioned, use slip-resistant tiles for stair treads. Special slip-resistant stair nosings and frontings are available to further reduce the danger of accidental slips on the stairs. These consist of an aluminum channel with replaceable anti-slip PVC nosing inserts.

BUILDING CONSIDERATIONS

Stair design and construction are beyond the scope of this book. But, here are a few tips for tiling stairs.

Sturdy Substrate. Be sure to provide a suitable substrate on which to lay the tile. Use exterior-grade plywood (3/4 inch minimum) to cover wood-frame stairs, steps, and platforms, and provide adequate structural support to prevent flexing of the wood. It is best to use two layers of 3/4-inch plywood on steps over 16 inches deep. Raised plywood platforms must meet the same structural requirements as plywood subfloors (see page 47), and the treads must be supported at the edges. Apply tiles with an epoxy mortar. Poured-concrete stairs also can be tiled (see page 120).

Level Transitions. When calculating the tread-riser ratios, do not forget to include the thickness of the tiles and any substrate. Plan the stairway so that the top tiled step will be flush with the adjoining floor, and so that all steps will be equal in width and height.

Mark vertical layout lines on each tread and riser so that any cut tiles at each end will be more than half a tile wide and equal in width. If the steps are level width-wise, you need not establish horizontal layout lines for each tread and riser.

Tiled Risers. Indoors, long flights of stairs often use a combination of wood and tile, typically hardwood treads and tiled risers (6x6 or 8x8 tiles are used, depending on the run and rise of stairs). Provide slight expansion gaps between the tiles and treads. Then, fill with flexible caulk.

Riser with Tiled Inlays. If constructing new stairs, consider installing risers with decorative tiles inset into them. Make a tile-sized router template from 1/8-inch hardboard, and rout recesses in the riser. Use epoxy adhesive to set the tiles.

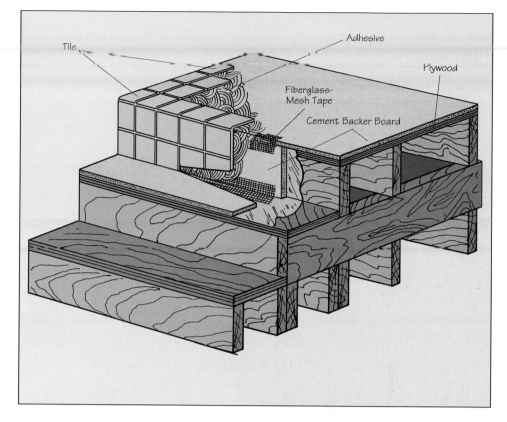

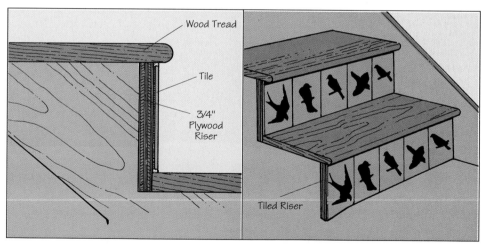

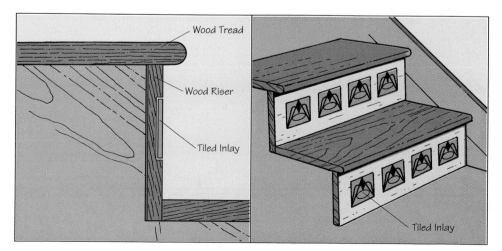

PATIOS, ENTRIES & POOL DECKS

eramic tile is one of the most elegant surfacing materials you can use for an outdoor patio, walk, or entryway. It also can be one of the most expensive. For this reason, you will want to protect your investment by providing a solid base on which to lay the tile.

It is best to choose the tile before beginning the layout for the patio so the layout will be based on the tile size chosen. Tile dealers can loan or sell you a few sample tiles for this purpose. Unglazed quarry tile and pavers are the most popular tiles for outdoor patios and walks. Glazed floor tiles are used in special circumstances, for instance, when the tiles on an interior floor are extended onto a connecting patio.

The type of tile you choose will be somewhat determined by the region in which you live. In warm, relatively dry regions, such as the Southwest, soft-bodied, nonvitreous pavers often are used. These include low-fired handmade Mexican pavers (patio tiles) and cement-based saltillo tiles. Both types are porous, and will not hold up in wet or cold climates. Even in areas with light to moderate rainfall, these unglazed tiles should be sealed with an appropriate sealer to help prevent moisture penetration.

In most areas of the country, you will need a hard-bodied vitreous or impervious tile, such as porcelain pavers or vitreous quarry tiles. In cold climates, the tile should be freeze- or thaw-stable. In extremely cold climates, tile is not a good choice for patios. Your tile dealer should carry a selection of outdoor tiles best suited to your particular region.

▶ *When you choose to install a tiled floor around a pool, make sure the tile is a nonslip variety.*

▼ *Terra cotta pavers are built up around the pool's perimeter, creating a defined ledge.*

TILING ENTRY STEPS

Steps and raised entries are poured, finished, and tiled in very much the same manner as a patio. Because steps require a thicker pour, the gravel-and-sand base may have to be deeper to support their weight. The steps also will require perimeter footings at least 2 feet below grade, or 6 inches below the frost line. The formwork will be more complex. It requires additional bracing to support the weight of the concrete. Typically, each step, no matter how deep or wide, should be no less than 4 inches high and no greater than 7½ inches high. Tread widths should be a minimum of 11 inches deep. For long flights of steps, you will need to figure out the tread-riser ratios (see page 117).

BUILD THE BASE

There is a typical formwork for entry steps. A release agent may be applied to the forms to make them easier to remove after the concrete sets. Ordinary motor oil may be used as a release agent, and then cleaned off the concrete later with a mild detergent before tiling. Tie the steps to the foundation walls with anchor bolts or short tie rods.

Typically, the steps are poured first. Let the concrete partially cure, remove the forms, and then pour the patio. You will need to install an isolation joint between the steps and the house foundation or exterior wall. Provide controls joints around the base of the steps where they meet the patio.

TILE THE STEPS

You can use the same tiles as those for outdoor patios. Step treads should be slip-resistant. Glazed decorative tiles can be used for the risers. These must be vitreous to prevent water penetration, and, in cold climates, freeze- or thaw-stable. Finish off the front edge of the step with bullnose tiles or stair-tread tiles (see page 22).

▲ *The tiles used for the patio are continued up these elegant double-entry steps.*

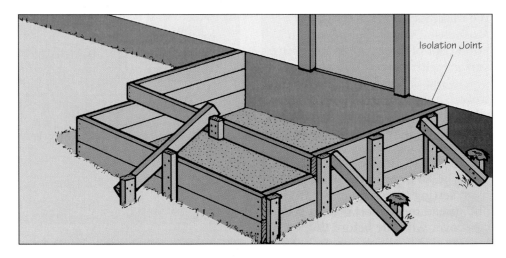

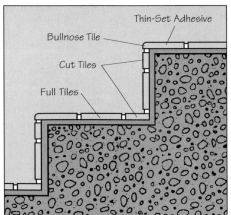

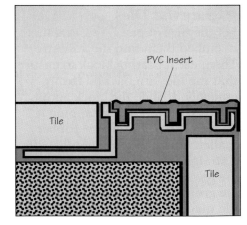

Note: *You can economize on the amount of concrete needed by partially filling the forms with field stones, chunks of concrete, or similar rubble. Wash the rocks thoroughly to remove all dirt, and*

place the pieces at least 4 inches away from the form edges and 6 inches below the finished surface of the concrete. When the concrete is poured, make sure it fills all voids between the rubble.

Unless you know how to build swimming pools, we recommend that you let the pool contractor tile the inside of your concrete pool. We also suggest that he or she install the perimeter coping tiles as part of the overall project. (Most pools are tiled around the water line to facilitate cleaning and may include numbered depth-marker and lane-marker tiles. Some prefabricated fiberglass pools come with tiles already set into the fiberglass shell.)

However, once the pool and coping are installed, you can tile the deck surface around it. The requirements and building procedures are the same as those for a tiled concrete patio. A base is poured up to the edge of the pool coping, and an expansion joint is installed between the two, according to local building codes. The pool deck itself should slope away from the pool on all sides, and its outer perimeter should be raised a few inches above grade to prevent water-washed soil and other contaminants from flowing back into the pool.

▲ *This gently curved tile pattern mimics the curve of the swimming pool, creating a harmonious effect.*

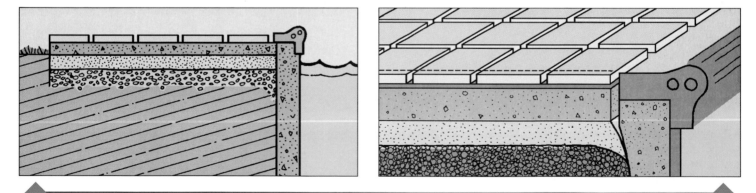

Tile Spas & Hot-Tub Surrounds

Tile surrounds for sunken tubs, spas, and garden pools employ the same principles and building procedures as for tiled pool decks, as outlined in the preceding section.

Fiberglass spas and wooden hot tubs can be sunk in the ground, above ground, or anywhere in between. A tiled surround or plat-form for raised tubs and spas can be built much as you would install

a tiled platform for a drop-in tub (see page 106).

Framing members for raised steps and platforms should consist of pressure-treated lumber rated for on-ground or below-ground use; even if installed above ground, the lumber will have to withstand a soggy environment. Use exterior-grade plywood to cover the steps and platform. In all cases, raised

tubs and spas need to be supported independently of the platform and to rest on a firm foundation. Also, do not place a hot tub or freestanding portable spa directly on a tiled patio—its weight (when filled with water) may crack the tiles. Check local codes and spa or hot-tub dealers in your area for additional building requirements.

9

TILE WITH STONE

Natural stone tile is becoming an increasingly popular surfacing material for floors, walls, and countertops in upscale residential architecture. The three most popular are marble, granite, and slate.

Granite, marble, and slate come in the form of gauged stone; that is, they are cut to a uniform size and shape, and then sawn and ground to a consistent thickness. The backside of the stone is ground smooth to provide an even adhesive bond; surface textures range from a rough, natural cleft appearance (slate) to a highly polished surface (granite and marble).

Slate, quartzite, and sandstone come in the form of cleft (hand-split) stones. These and many other types of cleft stones are commonly available as flagstones and dimensioned paving stones, which easily can be split or cleft to produce relatively thin, flat stones for paving and surfacing. Flagstones come in random sizes and shapes and are fitted together like a jigsaw puzzle. Dimensioned paving stones are sawn to uniform square or rectangular shapes to present a more formal appearance. With both types, thickness varies considerably from piece to piece and the cleft surface is usually too rough or irregular for most indoor applications. Flagstone and dimensioned pavers commonly are used outdoors for patios, entries, walks, garden walls, and exterior house siding.

The stones are available in a range of sizes. Larger slabs typically are set directly in a thick mortar bed and require specialized skills to be installed (a job best left to a professional). Thinner, gauged stone tiles can be set with a thin-set adhesive, much like ceramic floor tiles. By combining the information in previous chapters with that provided by the dealer or manufacturer, you should be able to set most types of gauged stone tiles yourself. Also consult your tile dealer for recommended adhesives, sealers, and maintenance requirements for the type of tile you have chosen.

◀ As an alternative to ceramic tile, stone tiles create an opulent scene wherever they are used.

▶ Marble tiles are the perfect answer to this fancy living area. The addition of majestic columns creates an even more formal air.

▲ *Since it is prone to stains, marble tile must be sealed when used in the bathroom or other wet areas.*

MARBLE TILE

Marble tile lends an air of opulence to practically any room in the house. It can be used for floors, walls, stair treads and risers, tabletops, and fireplace surrounds.

True marble is a relatively hard, metamorphic form of limestone. Usually it is white or off-white, but marble comes in a broad range of color. Often marble has subtle streaks of grey, brown, pink, or other colors. This is sometimes called statuary marble. Expect variations in color and vein patterns between individual tiles of the same type of stone.

Any stone (except granite) that can be machine-polished is classified as marble. Most marble actually is limestone in one form or another. Some forms are relatively soft and absorbant whereas others are quite hard and nearly impervious to water. Common tile sizes are 12 inches x 12 inches and 12 inches x 18 inches, from 3/8 to l/2 inch thick.

The surface of marble is either polished or honed. Polished marble is highly reflective and emphasizes the natural colors and markings of the stone. Use polished marble on low-wear surfaces, such as walls, tabletops, fireplace surrounds, and floors in low-traffic areas. Honed marble has a dull, matte finish. Choose this finish for floors, thresholds, transition strips, or stair treads where heavy foot traffic is likely. Honed marble provides a more slip-resistant surface and is less likely to reveal scratches. Marble is susceptible to abrasions, but it can be repolished as needed (see page 165). Also, please note that any dark-color stone tile will show scratches more vividly than a light-color one.

GRANITE TILE

In homes, granite-tile floors, walls, and countertops result in a high-tech look. Most granite tiles have a highly polished surface. It is a hard, dense stone, nearly impervious to stains, scratches, and abrasion. If granite does take a stain, it usually is much harder to remove. Grit and dirt can make granite floors slippery.

Common tile sizes are 12 inches x 12 inches x 3/8 inch and 18 inches x 18 inches x 1/2 inch. Although most granite tiles are of the characteristic mottled grey or black-and-white speckled variety, they come in other colors, including tans, pinks, and greens. A stone called gabbro often is sold as "black granite." Not a true granite, this softer stone is susceptible to scratches. It is not recommended for high-traffic areas, and often is used as a decorative border tile on granite floors.

SLATE TILE

Most slate tiles have a rough, cleft surface, which precludes their use in some applications, such as countertops and floors where a smooth surface is desired. On the plus side, if a slate tile cracks or breaks, you can use epoxy to put it back together, and the crack will be hidden by the cleft-surface texture. Slate comes in a wide variety of natural colors—not just grey. Most slate is highly resistant to water penetration. Although it is not as soft as marble, slate can be scratched.

Common tile sizes are 12 inches x 12 inches, 12 inches x 18 inches, and 12 inches x 24 inches, from 1/4 to 1 inch thick. Tiles can be set with or without wide grout joints. The backs of the tiles are ground flat, whereas the face retains a cleft appearance. Slate tiles are either hand-gauged or machine-gauged. Hand-gauged slate tiles vary in thickness and are usually set directly in a thick mortar bed. Machine-gauged slate tiles are uniform in thickness, so you can install them with a thin-set adhesive. For floors, choose a relatively smooth-surfaced tile from 3/8 inch to l/2 inch thick.

▶ *Marble tiles are available in a range of colors, as shown here.*

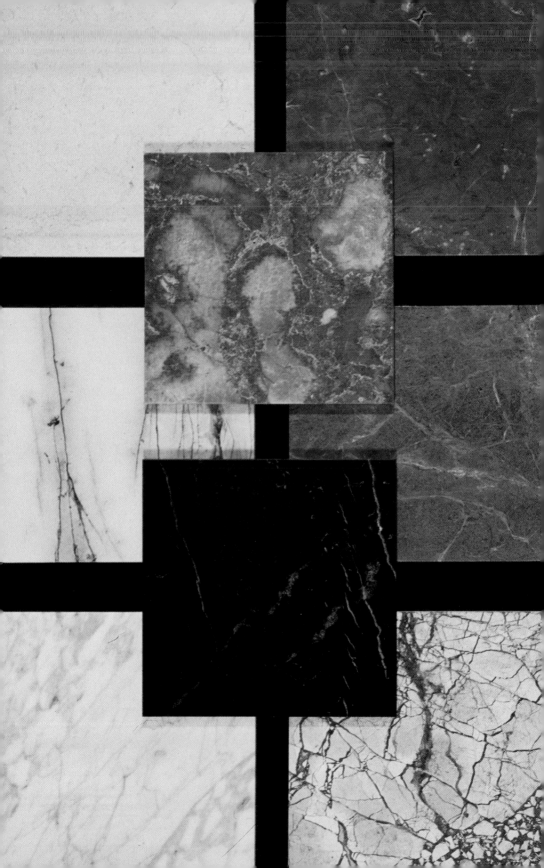

As mentioned, gauged stone tiles are installed much the same way ceramic floor tiles are installed. Following are some general guidelines for installing stone tiles. See details on page 135 for general step-by-step instructions. For more specific details, be sure to read all manufacturer's instructions.

SUBSTRATE REQUIREMENTS

Because most stone tiles are more brittle than ceramic tiles, it is essential that you provide a sound, rigid substrate on which to lay them. The floor, wall, or countertop must be solid and free of any deflection; otherwise, the tiles may crack. The substrate also must be perfectly smooth and level, especially if you are setting the tiles without wide grout joints. In new construction, a thick-set mortar bed (at least 1 inch thick) or tile backer board applied over a 3/4-inch plywood substrate provides a sufficiently smooth and rigid backing on which to lay gauged stone tile. The tiles are set over the bed with a thin-set epoxy adhesive. However, the addition of a mortar bed or backer board is not always possible when an existing floor is to be tiled. Sometimes the subflooring or framing will not support the weight of the added materials, and sometimes the extra thickness creates an undesirable change in floor level. If you are not sure whether the existing floor is rigid enough to support the tile, have a structural engineer or architect conduct a deflection test to determine its rigidity. Also check local building codes for specific subfloor requirements.

ADHESIVES

The type of stone you have chosen and the substrate on which you lay it will determine what type of adhesive you need. Machine-gauged stone tiles are often set with a latex-portland cement or preferably epoxy thin-set adhesive. Special adhesives are formulated specifically for setting stone tiles. Organic adhesives usually are not recommended. Petroleum-based organic adhesives can stain stone tiles. Water-based organic adhesives tend to leave voids under the tiles, which can crack and cause curling. Water-based adhesives of any type should not be used with green marble (serpentine) tiles because the water in the adhesive causes these tiles to warp.

Use only white-color adhesives with light-color translucent marble tiles such as onyx; darker adhesives will change the tile color. Your tile dealer can recommend the appropriate adhesive for the particular tile you have chosen.

CUT STONE TILES

Because stone tiles tend to fracture along natural cleavage lines or fissures, you will need to cut them rather than using the score-and-snap method used for ceramic tiles.

Straight Cuts. For straight cuts, use a wet saw (available from a tool-rental shop or tile dealer). Cutting stone tiles on a wet saw is slow, tedious work so you may want to have the tile dealer cut them for you. After laying all the full tiles, mark the tiles to be cut. Then, number each tile and mark corresponding numbers on the floor to indicate their locations. After the tiles are cut, position them so the cut edges will be hidden by base molding.

Irregular Cuts. To make curved or irregular cuts, use a tungsten carbide rod blade fitted in a hacksaw frame. Mark the outline of the cutout on the tile as for resilient tiles (see page 146). Then, with the tile firmly supported on a flat surface, cut along the line with the saw. Work slowly to avoid cracking the tile. After making the cutout, smooth the edges with a carborundum stone.

SET THE TILES

If the tiles you have bought vary in thickness by more than about 1/4 inch, you will need to set them directly in a wet mortar bed that is at least 1 inch thick. This method requires considerable skill to ensure that, once the tiles are installed, the surface will be perfectly smooth and flat. Proper and timely compaction of the setting bed is a must. Consider hiring an experienced tile-setter to do the work. If the tiles vary only slightly in thickness, you can set them with a special latex thin-set adhesive that can be applied in a coat up to 1/2 inch thick. As mentioned, machine-gauged stone tiles are cut to exact thickness and can be set with a thin-set adhesive.

Unlike ceramic tiles, marble and granite tiles usually are set without wide grout joints. However, you must allow some tolerance (between 1/16 and 1/8 inch) between the tiles to allow for minor out-of-square conditions resulting from inaccurately cut tiles. Also, if you butt the edges of stone tiles tightly together, any movement in the subfloor will cause spalling (chipping) along the tile edges.

Slate can be set with or without wide grout joints, depending on the look you want to achieve. Because slate often does have a rough, uneven surface, wider grout joints serve to make a smooth transition between adjoining tiles, creating a smoother walking surface on floors.

GROUTS

In most cases, you will want to choose a grout color that matches the stone color as closely as possible. Unlike ceramic tiles, the idea with marble and granite tiles is to de-emphasize the joints (as much

▲ *Machine-gauged slate tiles are uniform in thickness and can be installed like other stone tiles.*

as possible) to give the installation a "monolithic" appearance. As mentioned, slate tiles can be set with or without wide grout joints.

For marble and slate tiles, fill the joints with an unsanded cement grout; a sanded grout may scratch the stone surface when applied. Narrow joints between granite tiles are best filled with an epoxy adhesive, which makes for a virtually waterproof installation.

SEALERS

A variety of clear sealers, from low sheen to a mirror-like gloss, are available for all three stone types. Sealers are used to enhance the appearance of the tile and to protect it from dirt, stains, and moisture penetration (a sealer is usually recommended in wet areas). Low-sheen penetrating sealers are commonly used on floors because they need not be applied as frequently as glossier surface sealers. Although it is not a real sealer, a simple mixture of turpentine and sawdust rubbed over slate gives it a nice sheen. Generally, sealers are not recommended in food-preparation areas, because most leave a toxic residue.

Note: Granite should not be sealed or waxed.

Because the mineral composition of stone tiles varies widely, you cannot always predict how the chemicals in any given sealer will react with any given tile. Also, some clear sealers, such as silicone, will eventually turn yellow when subjected to sunlight. Clear sealers will usually darken the tile color, which may or may not improve its appearance. Generally, an experienced tile dealer can recommend the appropriate sealer for the stone tile you have chosen. Before applying any sealer, however, test it on a sample tile or in an inconspicuous spot on the installed surface. All sealers require periodic reapplication to maintain their effectiveness. Follow the manufacturer's guidelines.

Caution: Be careful when applying colored grouts. They may stain the tile surface, especially on porous stones.

A marble or other type of gauged stone, such as granite and slate, is an elegant addition to any room.

1. Spread Adhesive

The surface that you want to tile must be clean and level. If you are dealing with an uneven surface, create a subfloor out of plywood.

Using a notched trowel, spread some thin-set adhesive on the floor surface. It should be applied thinly and evenly. You will have to work on parts of the floor, rather than attacking it all at once. Refer to the manufacturer's instructions for advice on how much adhesive you will need to complete the job.

2. Cut Tiles

Most likely, some of the tile will have to be cut to fit to the wall and around corners. The problem with cutting stone is that the tiles often break along existing fissures in the rock. Cut the tile three quarters of the way across; then turn it around and cut the last quarter. If the stone is extremely delicate, try wrapping it in masking tape before making the cut. A wet saw with a sliding carriage and a diamond blade is a very good marble or stone cutter and is available at tool-rental shops.

3. Lay Tiles in Place

Use a slight twisting motion when firmly laying the tiles. Do not slide the tiles into position as this will result in a buildup of adhesive within the joints. Take care not to get adhesive on the face of the tile.

4. Set Tiles

Keeping vertical and horizontal lines straight, set the tiles and the tile spacers. Allow the tile and adhesive to dry overnight before continuing work.

5. Fill Joints

Mix a batch of white portland nonstaining cement to a thick and creamy consistency. Use a moist sponge to dampen the joints

1. Spread Adhesive

2. Cut Tiles

3. Lay Tiles in Place

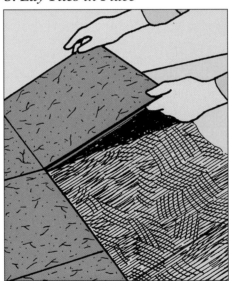

4. Set Tiles

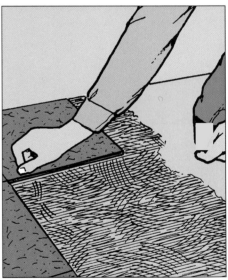

between tiles. Then, fill the joints with the cement, pouring the manufacturer's recommended amount on the tile. Use a squeegee to spread it evenly over the moistened area. Then, let the cement sit for 10 minutes. A layer of dry cement should be sprinkled over the area and rubbed into the spaces with a burlap rag.

Remove any excess grouting material or adhesive before it has time to harden. Wipe the joints smooth. Then, clean the stone surface with water. Tools may be cleaned with acetone.

5. Fill Joints

Cleft stones (those that have been hand-split) are available as randomly shaped flagstones and uniformly shaped paving stones. With both, thickness varies considerably.

When you are finished installing the stones, seal them with a sealer that has been recommended by the tile supplier. When the surface is tightly sealed, you can maintain the floor by sweeping and occasionally damp mopping it with a mild detergent. A light coat of wax heightens the texture of some stones. However, choose the wax and sealer carefully, because not all waxes and sealers are "friendly" to stone.

1. Lay Stones

Begin in a corner opposite your supply of masonry and mortar and an exit. Lay a couple of pieces dry to determine how they will sit. Then sprinkle the slab with water so it is damp, and apply mortar evenly for two or three stones. Tap each stone in place with a rubber mallet, and check to see if it is level with neighboring stones.

2. Trim Stones

Trim stones to fit along walls and other obstructions. Trimming is done by laying a stone over its neighbor and marking lines where it will be trimmed. Score it with a brick set or stonemason's chisel. Prop the stone and strike the scored line with brick set and hammer.

3. Grout the Joints

After the stones have set for at least 24 hours, prepare grout (three parts sand and one part cement) and mix it to a soupy consistency, not as stiff as mortar. Pour it from a coffee can or trowel it into the joints between the stones. With a wet sponge, wipe up grout that spills onto the stone surface. Before the grout sets hard, smooth it with a trowel. When the floor is completely dried, finish with a sealer, if needed, as recommended by your stone supplier.

1. Lay Stones

2. Trim Stones

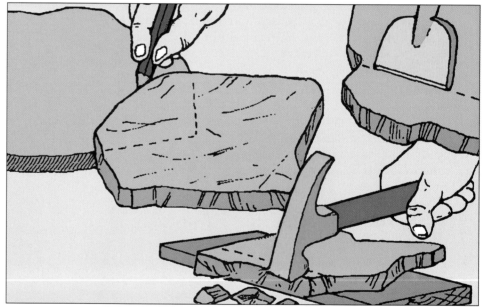

3. Grout the Joints

10

RESILIENT TILE

Today's resilient tile offers a vast selection of styles, patterns, and colors. Most designs still simulate other flooring materials—ceramic tile, brick, stone, and wood parquet. But thanks to modern computerized engraving techniques, these tiles are much more realistic in appearance than the ersatz designs of a decade ago. You also will find a plethora of designs and patterns unique to resilient tile, with smooth or embossed surfaces. Colors and patterns range from subtle to bold to fit practically any decor, and manufacturers are continually introducing new styles to keep up with decorating trends. Don't forget that solid-color tiles can be mixed and matched to produce unique floor patterns.

Durable, easily maintained, and attractively designed, the new resilient tiles wear longer and are especially good in rooms prone to splashes and spills.

▶ *Use your imagination when it comes to creating a floor design. With resilient tiles from Armstrong the possibilities are endless.*

▼ *Resilient tiles are available in a broad range of colors, such as these from Armstrong.*

SELECT RESILIENT TILE

The term "resilient" tile has become synonymous with vinyl tile. Vinyl tiles fall into two basic categories: vinyl composition tiles and solid vinyl, or luxury vinyl tiles. Some people still refer to resilient tiles as vinyl asbestos (VA) tiles because asbestos fibers once were used as the filler-binder material in vinyl tiles, sheet flooring, and adhesives. Because of environmental and health concerns, manufacturers no longer make VA products. Even so, many homes still have VA tile floors, and, as a result of the hazards involved in working with asbestos products, special precautions are needed when preparing or removing these materials for new floor coverings (see page 140).

Standard tile sizes are 9 inches x 9 inches and 12 inches x 12 inches, although other sizes are available, often depending on the flooring material the tile simulates (wood planks, for example). Companies also offer decorative feature strips in various widths and lengths, as well as small insert tiles, called spots.

VINYL COMPOSITION TILES

This type of tile is made up of a mixture of vinyl, plasticizers, and filler materials (typically limestone). The quality of the tile is largely determined by the overall thickness, 1/16 to 1/8 inch, and the percentage of vinyl used in relation to filler materials. Better tiles have a higher vinyl content, which make them more durable and less brittle than cheaper tiles. Most vinyl composition tiles have a no-wax surface.

▲ *The same design ideas used for ceramic tile can be replicated with resilient tiles, such as these from Armstrong.*

SOLID VINYL TILES

Although not really made of solid vinyl, these tiles have a very high percentage (at least 85 percent) of it in relation to fillers, binders, and pigments. This makes them much more durable, flexible, and resilient than vinyl composition tiles. The color and pattern extend completely through the thickness of the tile, so they will not "wear off" in high-traffic areas. Solid vinyl tiles often exhibit brighter colors and a deeper gloss than most vinyl composition tiles. They also are more expensive and require special adhesives for installation.

Most vinyl tiles have no-wax surfaces, which make them easy to clean and maintain. Should the surface ever become dull, a special no-wax conditioner (available at most supermarkets or from the flooring dealer) can restore the shine.

CUSHIONED VINYL TILES

Cushioned vinyl tiles consist of a resilient foam core or backing covered by a vinyl wear layer. Think twice before buying these, however. Although they are softer underfoot, they also are prone to dents from furniture legs and sharp objects such as spiked heels.

SELF-STICK TILES

Self-stick resilient tiles take much of the work out of installation. Simply peel off the paper backing, place the tile, and adhere it to the floor (see pages 142-143). On the downside, once the paper backing is removed, the adhesive can become contaminated with dirt, resulting in a poor bond.

RUBBER TILES

These tiles are extremely durable and naturally resilient, making them an excellent choice for high-traffic areas. Their studded surface provides excellent slip resistance in wet areas. However, a limited range of colors and patterns gives them an institutional look, which is why they are found mostly in commercial applications. Even so, rubber tiles often are used to complement a high-tech or Euro-style decor in kitchens, bathrooms, and entries.

VINYL COVE BASE

Usually, a flexible vinyl cove base is used to seal the joint where the floor meets the wall, although wood base molding can be used. Available in a variety of colors, the base eliminates dirt accumulation in the joint and provides a smooth, tough surface that never needs painting and is easily cleaned. Both straight strips and preformed inside and outside corners are available.

Most resilient tile can be laid above or below ground level, over most clean, smooth, sound, dry flooring material. Because resilient tiles are relatively soft and thin, they will follow any contours in the floor. Although this enables you to install resilient tiles over slightly wavy floors, it also means that any irregularities in the subfloor, such as cracks, open joints, knotholes, or popped nail heads, or small pieces of debris, will eventually sculpture through the tile surface. You must take extra care to make sure the surface is perfectly smooth and clean, even though it need not be perfectly level.

Following are some general guidelines for preparing various floor surfaces for resilient tile. However, some tiles may require additional preparation, so check manufacturer's instructions.

INSTALL TILE OVER EXISTING FLOORS

Follow the procedures that apply to your specific floor type.

Wood. A wood subfloor should be at least 24 inches above ground level and well ventilated. If the subfloor is of single-wood construction (a single layer of wood board nailed directly to the joists), install a suitable underlayment (at least 3/8 inch thick).

Floors and subfloors of double-wood construction can be tiled over, provided the surface is smooth and firm. Minor surface imperfections can be patched with a floor-patching compound or a filler. Slightly cupped or warped boards can be sanded smooth with a floor sander. If the boards are very rough, loose, broken, or warped, cover them with an underlayment. Install an underlayment if the boards are over 4 inches wide.

New Concrete. This type of subfloor should be finished with a steel trowel to provide a perfectly smooth, even surface, free of score marks, grooves, or depressions.

Concrete subfloors on or below grade require a waterproof membrane, such as 6-mil polyethylene sheeting, installed between the concrete slab and the ground. Be sure the slab is fully cured and dry before installing resilient tile (wait at least 45 days). To check for moisture, tape squares of kitchen plastic wrap to various parts of the slab surface. If moisture collects under any of the squares after several days, the slab is too damp to be tiled.

Do not use curing compounds or concrete sealers, as these may interfere with a good adhesive bond. If one was used, it will have to be removed. (If water beads up on the concrete surface, it is likely that a sealer has been used.) Similarly, be sure any alkali deposits on the concrete surface are neutralized before installing resilient tile.

Old Concrete. Old concrete floors must meet the same basic requirements as new concrete. First, use a heavy-duty detergent or concrete cleaner to remove any oil, grease, wax, or dirt from the floor. Rinse thoroughly with water and allow to dry. If the floor is covered with paint or another coating, clean and roughen the surface with a floor sander; then vacuum up the sanding dust. Wear safety goggles when grinding off any high spots with a carborundum stone or a grinder attachment chucked in an electric drill.

Fill cracks and other depressions with a latex filler. For detailed instructions, see page 49.

Ceramic Tile and Terazzo. This type of flooring must meet the same basic requirements as a concrete floor.

First clean the floor to remove any wax or sealers. Re-adhere any loose tiles with a ceramic tile adhesive (see page 46). Then, fill and level the floor with a latex filler.

Old Resilient Tiles. Most new resilient tiles can be installed over old asphalt tile or vinyl-asbestos tile floors provided they are sound, smooth surfaces (not embossed or textured), firmly bonded to the subfloor, and limited to one layer of old floor covering. Tiles with no-wax surfaces and solid vinyl tiles usually cannot be tiled over because these surfaces do not provide good adhesion. Do not tile over cushioned vinyl floors.

To prepare an existing tile floor, use a wax stripper to clean off all wax and dirt; then rinse thoroughly with warm water and allow to dry. If the floor has a few loose tiles, remove these with a wide putty knife, butter the backside with adhesive, and re-adhere using a rolling pin. Fill any cracks and uneven areas with a latex filler.

If you cannot tile over the existing floor, you can either add a layer of underlayment or remove the existing tiles. You would take the latter approach when a change in floor level would cause problems. When installing underlayment over existing resilient tile, make sure the nails are long enough to reach well into the subfloor beneath.

Vinyl and Linoleum Sheet. Generally, it is not advisable to install resilient tiles over vinyl or linoleum sheet flooring. If possible, cover with a thin (1/4- to 3/8-inch) plywood underlayment (see pages 47-48). Remove the old floor covering as a last resort—it is a messy, time-consuming job (next page).

Caution: To prevent any release of encapsulated asbestos fibers, never sand asphalt tile, vinyl-asbestos tile, or sheet flooring.

REMOVE TILES

To remove resilient tiles, you will need the following tools: stiff-blade floor scraper, wide-blade putty knife, hammer, electric heat gun, wet-dry vacuum, garden sprayer, water and liquid dishwashing detergent, Ground Fault Circuit Interrupter breaker, heavy-duty trash bags and labels to identify the hazardous contents, safety glasses, heavy gloves, and a respirator.

Remove all appliances from the work area; then remove all base moldings and thresholds.

1. Remove Tiles

Begin at a corner of the room. Work the putty knife under a tile and pry it up. Try to remove the tile in one piece. Tiles in high-traffic areas will be harder to remove: Wear goggles and strike the knife with a hammer, or soften the adhesive with a heat gun. As you remove each tile, place it into the trash bag.

2. Remove Old Adhesive

Remove any residual adhesive by wetting down one section at a time with detergent solution and scraping it off until no more than a thin residue is left. After wet-scraping, vacuum up the debris with a wet-dry vacuum. Tiles that require latex or epoxy adhesives may require that you cover any remaining adhesive with a trowel on the underlayment.

3. Clean Up

Empty the vacuum and place its contents in a trash bag along with the tiles. Seal the bags and label each with a sticker that reads "Caution: Contains Asbestos"; then dispose of them according to local landfill regulations (see above).

Caution: Heat guns can cause severe burns within seconds. Wear heavy gloves and never place your hand in front of the gun. Allow tiles to cool before handling them.

Asbestos Warning

Resilient flooring that was installed prior to 1985 is likely to contain asbestos. This includes asphalt tile, linoleum, vinyl-asbestos tile, vinyl sheet flooring, and asphalt "cutback" adhesives. If at all possible, you should leave them in place and cover them with underlayment or new flooring adhered directly to the old. If you have to remove these flooring materials, never sand or dry-scrape them, and never dry-sweep the residue. In short, avoid any removal procedure that creates dust. You will need to dispose of these materials in accordance with local ordinances. Check with your local landfill for proper disposal methods.

General procedures for removing tiles and sheet flooring are outlined here. For more comprehensive instructions, the Resilient Floor Covering Institute (RFCI) offers an excellent free pamphlet, entitled "Recommended Work Practices for the Renewal of Resilient Floor Coverings." To obtain a pamphlet, write to: RFCI, 966 Hungerford Drive, Suite 12B, Rockville, MD 20850 (301/340-8580).

If you are not sure whether or not the existing flooring or adhesive contains asbestos, treat it as if it does.

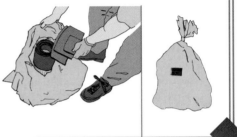

1. Remove Tiles

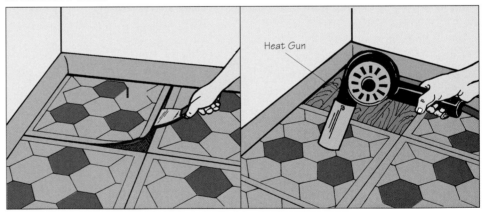

Heat Gun

2. Remove Old Adhesive

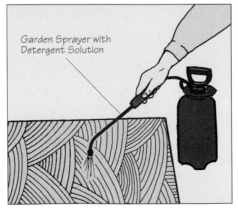

Garden Sprayer with Detergent Solution

3. Clean Up

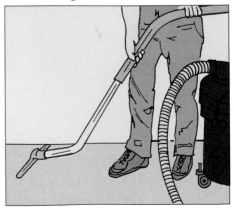

REMOVE SHEET FLOORING

In addition to the tools listed for removing tile, you will need a sharp utility knife.

1. Remove a Strip

Make a series of parallel cuts 4 to 8 inches apart crossing the entire floor. Pry up the first strip, separating it from its felt backing. If the flooring is adhered only around its edges, most of it will come up in one piece; otherwise, remove all of the felt backing by wet-scraping (see next step). As you pull off a strip, roll it up tightly as a helper sprays a constant mist of detergent solution under the strip. Then, secure it with tape and place it in a heavy-duty trash bag. Avoid contact with the exposed backing.

2. Wet-Scrape the Backing

After removing several strips, moisten the exposed felt backing with detergent solution and scrape it off the floor. Put residue in a trash bag. Vacuum the exposed floor with a wet-dry vacuum cleaner. Allow the floor to dry and vacuum again. Remove the vacuum dust bag and place it in a sealed trash bag. Dispose of all waste as described on the previous page.

1. Remove a Strip

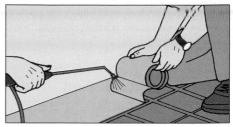

2. Wet-Scrape the Backing

INSTALL UNDERLAYMENT

1. Stagger Joints

Recommended underlayments include 1/4-inch or thicker C-C underlayment-grade plywood (exterior grade for wet areas), with one plugged and sanded face or untempered hardboard. Butt the sheets tightly together; stagger the joints. Do not align the new joints with the joints of the existing underlayment.

2. Attach Underlayment

Use 1½-inch ring-shank nails or drywall screws, spaced 6 inches apart along the seams, 1/2 inch from the edges, and 8 to 12 inches apart across the face of the panel. Drive the nails or screws flush with or slightly below the panel surface.

3. Patch & Sand

Fill all cracks and holes with a floor-patching compound or filler, and sand smooth.

4. Seal

You may need to apply a light coat of shellac or a wood sealer to the plywood. This prevents the wood boards from absorbing liquid from the tile adhesive, causing them to cure improperly.

1. Stagger Joints

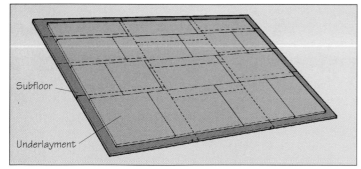

Subfloor

Underlayment

2. Attach Underlayment

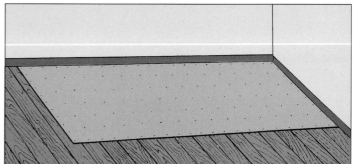

3. Patch & Sand

4. Seal

LAYING THE TILE

In most cases, laying the tile itself is much easier than preparing the floor to accept it. At this point on, the rest of the job should be easy. The tile, adhesive, and the room in which you will be installing should be kept at a temperature of at least 70 degrees for 24 hours before and after the tile is laid.

1. Room Preparation

Remove all existing base moldings or shoes, thresholds, floor registers, doors, and similar obstructions. Sweep or vacuum the floor to remove all debris.

1. Room Preparation

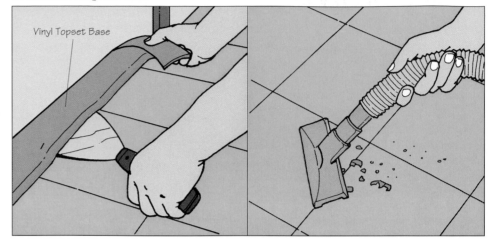

Vinyl Topset Base

Tools & Supplies

Different adhesives require different application methods, so be sure to follow instructions on the adhesive container label. Some adhesives are brushed on whereas others are applied with a notched trowel (notch size is indicated on the container label). The label also will tell you the adhesive's open time (the amount of time you can work with the adhesive). Tools required to lay resilient tile include: pencil, metal straight-edge, utility knife (or heavy scissors for thin tiles), and notched trowel. In addition, you will need a kitchen rolling pin to bed the tiles (for large floors use a heavy floor roller found at tool-rental shops).

Estimate Materials

Use a scale drawing to determine the number of tiles you will need. If you are using 12-inch tiles, one tile will equal 1 square foot. For example, a 10-foot x 16-foot floor will require 160 tiles. If you use 9-inch tiles, multiply the number of square feet by 1.78 (10 feet x 16 feet = 160 square feet x 1.78 = 284.8 tiles). You also can convert square feet to square inches; then divide by 81, the number of square inches in a 9-inch x 9-inch tile (120 inches x 192 inches = 23,040 square inches ÷ 81 = 284.4 tiles). Coverage rates for adhesives are listed on the container label.

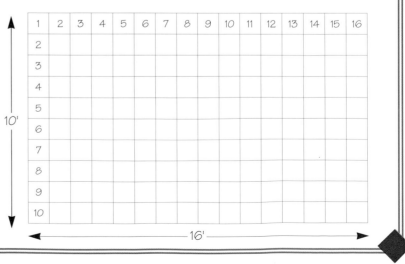

2. *Establish the Layout*

Resilient tile floors are laid out much like ceramic tile floors. You can use the basic procedures described on pages 40-42 to plan the design, make your scale drawing, and establish the working lines on the floor. However, there are a couple of minor differences. First, because resilient tiles don't require grout joints, you need not allow for these in the layout. In fact, with some tile patterns, the joints between tiles are nearly invisible once the tiles are laid.

Second, if your design is to include feature strips, you will want to indicate the locations of these on both your scale drawing of the floor layout and the floor itself (by snapping additional working lines).

3. *Mark Guidelines*

Measure and mark the center points of two opposite walls, and stretch a chalk line between nails driven into them. Do the same on the other walls. Do not snap the lines yet. Use a carpenter's square to determine that they intersect at a true 90-degree angle.

If the pattern is to be laid on a diagonal, measure the shorter chalkline from the intersection to the wall. Then measure that distance on either side of the nail. Do the same on the opposite wall, and drive nails into the four new points. Stretch chalk lines between these nails so that they intersect in the middle.

4. *Adjust Guidelines*

Lay dry tiles in one quadrant. Begin at the intersection and extend them at 90 degrees along the chalk lines all the way to the two walls. Duplicate the color combination on the graph paper. If you discover the last tiles are less than one-half tile width from the wall, move the chalk line to make a wider border at the wall. If the last tile is more than one-half width from the wall, leave the

chalk line where it is. In either case, the chalk line should be snapped.

For a diagonal pattern, lay dry tiles along two perpendicular lines point to point and a row of tiles along the intersecting diagonal line. If the places where the border tiles butt the walls are not aesthetically pleasing, adjust the chalk lines before snapping them again.

2. *Establish the Layout*

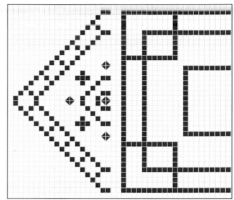

3. *Mark Guidelines*

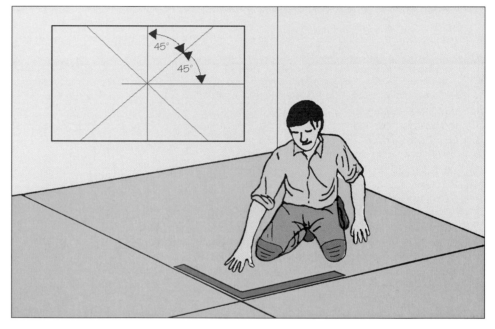

4. *Adjust Guidelines*

Diagonal Layout

5. Spread the Adhesive

Starting at the intersection of your working lines, spread adhesive along one line with a notched trowel angled 45 degrees to the floor until you reach one wall. Be careful not to obscure the working line with adhesive. If you are installing self-stick tiles, skip this step (see page 145).

6. Fill a Quadrant

Set a row of tiles along the line, butting each tile tightly against the preceding one. Drop the tiles into place; do not slide them. Set a row of tiles perpendicular to the first; then fill in the tiles between the two rows in stair-step fashion. Note that some patterned tiles (such as floral designs) have arrows printed on the back to show the direction they should be positioned when laid. Other tiles with strong directional patterns often look best if you alternate the pattern direction with each successive tile.

For a diagonal pattern, begin at the intersection of your diagonal working lines and lay one row along one diagonal. Use this row as a baseline on which to build your pattern.

7. Roll the Tiles

After filling in one quadrant, roll the tiles with a rolling pin or floor roller.

8. Clean off Adhesive

Use a cloth dampened with adhesive solvent to clean off any adhesive that squeezes out between the joints.

9. Repeat the Process

Fill in the remaining three quadrants using the same procedure. Avoid stepping on newly laid tiles until the adhesive dries (see label instructions).

5. Spread the Adhesive

6. Fill a Quadrant

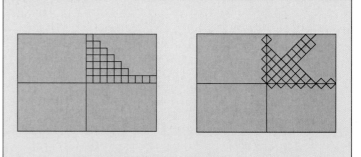

7. Roll the Tiles

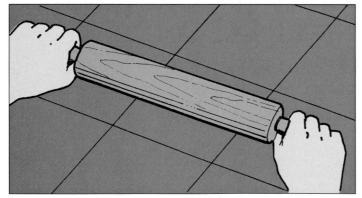

8. Clean off Adhesive

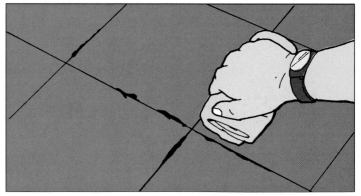

9. Repeat the Process

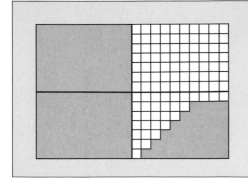
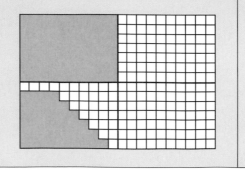
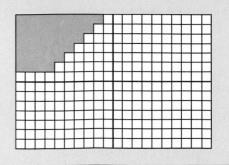

BORDER TILES

Align a dry tile over the last set tile from the wall. Then place a third tile over these two and push it to within l/8 inch of the wall. Using the top tile as a guide, score a line with a utility knife on the tile immediately under it. Cut the tile on the scored line, and fit into the border the piece that was not covered by the top tile.

For a diagonal pattern, use a straightedge and utility knife to score and snap the tiles from corner to corner to make triangular halves. If the tiles themselves have a directional pattern, you will need to cut "left-half" and "right-half" tiles to fit the border (see next page).

To fit tiles to outside corners, align a tile over the last set tile on the left side of the corner. Place a third tile over these two and push it to within 1/8 inch of the wall. Mark the edge with a pencil. Then, without turning the marked tile, align it on the last set tile to the right of the corner and mark it in a similar fashion. Cut along the marked lines to remove the corner section.

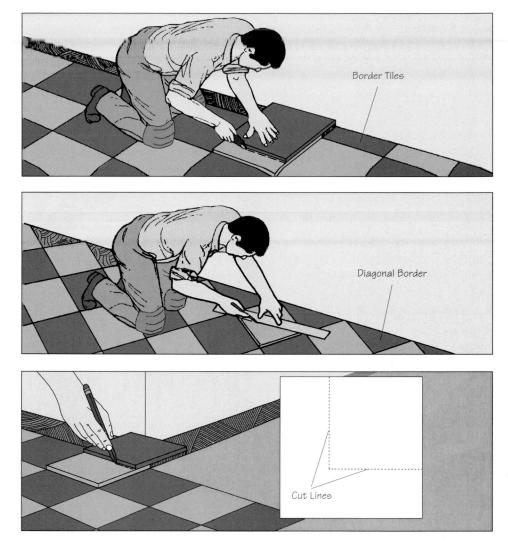

Install Self-Stick Tiles

Peel off Backing. The tiles come with a protective paper backing, which you will peel off just before setting. Generally, self-adhesive tiles are thin enough to cut with a pair of heavy household scissors. Do not remove the paper backing before you cut the tiles. Since they are very slick, you should place them in a trash bag after they have been removed.

Press into Place. To lay the tiles, simply position them and press them into place with your hands (no roller is needed). Butt each tile tightly against the adjoining ones, dropping it into position and pressing it firmly in place with the palms of your hands. Once pressure is applied, the adhesive back bonds tightly to the floor. Lay the tiles carefully, because if you make a mistake in positioning one you cannot simply lift it back up.

Peel off Backing

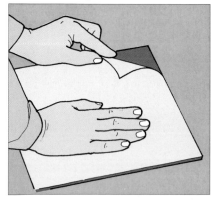

Press into Place

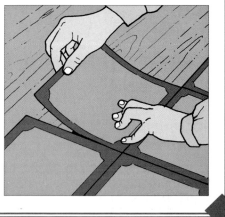

IRREGULAR CUTS

There are several ways to cut an irregular shape. Choose the best method for your particular situation.

■ Use the same procedure that is used for corners, but move the top tile along the irregular shape to locate its surfaces on the tile to be cut. For curves, bend a piece of solder wire and transfer the curve to the tile being marked.

■ Make a simple paper pattern to fit around the obstruction. Use the paper to trace it onto the tile.

■ Use a compass to draw an outline onto the tile. One leg runs

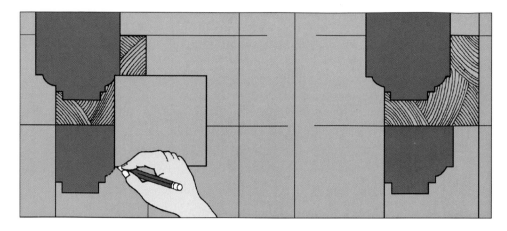

along the molding, whereas the other draws the outline on the tile.

■ Use a contour gauge to provide an accurate copy of the profile or ornate moldings.

■ At curved surfaces, bend a piece of solder wire around the curve to match the profile; then transfer to the tile being marked.

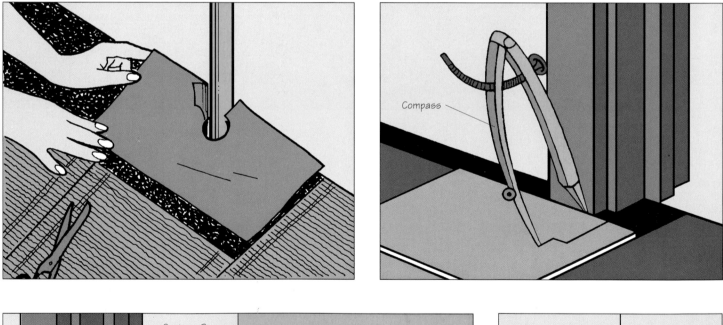

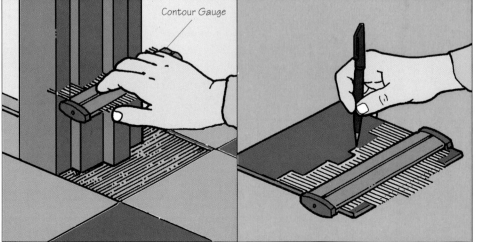

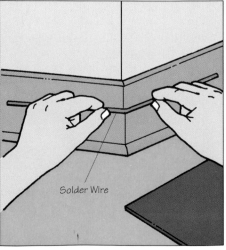

FINISHING TOUCHES

Feature Strips. Vinyl feature strips and ceramic tiles are installed in a similar way. Fill in all tiles bordering the strips before you lay them. Make sure that no part of the strip extends beyond the rows of tiles you have laid. When laying down strips, do not slide them into position, but place them firmly against the row of tiles and lower them into position.

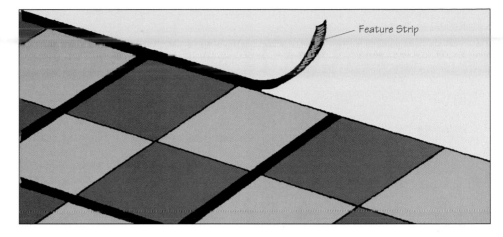

Feature Strip

VINYL COVE BASE

When installing vinyl cove base, the wall must be dry and free of all dirt, grease, oil, and loose paint. The base may not be installed over wallpaper of any kind.

Install all inside and outside corners first; then cut strips to fit between these.

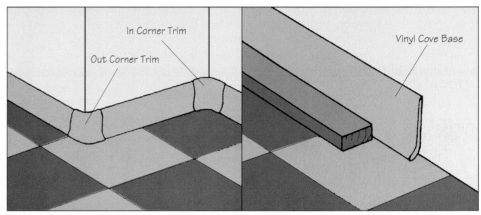

Out Corner Trim

In Corner Trim

Vinyl Cove Base

With a notched trowel or wide putty knife, apply cove adhesive to the ribbed back of the base. Leave a 1/4-inch bare space along the top edge of the base so that the adhesive will not ooze above the base. Immediately, press the base firmly against the wall—the toe must fit tightly against the floor and wall. Roll the base with a rubber or steel J-roller or other smooth, cylindrical object. After rolling, use a short length of 1x2 to press the toe of the base firmly against the wall.

Clean Up. Once you have laid all the tiles and base, use a solvent-dampened rag to clean any remaining traces of adhesive off the floor and off your tools. Allow the adhesive to set for at least 24 hours before washing or waxing the floor.

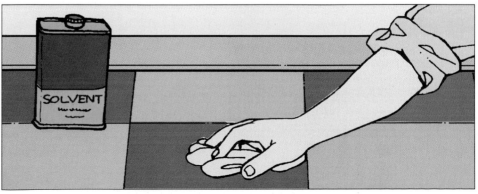

SOLVENT

11

WOOD PARQUET TILE

U p until the latter part of this century, wood parquet floors were painstakingly assembled from small, individual strips of wood called "fillets" into elaborate designs. Consequently, such floors were found only in the homes of the wealthy. Prefabricated wood parquet tiles make the job considerably easier and more economical. In fact, wood parquet tile is laid much in the same manner as resilient tile.

Before you decide to install wood parquet tiles, be aware that there are several situations in which they cannot be used. First, wood tiles are especially sensitive to moisture: Do not install them in a bathroom or on a concrete floor below grade, or in any area where high humidity or subsurface (ground) moisture exists. In all other situations, the subflooring must be completely dry (vapor barriers must be installed on concrete floors on or above grade). Also, wood tiles should not be installed over radiant-heated floors because extreme changes in heat or humidity will crack or warp the tiles, loosening the adhesive bond. Keep these considerations in mind before choosing wood parquet tiles for your floor.

▶ *Parquet wood tiles make a smooth surface for a children's play room. Do not install them in any room that contains high humidity.*

▼ *Used in the kitchen, parquet wood tiles create a warm, inviting atmosphere.*

Parquet tiles come in a variety of patterns and woods, including oak, ash, walnut, and teak. Tiles are either solid or laminated and either prefinished or unfinished. On solid wood tiles, splines or mesh backing fasten the individual hardwood fillets together to form the tile.

Wood parquet tiles come either with square edges (butt-edge tiles), or tongue-and-groove edges. The top edges of the tile may either be flat or beveled. A flat edge provides a smooth continuous walking surface. Beveled-edged tiles add dimension to pattern, and the crevices catch dirt, preventing the dirt from being ground into the surface.

Although most tiles have a wood or thin-mesh backing, some come with cushioned, foam backings that serve as a moisture barrier and make the tiles softer underfoot. Self-stick tiles, which eliminate the need for setting in an adhesive, also are available. As with resilient self-stick tiles, simply peel off a backing and press into place.

PREFINISHED TILES

Most prefinished tiles have a hard, durable, factory-applied acrylic or polyurethane finish. Some have no-wax surfaces; others are coated with a thin layer of factory-applied wax. Because the baked-on finish penetrates the wood, it is usually much more durable and scratch-resistant than finishes applied on-site. For a natural, hand-rubbed look, some tiles are factory-treated with a tung-oil sealer/filler followed by a penetrating stain or finish and factory-applied, hot-melt carnauba wax. These tiles have a mellow sheen that enhances grain pattern and wood color. Although more expensive than unfinished tiles, prefinished tiles are a good choice for the do-it-yourselfer. Finishing a wood floor is a time-consuming task and requires experience to ensure a smooth, even surface. For tips on finishing wood floors, see page 157.

UNFINISHED TILES

Because unfinished tiles require finishing, they are most often used by professional flooring contractors. Although less expensive than pre-finished tiles, parquet patterns are usually more limited. However, unfinished tiles afford much more versatility in terms of color—you can stain and finish them any way you want. For example, you can stain or finish the tiles to match existing woodwork in the room, or use pastel "pickling" stains of various colors to create a contemporary or Southwestern look. You also could use an aniline wood dye to stain the tiles with bold, brilliant colors. The possibilities are limitless.

COMMON SIZES

Most wood parquet tiles are 12 inches x 12 inches and range in thickness from 5/16 to 3/4 inch, although other sizes and shapes (rectangles and octagons) are available. You also can buy individual wood blocks or fillets of various widths and lengths to create your own parquet design. Wood feature strips are available for use as borders and for setting off blocks or groups of tiles on the floor. Wood reducer strips (to make smooth transitions where floor is nchange levels at entryways) can be found, as well as matching wood base moldings and stair nosings in various profiles.

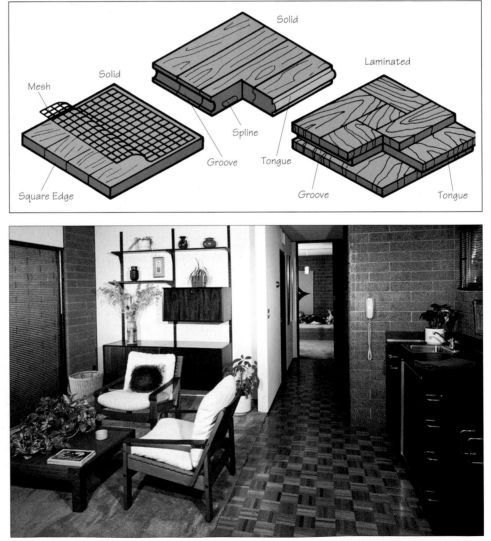

▲ *Choose from a broad range of colors, from light blond (used here) to dark mahogany.*

▶ *Spice up an ordinary parquet wood with an elaborate design.*

You can install wood parquet tiles over plywood, medium-density particleboard, hardboard, and woodboard or concrete subfloors and underlayments. Some finish flooring materials, such as polished stone, wood strip floors, and most resilient tiles and sheet flooring, also provide suitable underlayments for wood tiles. Generally, wood parquet tiles cannot be laid over cushioned vinyl or urethane no-wax surfaces. Check with the manufacturer or dealer for specific requirements for the tile you have chosen.

MOISTURE REQUIREMENTS

In all cases, the existing surface must be smooth, sound, rigid, and, above all, dry. More than any other flooring material, wood is sensitive to moisture—even relatively small amounts in subfloor materials can warp, cup, delaminate, crack, or even rot the tiles. Manufacturers generally recommend that you do not install the tiles on floors below grade or in damp or humid areas, such as bathrooms or laundry rooms. Subfloors and underlayments on or above grade should be checked with a moisture meter or other precise testing method to determine the percentage of moisture in the subfloor material. Typically, the moisture content should be about 7 percent and should not exceed about 15 percent. Conduct these tests during the rainy season. Moisture specifications, testing methods, and other subfloor requirements usually are included in the installation manual provided by the flooring manufacturer. The manuals also specify appropriate moisture barriers, if required. Wood parquet tiles should not be applied over radiant-heated floors, as extreme changes in temperature will dry out the wood, causing the same problems caused by moisture.

Extreme changes in atmospheric humidity and temperature can also

General Room Preparation

Remove all existing base moldings or shoes, thresholds, floor registers, doors, and similar obstructions. Using a handsaw, undercut or notch the bottoms of all door casings so the finish tiles can fit underneath them when installed (see page 156). If you are going to be installing unfinished tiles that require sanding, tape polyethylene sheets over entryways to prevent airborne sawdust from migrating to adjacent rooms. Also tape pieces of cardboard over heating outlets and cold-air returns. Sweep or vacuum the floor to remove loose dirt and dust.

▲ *Consider continuing the parquet tiles up stairs and on landings.*

affect wood parquet tiles. Typically, you want to keep the room humidity relatively constant (between 40 and 65 percent). During the heating season, you can increase humidity levels with a vaporizer, humidifier, or similar device. Wood stoves and electric heaters create an especially dry atmosphere during winter months. During the wet, humid season, you can reduce room humidity by means of a refrigerant-type air conditioner or dehumidifier.

WOOD SUBFLOORS

These must be smooth, rigid, and securely nailed to joists spaced 16 inches on center. Plywood subfloors should be a minimum of 3/4 inch thick (or 5/8 inch for tongue-and-groove). If the floor flexes, install bridging (see page 47).

1. Sand Floor
On finish wood floors, rough-sand the surface to remove any varnish, paint, or wax.

2. Renail Loose Subfloor
Secure a loose subfloor with nails. Set the nail heads, and fill nail holes, cracks, and other defects with wood putty or filler.

3. Sand Irregularities
Sand ridges or rough spots to provide a smooth surface on which to set tile. If the floor proves to be excessively damaged, cover it with a new underlayment.

4. Finish Cleanup
Vacuum all sanding dust that has been created.

1. Sand Floor

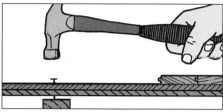

2. Renail Loose Subfloor

3. Sand Irregularities

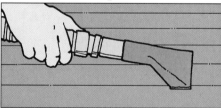

4. Finish Cleanup

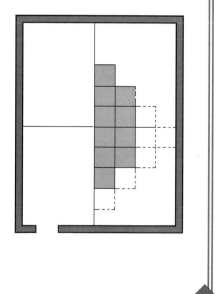

CONCRETE SUBFLOORS

To install the tiles, these must be smooth, even and waterproof. If not, see page 49.

1. Wash Floor
Remove grease and oil stains with a concrete or driveway cleaner. Rinse thoroughly.

2. Fill Cracks
Fill all cracks and low spots with a latex concrete-patching compound.

3. Grind High Spots
Wear safety goggles while grinding off high spots with a carborundum stone or a terrazzo grinder chucked in an electric drill. Remove any paint or sealer with a floor sander.

4. Finish Cleanup
Vacuum the floor to remove all dust.

1. Wash Floor

2. Fill Cracks

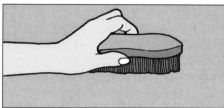

3. Grind High Spots

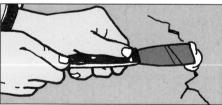

4. Finish Cleanup

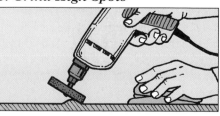

Layout

Use the layout methods described on pages 142-143 for resilient tiles. If you are installing feature strips, indicate their locations on the floor when you snap the working lines. If you are using solid-wood tiles, allow for a 1/2-inch expansion joint between the tiles and all vertical surfaces (walls, built-ins, raised fireplace hearths, etc.). Laminated tiles usually do not require an expansion space, but read manufacturer's instructions to make sure. The joints are covered later by base molding, or, in the case of exposed joints, filled with a cork filler strip stained to match the tiles (available from the flooring dealer).

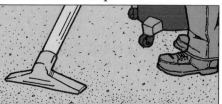

Before you lay the tiles, mix up the tiles from several cartons to assure a good mix of colors and grain patterns over the entire floor. Tools needed are shown to the right.

1. Establish Working Lines

Mark the working lines by measuring the center points on opposing walls. Drive a nail into each and stretch a chalk line between them. Do the same on the other walls, but do not snap the chalk lines yet. With a framing square, check that they form a true 90-degree angle. If this is done accurately, the tiles form a grid perfectly centered in the room. If the room is irregularly shaped, or if there are various entrances or bowed walls, you may want to adjust the working lines to minimize the visual effects on the grid pattern. If one wall is usually hidden by furniture, make the adjustment there.

2. Make a Trial Run

Practice laying out several tiles along two work lines that form a quadrant. Get used to the tongue-and-groove construction of the tiles. There will be two adjacent edges with tongues, and two adjacent edges with grooves. If you place them correctly, tongue into groove, you will create the basket-weave pattern of the parquet floor. Alternate the grains from wood tile to wood tile, placing the tongues into the grooves.

3. Spread the Adhesive

Starting at the intersection of your working lines, spread adhesive with a notched trowel, being careful not to cover the working lines. Spread only as much adhesive as you can cover with tile before the adhesive dries. Some adhesives should be tacky before the tile is laid.

With self-stick tiles, this step is eliminated. These tiles bond instantly when pressed into place, so be careful to position them correctly.

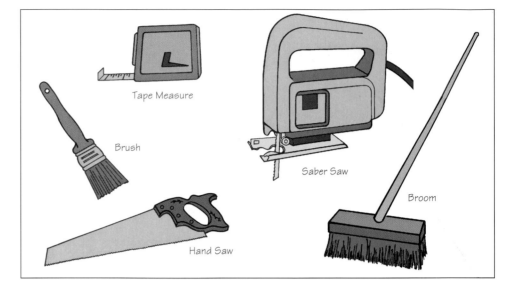

Tape Measure
Brush
Saber Saw
Broom
Hand Saw

1. Establish Working Lines

Knee Pads
Framing Square

2. Make a Trial Run

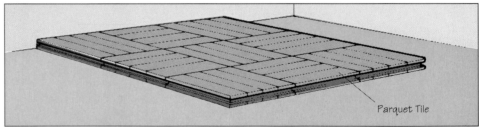

Parquet Tile

3. Spread the Adhesive

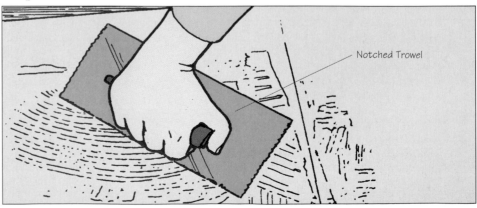

Notched Trowel

4. Set the First Tiles

Before you begin to spread the adhesive, read the instructions and note how much time you will have to work before it dries. Apply the adhesive along one chalk line, with a notched trowel angled at 45 degrees to the floor. Begin at the intersection and work toward the wall, leaving part of the chalk line exposed for guidance. Lay the first tile into a corner of the intersection. Align the edges of the tiles, not the tongues, with the lines. Place the second tile against the first one, engaging the tongue and groove. Make sure each tile interlocks fully with the adjacent tiles. Avoid sliding the tiles any more than is necessary. If you have to walk or kneel on newly laid tiles, put down a piece of plywood to distribute your weight; otherwise, the tiles may slip out of place. The first 10 or 12 tiles determine the alignment for the rest of the floor. Lay additional tiles in a stair-step fashion.

5. Bed Tiles

When you have filled in one section of the floor with full tiles, strike over the entire surface with a rubber mallet to bed it firmly into the adhesive (do not use a floor roller or rolling pin). Follow the same procedure to lay the remaining full tiles.

6. Create the Border

Cut and fit all partial tiles around the border and room openings. For straight cuts, use a fine-tooth handsaw or jigsaw equipped with a fine-tooth blade. You also can use the jigsaw to make curved or irregular cutouts.

To make a border, align tile 2 (refer to drawing) over tile 1 and place tile 3 over tiles 1 and 2, pushing it 1/2 to 3/4 inch away from the wall. It helps to place a wood spacer of that width between the top tile and the wall. This gap is needed for the cork expansion strip that comes with the tiles. Mark tile 2, using tile 3 as a guide. Then saw along the mark. Tile 2 will be the piece to place in the border.

Remember to leave at least 1/2 inch between the tiles and the wall or other vertical surfaces. When marking tiles for cutting, use a wood spacer to maintain the appropriate gap.

To avoid scratching the finish on prefinished tiles, use a low-tack spray adhesive (available at art supply stores) to apply a piece of thin felt or similar fabric to the underside of the jigsaw shoe. Coat both surfaces, allow the adhesive to become tacky, and then press the fabric in place.

4. Set the First Tiles

Working Lines

5. Bed Tiles

6. Create the Border

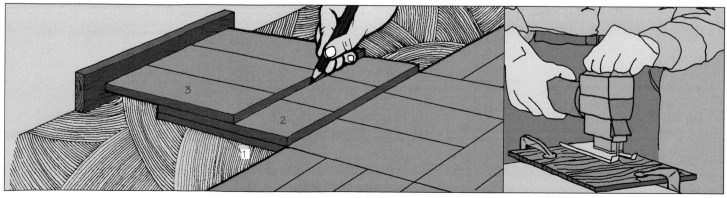

7. Cut under Doorjambs

Using a tile for a guide, mark how much of the doorjamb must be removed to allow the tile to fit under it. Then trim the bottom of the jamb with a saw. Generally, the width of the sawblade will provide a sufficient gap to allow for the tile and tile adhesive.

8. Clean, Replace Moldings, Finish & Wax

Use a clean rag dampened in adhesive solvent to clean any excess off the floor. Let the adhesive dry overnight, or as specified on the container label; then insert the cork expansion strip before replacing the baseboard, shoe molding, heating registers, and so on. Drive nails into the baseboard, not down into the tile. If you have installed unfinished tiles that require sanding, use a drum sander and edging machine equipped with a 150-grit paper. Hand-sand areas that the machines miss. Finish the floor with a reliable paste wax (if required) and buff it twice a year. Wet-mopping or scrubbing will ruin the finish.

7. Cut under Doorjambs

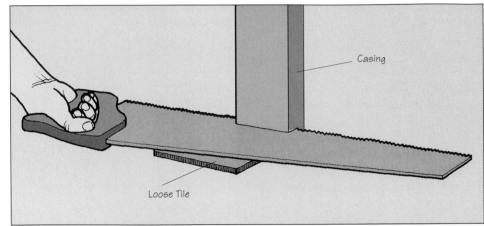

Casing

Loose Tile

8. Clean, Replace Moldings, Finish & Wax

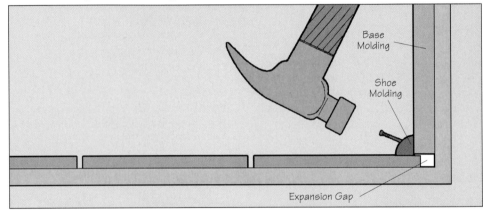

Base Molding

Shoe Molding

Expansion Gap

▲ *Wood tiles create an elegant feeling in this entryway.*

Unfinished parquet tiles will accept a variety of stains and finishes, although a durable, floor-grade polyurethane—either oil-based or water-based—is often the finish of choice. Traditional oil-based floor varnishes (called short-oil or bar-top varnishes) are rarely used anymore, because they are not as durable, are harder to apply, and impart a distinct amber cast to the wood.

Another finishing option is a group of products called gel stains and clear gel finishes. These vary in consistency from that of a thick latex paint to toothpaste. They are applied easily with a clean cloth or sponge mop. Although most are solvent-based, at least one water-based brand is available. Gel stains and clear finishes dry within 3 to 4 hours, considerably speeding up application. Some clear gel finishes are durable enough for wood floors; others are not. Most gel stains, however, are compatible with polyurethane topcoats.

POLYURETHANE FINISHES

As a group, polyurethanes provide greater protection than other clear finishes. Polyurethanes are available clear, colored, or tinted. They come in gloss, semigloss, and matte finishes. The amount of protection depends on the formula. The tougher polyurethanes have a higher resin or solids content, which also makes them more costly than the less-durable grades. Use a top-grade interior polyurethane rated for floor use. Although the surface film is not as flexible as that of an exterior polyurethane, it is harder and more resistant to scratches. If you do not like the "plastic over wood" effect of a heavy polyurethane surface coating, you can use a penetrating polyurethane. This allows more of the natural grain texture and pattern to show through, giving the floor a "hand-rubbed" look.

Oil-Based. The oil-based finishes are readily available at any paint dealer or hardware store, and usually cost less than the water-based finishes. Generally, you need to apply only two coats of a premium oil-based polyurethane, whereas the thinner water-based polyurethanes may require up to five coats to offer the same protection. On the down side, these polyurethanes have relatively long dry times (12 to 24 hours between coats) and require a solvent, such as mineral spirits, for cleanup. Also, oil-based polyurethanes rely on a mechanical bond for good adhesion, which means you must scuff the surface with 150- 180-grit sandpaper between each coat. Oil-based polyurethanes can be applied over oil varnishes and other sanded polyurethanes, but not over lacquer, shellac, or any finishing products (stains, fillers, sealers, waxes) that contain silicone or stearates. Doing so causes "fisheyes" in the final finish. Clear oil-based polyurethanes have a slightly yellow cast, which will darken over a period of time after exposure to sunlight, though not as much as oil-based varnishes.

Water-Based. These polyurethanes dry much more quickly than oil-based ones (2-3 hours between coats). They clean up with water. They do not rely on a mechanical bond between coats. Sand lightly with a fine 220-grit paper just to knock off dust specks. Because each coat goes on thinner than oil-based polyurethane, you will need to apply at least three to five coats. Since they dry quickly, you should be able to apply several coats in a day. Unlike oil-based polyurethanes, water-based types dry crystal clear and will not yellow over time. Make sure you like the result of a clear finish; it may look different than expected.

Water-based polyurethanes have several drawbacks. Aside from the higher cost, only a few are durable enough for floors. Also, application can be tricky and it is easy to introduce bubbles when you mix and apply it. Manufacturers recommend using a paint pad applicator (rather than a brush or roller) to apply the finish. Apply the finish using long, even strokes, while keeping a wet leading edge at all times.

▲ *Not only does polyurethane protect your wood floor, it also gives it a beautiful shine, bringing out the best in the wood.*

APPLY POLYURETHANE

On open-grained woods such as oak, you may want to use wood filler to fill the pores before applying polyurethane.

Do not "brush in" the polyurethane as you would a penetrating oil finish. Agitating the finish in this way will introduce air bubbles that may not work their way out before the finish cures. Instead, lay the finish in long, even strokes.

You can apply polyurethane with a good-quality natural bristle paintbrush, but it takes some skill not to leave brush marks. It is much easier to get good results with a lamb's wool applicator. This applicator consists of a piece of soft wool clamped to a wooden block. Attach the block to a broomstick. The stick lets you make longer strokes than you could with a brush. It also makes the job quicker and easier.

No matter how careful you are, you may find that you get tiny, trapped air bubbles after the first or second coat. Sometimes this happens because the polyurethane was too cool when applied. If this happens to you, sand the bubbles out with 220-grit sandpaper. You may have to sand a little more aggressively than the normal scuffing between coats, but be careful not to sand through to the wood. Sanding scratches in the finish will become invisible with the next coat.

Scatches in the wood will remain visible. Then, instead of applying one or two more coats of full-strength polyurethane, thin the finish with about one-quarter part solvent, and put on three or four more coats. Thinned polyurethane will spread more easily and will be much less likely to trap bubbles.

Because specific application methods, solvents, and dry times vary between different brands, make sure you follow label directions.

1. *Vacuum Area*
Before the final finish is applied, thoroughly vacuum the floor and all moldings, door frames, and anywhere else dust may have collected. Then, wipe the floor lightly with a tack cloth. You can buy a tack cloth at the paint store or at any hardware store or home center. A tack cloth is a piece of cheese cloth that has been soaked in varnish and then allowed to dry just until the finish becomes sticky. Then it is packaged in plastic to keep it from drying out. You do not want to rub the floor with the tack cloth, because you do not want the finish from the cloth to get on the floor. You just want to pass it lightly over the floor to pick up any bits of dust that may remain. If you have a lamb's wool applicator, you can wrap the cloth around the applicator and then wipe the floor with no more pressure than the weight of the applicator.

2. *Apply Sanding Sealer*
A sanding sealer is never required, but there are three reasons you might want to use one. One reason is to save time, because sealers cure more quickly than polyurethane. Another reason is that sealers are softer, making the sanding easier. The final reason applies only to matte-finish polyurethane. To achieve the matte finish, manufacturers add tiny particles to the polyurethane. The particles break up the light when it hits the surface. Because the porosity of wood varies, the first coat of finish may soak in unevenly. With a matte finish, the particles are distributed unevenly, and this can make the finish look blotchy. If you choose to use a sealer, follow manufacturer's instructions. Begin in a corner and work outward so that you do not step on wet sealer.

3. *Apply Polyurethane*
Apply the polyurethane using a brush or lamb's wool applicator. Let the first coat dry completely before scuffing it with very fine sandpaper or with #2 steel wool. Vacuum the area and wipe with a moist mop or tack cloth. Any dirt or dust that remains will be sealed in the final coat. Apply the final coat. Do not sand the final coat.

▶ *Parquet tile patterns range from simple to elaborate in design.*

1. *Vacuum Area*

2. *Apply Sanding Sealer*

3. *Apply Polyurethane*

TILE CARE & REPAIR

Undoubtedly ceramic tile is popular for its beauty and resilience, however in addition to these attractive qualities, tile also is extremely easy to maintain. With a few simple tools, you can keep your tile looking like new. Almost everything you need can be found around the house, such as a toothbrush and an awl (or similar sharp tool), clean rags, a broom, and some household cleansers. You will need to purchase the proper grout.

Occasionally, you may find that it is necessary to remove a tile or two, if they become scratched or cracked, for instance, or you may need to reset loose tiles. These are not difficult jobs.

In addition to ceramic tile, the care and repair of stone, resilient, and wood parquet tiles are addressed, including a thorough guide to removing stains from stone and removing scuffs from resilient tile.

◀ *A ceramic tile floor requires little more maintenance than cleansing with a mild detergent.*

Ceramic tile is durable and easy to maintain. However, tile and grout joints require periodic cleaning. If you are dealing with an older installation, you may be faced with a few cracked or broken tiles and deteriorating grout joints.

ROUTINE CLEANING

Glazed Tiles. For day-to-day cleaning, simply wipe the tile down with warm water and a sponge. On floors, sweeping or vacuuming every few days will prevent grit from scratching the tile surface and dirt or grime from being ground into grout joints. Wiping up spills as soon as they occur will prevent stained grout joints.

Cleaning Agents. A mild solution of white vinegar and water (or window cleaner) removes light buildups of dirt, grease, soap scum, and water spots. For more stubborn cleanups, use a strong solution of soap-free, all-purpose cleaner or a commercial tile cleaner. Rinse thoroughly with clear water.

Ceramic tiles with metallic glazes should be cleaned and polished with a metal polish. If you need to scour the surface, use a woven-plastic pot scrubber rather than steel wool, which sheds tiny hairs that leave rust stains in grout joints. Metal scouring pads or brushes leave behind black marks that are hard to remove. Avoid using soap-based detergents because they dull the tile surface. No matter what cleanser is used, always rinse thoroughly with clear water. Avoid mixing different types of cleaners, and never mix ammonia with bleach or products that contain it.

Unglazed Tiles. Unglazed floor tiles are cleaned in the same manner as glazed tiles.

Outdoor Tiles. Other than an occasional sweeping or washing down with a hose, outdoor tiles do not require much maintenance. To remove stubborn dirt or stains, apply a solution of all-purpose cleaner, and scrub vigorously with a stiff-bristle plastic brush or push broom. Rinse thoroughly with clear water, and avoid letting runoff water enter garden areas. Grease and oil stains can be removed with a commercial driveway cleaner. Mold and mildew are removed with household bleach. (See table, right.)

REMOVE STAINS

Strong solutions of all-purpose cleaners or commercial tile cleaners will remove most stains. Always try these cleaners first before using other agents. If they do not work, try one of the stain-removal agents listed in the chart.

Stain Removal Chart

Stain	Removal Agent
Grease & Fats (animal cooking)	Concentrated solution of household cleaner
Tar, Asphalt, Oil, Grease, Oil Paints, Petroleum-Based Products	*Indoors:* Charcoal lighter fluid followed by household cleaner, water rinse *Outdoors:* Concrete or driveway cleaner
Ink, Mustard, Blood, Lipstick, Merthiolate, Coffee, Tea, Fruit Juices, Colored Dyes	*Mild:* 3% hydrogen peroxide solution. *Deep:* Full strength household bleach
Nail Polish	*Wet:* Charcoal lighter fluid *Dry:* Nail polish remover
Liquid Medicines, Shellac	Denatured alcohol
Rust	Commercial rust remover, followed by household cleaner, water rinse
Chewing Gum	Chill with ice cube wrapped in cloth, peel gum off surface

Caution: Some of these removal agents are highly toxic, caustic, or flammable. Exercise extreme caution when using them. Protect skin and eyes, avoid inhalation or ingestion, provide sufficient ventilation, and follow all label precautions.

Showers & Tub Surrounds

Shower and tub surrounds are prone to mildew and buildups of soap scum and body oils. Commercial tub-and-tile cleaners will take care of both problems, but there are some more economical alternatives: To remove mild soap deposits and hard water spots, scrub the tile weekly with a solution of 1 cup white vinegar to 1 gallon of water. This will also help keep mildew at bay. To clean grout joints, first rinse the area with water. Then use a toothbrush dipped in household bleach to remove stubborn mildew stains on grout joints. If the grout is colored, test first to make sure the bleach will not affect it. If so, use a commercial tub-and-tile cleaner.

Caution: When working with household bleach and other chemicals, provide room ventilation, wear rubber gloves and safety goggles, and avoid contact with the skin and eyes.

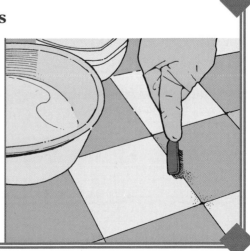

SEAL GROUT JOINTS & UNGLAZED TILE

A clear sealer may be applied to grout joints and unglazed tiles when the tile is installed to protect the surface from stains and moisture penetration (see page 33). As part of tile maintenance, you will need to reapply the sealer every 2 years (or as specified on the container label) in order to maintain that protection. If you find that the tile or grout is becoming harder and harder to keep clean, it is time to apply more sealer. Clean the tile

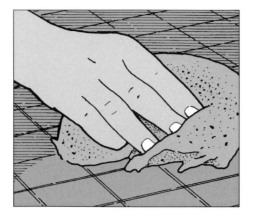

and grout thoroughly and allow to dry for several days. If the tile is waxed, remove wax with an

appropriate wax stripper (available at your tile dealer). Apply sealer according to label instructions.

WAX & BUFF

A variety of tile waxes and buffing compounds are available for unglazed tile floors. Some tile waxes are colored to enhance the appearance of unglazed terra cotta tiles or pavers. You need not apply wax each time the floor becomes dull. After cleaning the floor with a soap-free floor cleaner and rinsing thoroughly with clear water, allow to dry and then buff out the existing wax to restore the shine.

Whether using wax or a buffing compound, the simplest way to buff the floor is to rub it by hand with a soft cloth or buffing pad on an ordinary floor mop. You also

can rent a floor buffer equipped with a lamb's wool buffing pad. Operating instructions usually come with the machine.

When it is time to reapply wax, follow label instructions. To prevent wax buildup, strip off any old wax. Then wash the floor with a mild detergent and rinse thoroughly with clear water. Two or three very light coats of wax are better than one heavy coat. Spread the first coat thinly and evenly, allowing it to dry thoroughly; then buff. Repeat the procedure for each successive coat. Although this process involves more work, it achieves a higher gloss and prevents wax buildup.

Floor Buffer

REPLACE GROUT

Cracked or crumbling grout joints may indicate problems in the wall behind the tile. In fact, deteriorating grout joints usually are the first sign of water damage or excessive movement in the substrate. On the other hand, the grout itself may be at fault. In any case, try to determine the cause of the problem and fix it before you regrout.

1. Remove Old Grout

The easiest way to remove grout is to use a grout saw. For wide grout

joints, a dry diamond blade or carborundum masonry blade in a circular saw works best (wear safety goggles). For narrow joints, a pointed object such as an awl or a nail in a dowel works well.

1. Remove Old Grout

Wood Dowel

Nail

2. Clean & Regrout

After removing all of the old grout, wipe off the joints with a damp sponge and vacuum up debris. To apply new grout, see page 59.

2. Clean & Regrout

REPLACE LOOSE TILES

Loose tiles most commonly occur on walls, especially in areas subjected to moisture, such as bathrooms and backsplashes. A poorly prepared substrate, the wrong adhesive or backing, and cracked grout joints often result in moisture buildup behind the tile, breaking down the adhesive bond. In dry installations, excessive vibration, such as frequent slamming of doors, could be another possible source. If just a few tiles are loose, first fix the cause of the problem, and then replace the tiles.

1. Remove Tiles
To remove the tiles, use a hammer and a short length of hacksaw blade, an ice pick, beer-can opener, small cold chisel, or similar object to dig out the grout around the loose tiles.

2. Pry out Tile
Use a putty knife to carefully pry out each tile.

3. Scrape off Adhesive
Scrape off the dried adhesive with a putty knife from the wall and from the back of the tile.

4. Apply New Adhesive
Allow the wall to dry thoroughly; then apply tile adhesive, using the putty knife, to the back of the tile and to the wall and press the tile tightly into place. Clean off any excess adhesive.

5. Tape Tile in Place
On vertical surfaces, hold the tile in place with masking tape and spacers, such as matchsticks or plastic tile spacers.

6. Grout
Allow the adhesive to cure fully; then regrout with a plastic putty knife. When the grout dries, apply a grout sealer (see page 59).

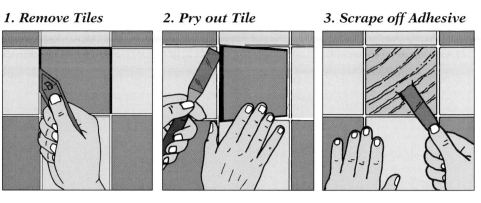

1. Remove Tiles **2. Pry out Tile** **3. Scrape off Adhesive**

4. Apply New Adhesive **5. Tape Tile in Place** **6. Grout**

Replace Many Tiles

If many of the tiles on the wall are loose, it is best to remove all of them, starting from the top and working down. If, after removing a few tiles, you find that the drywall backing also is wet or damaged, it will have to be replaced. In wet areas, ordinary drywall should be replaced with water-resistant drywall or cement backer board. See page 100 for instructions.

If you are removing wall tiles, first lay down a heavy tarp on the floor or counter to cushion the fall of tiles on the floor, counter, or tub. Use a utility knife to separate border and trim tiles from caulk beads.

With a hammer and wide-blade chisel or putty knife, carefully tap and pry the tiles away from the wall, starting with the top row and working down. Try to catch each tile as it falls off. If some of the tiles are still stuck tight, scrape out the grout between them as described, and pry them off the wall, one at a time. The whole point of this

exercise is to save as many full tiles as possible—work slowly and carefully. A few broken tiles will be inevitable, though. If you do not have spares, you can install decorative insert tiles or a pattern of contrasting tiles to take their place where appropriate.

After all the tiles have been removed, clean the adhesive off the tile backs, repair or replace the substrate as needed, and then re-adhere the tiles with an adhesive recommended by the tile dealer.

BROKEN TILES

A large number of cracked or broken tiles usually indicates structural problems. In this case, remove all tiles, install a rigid backing, and set new tiles.

If only a few tiles are cracked, remove them carefully.

1. Remove Damaged Tile

Scrape away the grout surrounding the tile. Glazed wall tiles will break easily if you score an X across the surface with a glass cutter. Wearing safety glasses, use a hammer and cold chisel to break the tile into small pieces and chip it out. Work outward from the center of the tile to avoid damaging other tiles.

2. Replace Tile

Use a putty knife to scrape dried adhesive off the substrate. Spread

1. Remove Damaged Tile

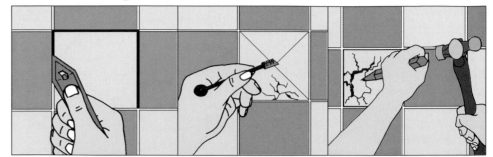

2. Replace Tile

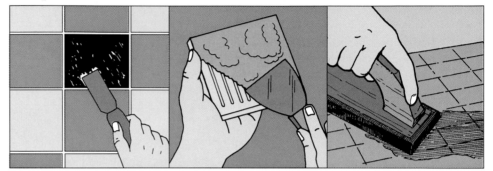

fresh adhesive on the back of a new tile and into the empty space. Press the new tile in place; then grout and seal (see page 59).

TRAPPED TILES

Often a portion of a broken tile extends underneath a permanent floor fixture. To repair the tile, you will not have to remove the fixture.

1. Remove Grout

Scrape out grout (see step 1 above).

2. Score the Tile

With a glass cutter, score the tile along the base of the fixture; then score an X on the exposed portion of the tile, from corner to corner.

3. Remove Tile

Chip out the broken tile and scrape the adhesive off the floor.

4. Cut New Tile to Fit

Mark the new tile to fit the space by placing it over an adjacent tile and marking it with a pencil compass fitted with a thin grease pencil. With a glass cutter, score the cutline and then a grid of criss-crossed lines in the waste area of the tile, and carefully nibble away.

1. Remove Grout

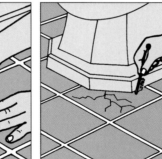

2. Score the Tile

3. Remove Tile

4. Cut New Tile to Fit

5. Tile & Caulk

6. Apply Caulk

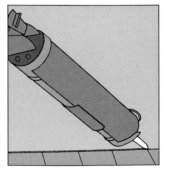

5. Tile & Caulk

With a putty knife, spread adhesive on the tile back and on the exposed subfloor. Set the tile.

6. Apply Caulk

Apply a bead of silicone caulk between the tile and the base of the fixture.

The maintenance techniques for stone tile vary for the different types of stone. Marble, for instance, is an alkaline material that can be etched by acids. Many common foods (especially citrus juices, vinegar, and alcoholic beverages) contain acids. Granite and slate are nearly impervious to acids, but all stones are porous and vulnerable to stains. Also, chemicals in cleaning solutions can interact with minerals in stones, causing discoloration or a dull finish. Use only cleaners, polishes, and sealers recommended by a stone tile dealer.

ROUTINE CLEANING

Daily maintenance of stone floors includes sweeping or vacuuming. A weekly damp mopping with soft water will pick up remaining dirt. For more stubborn dirt on granite or slate, use a light solution of all-purpose detergent in warm water followed by a clean-water rinse. For marble, use a liquid dishwashing detergent, or other neutral cleaner that has a pH of 7. Avoid scented detergents such as lemon or pine.

Tiled walls and countertops should be cleaned with a soft cloth moistened with warm water. For more stubborn dirt, use a mild solution of household cleaner or dishwashing detergent. Rinse thoroughly with water. Do not use abrasive cleaners, or those that contain oils, organic solvents, acids, or other chemicals that can discolor or etch the surface.

Preventive Maintenance. Sweep floors frequently to keep grit from scratching the tiles. Place floormats at entries and cover high-traffic areas with rugs. Use nonscratching casters, glides, and cups under furniture legs. Do not walk on the floor with spiked heels. Do not use a stone countertop as a cutting board or chopping block. Use placemats under plates and place coasters under glasses. Wipe up spills right away, and rinse with clear water.

▲ *With all stone floors, you will want to sweep frequently to prevent grit from scratching the tiles.*

Polishes. Small scratches can be removed by rubbing a polishing powder in with a damp cloth or by using a buffing pad with a mix of powder and water. Deeper scratches can be removed by "sanding" them out with progressively finer-grit abrasive blocks or powdered abrasives. Badly scratched surfaces will need to be reground and repolished professionally.

REMOVE STAINS

A stone cleaner or cleaning kit is available at most tile dealers.

Oil Stains. These stains are caused by a variety of foods and substances. They appear as dark spots on the surface. Light stains can be removed with an all-purpose cleaner. Remove deep-seated stains with a cloth that has been dampened with acetone.

Organic Stains. These stains usually are a yellow, pink, or brown color and are caused by foods, plant matter, bird and animal waste, and other organic substances. Light stains can be removed with a poultice made from a chlorine-based abrasive kitchen cleanser (rinse thoroughly). For stubborn stains, use the peroxide or chlorine bleach poultice (see next page).

Rust Stains. These orange-brown stains often respond to scrubbing with a nonabrasive cleaner and stiff bristle brush or plastic scouring pad. For more stubborn stains, you may have to use a commercial rust remover. You may need to repolish after removing the stain.

Smoke Stains. You can buy "smoke-stain removers" to remove a buildup of soot on tiled fireplace surrounds. Light deposits can be removed with a solution of nonabrasive, all-purpose cleaner applied with a soft cloth. To prevent heavy buildups of soot, clean the tiles every two weeks during months of heavy use.

Paint Spatters. Chip off the paint spatters with a plastic putty knife. If this fails, use a "heavy" liquid paint stripper to remove hardened paint. Like rust removers, caustic paint removers will etch or dull polished marble finishes. Avoid strippers that contain organic solvents, such as toluene, xylene, and methylene.

Caution: Acetone is highly flammable, so keep it away from open flames. Provide adequate ventilation and wear rubber gloves.

COMMON STAINS

Daily maintenance of polished marble tiles is best done with ordinary soft water and a soft cloth. Household detergent will help clean up more troublesome spots. To deal with very stubborn stains, you may wish to purchase a marble cleaning kit that contains the proper chemicals and instructions for specific stains.

Cleaning Marble. For removing ground-in grime and even some oil and grease stains, use household powdered detergent and a little water to make up a thick paste. Spread this over the surface of the marble in a coating about 1/4 inch thick. Cover with a damp cloth; over this place a plastic sheet. Allow the mixture to sit covered for at least 24 hours. Then remove the plastic and the damp cloth, and allow the material to dry in place for at least another 24 hours. Scrape away the residue, flush the marble with clean water, and polish the surface with a soft dry cloth.

Organic stains on marble, such as tobacco, tea, coffee, or leached colors from flowers are best removed by bleaching. Lay facial

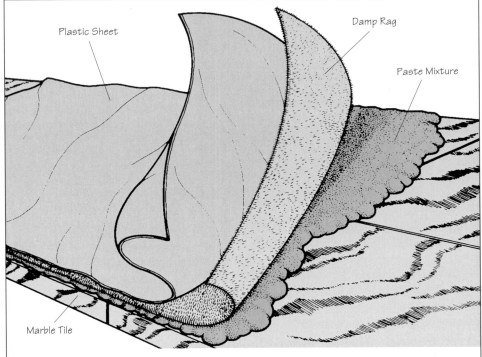

Cleaning Marble. *A paste made from household powdered detergent and water often removes stubborn stains. Apply it in layers and let sit overnight; remove the rag and let the mixture dry. Scrape it away, and then clean and polish the marble.*

tissues soaked in a 20-percent solution of hydrogen peroxide on the marble. Cover the entire marble surface with the soggy mass. Place a damp cloth over it, and cover this with a plastic sheet. Depending on how deep the stain is, up to 48 hours will be required to remove

it from the marble. Really stubborn oil stains are best removed using this method but substituting detergent for the peroxide.

Repair Stone Tiles

To replace damaged stone tiles or re-adhere loose ones, follow the procedures on page 164.

If you do not have replacement tiles and if you can remove the tile from the setting bed without additional damage, cracked or broken stone tiles can sometimes be glued back together. Use a special repair glue or an ordinary clear epoxy. With a small paintbrush, cover the edges to be glued; then clamp them together for the specified amount of time. Wipe away excess glue before it hardens.

Small missing pieces can be patched with a mixture of marble

dust combined with a clear, two-part epoxy. Some stone dealers carry marble dust for this purpose, or a small piece of marble can be pulverized to make the dust (wear goggles when doing this work). Prepare a stiff mixture of marble dust and epoxy (the consistency of dough) by mixing the dust with the epoxy resin, and then adding epoxy hardener. Use a plastic putty knife to force the mixture into the crack or depression; then smooth the surface.

For missing corners, construct a wooden form to hold the mixture. Cover the mold with wax paper and fill it with the paste. After the epoxy

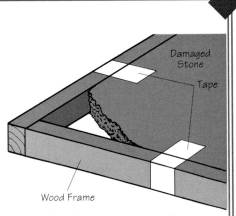

mixture is fully cured, remove the paper and the form. Sand the patch with successively finer grits of silicon carbide paper (down to 400-grit paper) and then polish.

Most modern resilient tiles have a no-wax surface, which simplifies cleaning considerably. Routine maintenance involves nothing more than sweeping or vacuuming the floor. A weekly damp-mopping with clear water will pick up most light dirt and stains. As with other surfaces, wipe up spills soon after they occur.

FLOOR CLEANERS

When damp-mopping no longer does an adequate job, it is time to use a cleaner. A variety of floor cleaners is available for resilient floors, both in supermarkets and from tile dealers. Avoid using abrasive cleansers or other cleaning solutions that will scratch or otherwise damage the vinyl wear layer. Cleaners containing caustics, harsh soaps, and powders or petroleum-based solvents such as kerosene, naptha, turpentine, and benzene can damage resilient tile floors. Most resilient tile manufacturers make cleaners and other floor-care products that are compatible with their tiles. No matter what cleaner you use, follow label instructions (some are not recommended for no-wax floors). Rinse thoroughly with clear water, but avoid flooding the floor with liquids, as they will seep through joints between the tiles and loosen the adhesive. Also, scalding water can discolor some resilient tiles.

REFINISH

If your flooring does not have a no-wax surface, you will have to refinish it periodically. Many clear acrylic-floor finishes are available. Floor strippers remove old floor finishes when they become discolored. Referred in the industry as "metal cross-linked acrylic finishes," they are resistant to neutral cleaners such as all-purpose cleaners. Follow label instructions.

▲ *Resilient tile floors, like this one from Armstrong, benefit from an occasional damp-mopping.*

On no-wax floors, you can restore the shine with special finishing products made by the tile manufacturer. Do not use paste waxes on resilient tile floors.

Preventive Maintenance. The best way to avoid damaging the floor is to take preventive measures. Place floor mats at all entrances to help keep out dirt and moisture. Place area rugs or mats in front of sink areas in kitchens and bathrooms. Note that some carpet dyes and rubber backings used for rugs or mats will discolor a resilient floor. Use nonstaining fiber mats or colorfast carpet mats.

All resilient tile is subject to indentations or gouges caused by heavy loads resting on small or uneven surfaces. Protect the floor by removing any small metal domes from furniture legs and substituting larger furniture rests or plastic furniture cups. Also place cups under the leveling feet of refrigerators, washers, dryers, and similar heavy appliances. Replace narrow casters with wider ones. Avoid walking on the floor in shoes with stiletto or spiked heels.

Wrong

Right

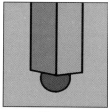
Wrong

Right

Wrong

Right

Wrong

Right

CLEAN SCUFFS, SPOTS & STAINS

You can remove most stains from resilient floors with a heavy solution of all-purpose household cleaner or commercial floor cleaner available from the tile dealer. To remove black scuff marks, rub lightly with fine (#0000) steel wool dipped in a light solution of all-purpose cleaner. Rinse thoroughly with clear water; then apply an acrylic floor finish or conditioner (available at supermarkets) to restore the shine.

If the spot or stain does not respond to the cleaners above, you may have to try one of the methods listed below. After removing stains by any of these means, apply a coat of floor finish or conditioner over the area to restore the shine.

Lipstick, Mercurochrome, Merthiolate, Ink, Mustard, Food, Beverages. Soak up excess with a dry cloth or tissue. Place a white cloth soaked in full-strength bleach over the stain, and cover it with household plastic wrap taped to the floor to prevent evaporation. Leave it in place for 10 to 15 minutes or until the stain disappears (but no longer than 1 hour). Wear rubber gloves when using bleach.

Note: *After bleaching, the surface of some dark-color tiles may appear milky. This condition usually disappears overnight.*

Oil, Oil-Based Paints, Grease, Tar, Asphalt. Remove excess with a plastic spatula or another tool that will not scratch the floor. Remove remaining residue with a clean cloth dampened in charcoal lighter fluid (follow label precautions). Immediately wash the area with a household cleaner; then rinse and dry.

Rust. Prepare a diluted solution of oxalic acid (1 part acid to 10 parts

Caution: Oxalic acid is highly toxic—wear gloves and avoid contact with skin and eyes, inhalation, or ingestion. Follow all label precautions.

water), and apply it to the stain with a clean cloth. Rinse with clear water and dry.

Nail Polish. If it's still wet, pick up residue with a cloth dampened in charcoal lighter fluid. Wash immediately with household cleaner; rinse and dry. If polish has dried, scrape off with a plastic putty knife or spatula. Remove any residue with a cloth dampened in nail-polish remover and rinse immediately. Avoid walking on the surface for at least half an hour.

Chewing Gum. Wrap an ice cube in a cloth or paper towel it and place on the surface for 10 to 15 minutes. Remove cloth and peel gum off the floor with a plastic spatula (do not use sharp utensils or tools that may scratch the floor).

Cigarette Burns. You can remove scorches caused by dropped cigarettes by carefully rubbing the spot with steel wool dipped in a paste of abrasive cleanser. Rinse with clear water and apply the appropriate floor finish or conditioner. If the burn has created a depression in the tile, you will have to replace it.

Repair Minor Damage

Remove light scratches by scrubbing with a lukewarm solution of resilient tile cleaner that is recommended by the manufacturer. Remove heavier scratches or cigarette burns by rubbing with # 00 steel wool dipped in cleaner. In both cases, rinse, dry, and polish.

For deeper scratches, use a knife or razor knife to make sawdust from a scrap piece of resilient tile. Then mix the residue with white glue. Press the mixture into small holes in resilient tile.

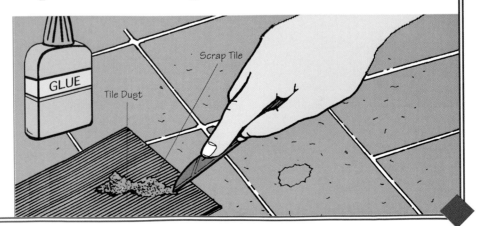

REPLACE DAMAGED TILES

If a resilient tile contains a noticeable cut, gouge, dent, or burn, usually it is easier to replace the whole tile than to try to patch the damaged spot. The same applies to cracked or broken tiles. If you do not have a spare tile for replacement purposes, you probably will not have much luck finding an exact match, even if the manufacturer is still making the same pattern. If this is the case, remove another tile from an inconspicuous place in the room (such as underneath a built-in cabinet or major appliance) and use it for the replacement.

1. Heat the Tile

Place a soft cloth or towel between an iron and the tile, and heat the tile to soften the adhesive. You also can use a blower-type heat gun to soften the adhesive. When using a heat gun, wear heavy gloves and work cautiously to avoid scorching the surrounding tiles.

2. Pry off Tile

To remove a damaged tile, insert a sharp, wide-blade chisel into the joint near one corner and gently pry up the tile. Be careful not to damage surrounding tiles. If the tile does not pry up easily, place a soft cloth or towel between an iron and the tile, and heat the tile to soften the adhesive. You also can use a blower-type heat gun to soften the adhesive. When using a heat gun, wear heavy gloves and work cautiously to avoid scorching the surrounding tiles.

If the tile is old and brittle, you will probably have to chip it out with your chisel. Wear safety goggles and try to avoid damaging surrounding tiles. Scrape all residual adhesive off the floor and from the edges of surrounding tiles.

3. Add New Tile

If the tile is dry-backed, coat the back of the tile and the floor with adhesive, press it in place, and roll with a rolling pin or J-roller. If using self-stick tile, remove the paper backing and simply press it into place. In some cases, you may need to use a hammer and wood block to tap the edges of the tile in place. Be careful not to bend or damage the new tile or any surrounding ones.

1. Heat the Tile

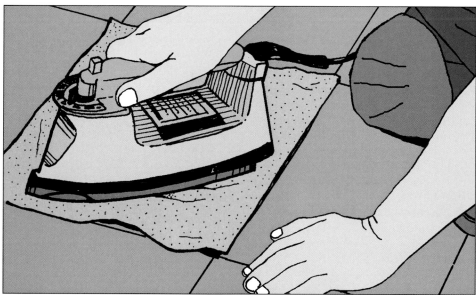

2. Pry off Tile

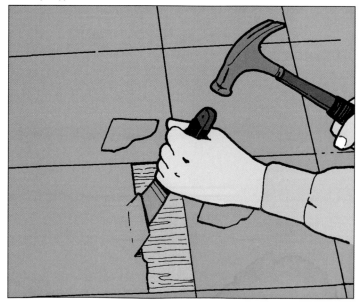

3. Add New Tile

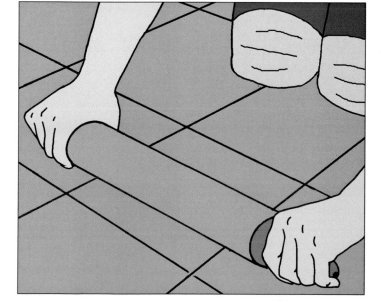

WOOD PARQUET TILES

Cleaning, polishing, and repairing wood parquet is the same as caring for fine wood furniture. Because different lines of wood flooring have varied finishes, it is best to use floor-care products recommended by the tile manufacturer. (Several manufacturers offer "repair kits" containing enough adhesive and finish to repair or replace a few damaged tiles.)

If yours is an older parquet floor and you are not sure what type of finish it has, chances are that it is either an oil-based varnish or polyurethane. Consult a flooring dealer for an appropriate "generic" floor-care product.

▲ *Wood floors should be treated like fine wood furniture. Never use water to clean a parquet tile floor.*

ROUTINE CLEANING

You should not damp-mop parquet floors—water is wood's biggest enemy. Wipe up spills as soon as they happen with a slightly damp cloth; then dry immediately with a dry cloth. Do not use cleaners that contain abrasives, water, caustic chemicals, bleach, or ammonia. For routine cleaning, it is best to use a solvent-based cleaner or a one-step cleaner/polish recommended by the manufacturer. Otherwise, use a solvent-based wood furniture cleaner available at supermarkets or hardware stores. (If you choose the latter, make sure the product is recommended for the finish on your floor, such as polyurethane.)

WAXING

On some prefinished floors, a floor wax may be applied over the surface finish after the floor is installed. When it is time to rewax, use only solvent-based wood floor waxes (or whatever is recommended by the flooring manufacturer). Acrylic "kitchen" floor waxes generally are not recommended for use on wood parquet floors. Also, some polyurethane finishes should not be waxed at all. Check label instructions.

PREVENTIVE MAINTENANCE

Vacuuming the floor will help keep tracked-in grit from scratching the floor and dirt from being ground into the joints. To protect the floor from scratches and dents, place slip-resistant nonstaining mats at entrances, use casters on furniture legs, and avoid walking with spiked heels. Floor mats in kitchen and bathroom areas will help protect floors from stains, as will area rugs in other rooms of the house.

Scratches and Burns. You usually can remove light surface scratches and burns by rubbing with very fine (#0000) steel wool dipped in a wood-paste wax and then buffing it out with a soft cloth. For deeper scratches or burns (that have penetrated the finish), sand with 240-grit sandpaper; then apply a touch-up stain and finish. When the finish dries, wax and buff. Minor scratches can be filled with colored-wood putty sticks.

Dents and Gouges. To fill minor dents and gouges, roughen the surface with fine sandpaper; then fill with a colored wood putty stick or a colored wood filler. To help conceal the patch, you can draw in "grain lines" with a dark-colored stain applied with a small artist's brush. Apply a touch-up finish, wax, and buff. Larger dents and gouges will require replacement of the whole tile (see next page).

White Spots or Water Spots. These are caused by standing water or other liquid that has penetrated the finish, turning it a milky color. If cleaner does not remove the spot, apply a stripper, followed by a touch-up finish. Then, wax and buff.

Stubborn Stains. If the stain has not fully penetrated the finish, you need only sand off the portion of finish containing the stain, and apply a touch-up finish. If the stain has penetrated the finish into the wood beneath, proceed as follows: Sand down to bare wood (be careful not to gouge the surface). Apply a full-strength bleach or a solution of oxalic acid (1 part acid to 10 parts water); wear rubber gloves and avoid spreading onto surrounding areas. Let stand about 1 hour. Rinse with a damp cloth and let dry. Sand again with 240-grit sandpaper until smooth; then use a tack cloth to remove sanding dust. Apply a touch-up wood stain, followed by a clear finish and wax.

REPAIR TILES

There are three ways to remove a damaged wooden tile. You can remove just one fillet or strip, you can saw the tile into sections and chisel it out, or you can saw through the tongue and groove.

However, no matter how the tile is removed, replacing the tile is always the same (see steps 3 and 4).

Method One: Remove Tile Fillet

1. Drill Holes. Drill a series of parallel, overlapping holes 5/8 inch in diameter along the length of the fillet (individual strip of wood), being careful not to damage adjacent fillets.

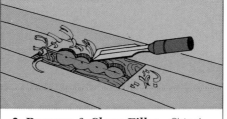

2. Remove & Clean Fillet. Chisel the fillet in half across the grain; then chisel lengthwise to remove all the fillet pieces. Scrape excess glue from the subfloor.

Method Two: Remove Butt-Edge Tiles

1. Cut into Tile. Adjust your circular saw to the thickness of the tile; then make several parallel cuts 2 inches apart across the tile. Be careful not to cut into the subfloor beneath.

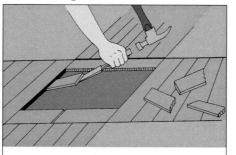

2. Remove Tile & Clean. With a hammer and chisel, remove the portion of the tile between cutlines. Remove the two sides of the tile and excess adhesive.

Method Three: Remove Tongue-&-Groove Tiles

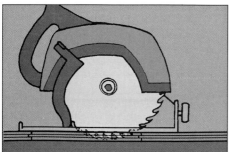

1. Remove Tile. To remove a tile, use a circular saw set to equal the thickness of the tile. Cut along the joint lines. Do not cut surrounding joints. Finish cutting the corners with a thin chisel.

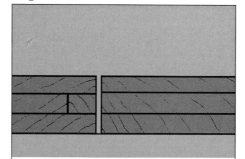

2. Pry out Tongue. Pry out the tongue of the old tile. Then, chisel off the bottom groove sides on the replacement tile. Leave one tongue and cut off the other.

Replace Tile

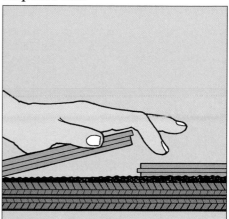

3. Set Fillet or Tile. If the replacement fillet or tile is a tongue-and-groove piece, remove the bottom part of the groove side (if any) and all tongues except one end tongue. Spread adhesive on the back side and fit it into place. Press down firmly until fillet or tile is flush with the surrounding tile.

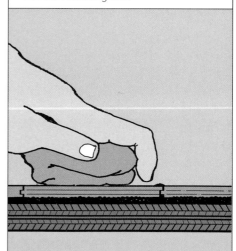

4. Clean & Refinish. Clean off any excess adhesive from the joints and off the surface with adhesive solvent, and weight down the tile with heavy books or similar objects. Do not use bricks or anything else that might scratch the tile. If required, sand, stain, and finish fillet or tile to match surrounding tile.

GLOSSARY

Apron tile Trim or facing on the side or in front of a countertop edge.

Back-buttering Applying adhesive to the back of a tile to supplement the adhesive spread on the setting bed. Any tile with an uneven back, button-backed tiles, sheet-mounted mosaic tiles, and small cut tiles must be back-buttered to provide a strong bond.

Backer board Cement-based panel with a fiberglass-reinforced coating; used as underlayment for tile. Also called cementitious backer units, or CBU's.

Backfill Dirt inserted behind concrete formwork for support.

Backsplash The tiled wall area behind a countertop, sink, or stove.

Base materials Layers of gravel, sand, and field stones laid beneath a footing, patio, or on slab to provide protection from ground heave and to aid drainage.

Base tile Tile that has a finished top edge; it is designed specifically for the floor line.

Battens Thin wood strips used to support ceramic tile and ensure straight courses.

Bedding block Block of wood covered with carpet or other protective material, used in conjunction with a hammer to bed tiles into adhesive.

Bisque The clay body of a tile, or the clay from which the tile is made.

Bleeding Condition in poured concrete in which water rises to the surface.

Bond coat Thin layer of adhesive applied over the substrate.

Bond strength The ability of the bond between the tile and setting bed to resist separation.

Brads Finishing nails no longer than 1½ inches; used to secure molding or other trim while minimizing its visibility.

Brick veneer tile Tile that simulates the appearance of real brick.

Bridging Cross-brace supports between floor joists used to reinforce the floor.

Bullnose tile A trim tile with one rounded edge, used to finish off outside corners.

Butt-edged wood tiles Tiles with flat edges along all sides.

Carborundum stone Coarse-grit, silicone-carbide whetstone used to smooth rough-cut edges of ceramic tile. Also called a Crystolon or India stone.

Caulk A waterproof material used to seal seams around plumbing valves, faucets, and expansion joints.

Cement-bodied tile Made of mortar rather than clay, this durable tile has the appearance of stone or pavers.

Chalkline Working line created by snapping a chalk-covered string pulled tightly between two nails.

Cleats Blocks used to support wood braces or other members.

Closet bolts Bolts that hold the toilet stool to the floor.

Cold chisel A heavy, blunt-edged chisel used in masonry work, typically for chipping or breaking up brick, stone, concrete, ceramic tile, and other masonry materials.

Contour gauge Device consisting of small metal rods between two metal pieces, and used to copy shapes of features of moldings.

Control joints Grooves cut into a concrete slab to confine cracking; cracks form along the joints rather than randomly across the slab.

Countertop trim tile Tile that is set on the outside edge of a countertop. It has a raised lip to prevent liquids from spilling over the edge.

Course One horizontal row of tiles or other material.

Cove tile A trim tile that creates a smooth joint between adjacent walls, a wall and a floor, or other surfaces.

Cross braces Supports (usually 1x3s or 2x4s) running between structural members or components.

Cure The period of time that concrete, tile adhesive, or grout must be left in order for it to reach full strength.

Dressing joints Smoothing and shaping grout lines.

Dry-set mortar A cement-based adhesive, so-called because it does not have to be kept constantly damp to cure.

Edger A tool for rounding off the perimeter edges of a concrete pour.

Expansion joint A planned break in a continuous field of tile that has been placed to absorb pressure when the setting surface expands and contracts; prevents buckling or crumbling.

Extruded cement-bodied tile Made from a mixture of portland-cement, sand, and a fine aggregate (concrete) that is extruded or cast under pressure, and then steam-cured. The result is an extremely dense-bodied tile.

Feature strip A long, narrow resilient tile trim piece often interspersed in a resilient tile floor to provide contrast and design.

Field tile A tile found in the main field of the installation.

Float A long-handled tool used to smooth (darby) a concrete surface after screeding; requires two handlers.

Floated bed A bed of mortar that serves as the setting surface for tile.

Forms Structures usually made of 2x4s, 2x6s, or other lumber to hold, shape, and support concrete as it cures.

Furring strip Narrow strips of wood attached to a surface to build it out. Provides nailing for the underlayment.

Gauged stone A stone tile (sometimes polished) that has been cut to uniform thickness and dimensions.

Glass cutter Pencil-shaped metal tool, at one end of which is a wheel-shaped cutter used for scoring glass or glazed ceramic tile.

Glaze A mixture of lead silicate and pigments applied to the surface of tiles, creating a colored, often glossy effect.

Grip (see Bond strength).

Grout A binder and filler applied in the joints between ceramic tile. May either be sanded (sand added) or unsanded.

Hearth A noncombustible horizontal surface in front of a fireplace; it may be flush with the surrounding floor or raised above it.

Impervious tile This dense-bodied tile is made from a bisque that is nearly waterproof and freeze-thaw stable.

In-corner tile Trim tile for turning a right angle in an installation in which the adjacent wall is also tiled and faces the horizontal tile surface.

Isolation joint Flexible material inserted between dissimilar floor or wall materials (e.g., concrete and wood) to allow for different expansion rates.

Isolation membrane Used on top of a setting bed to prevent seasonal movement.

Jack-on-jack Layout pattern in which courses of tiles align vertically.

Lath Either a wood slat or a wire-mesh base found in plaster walls.

Layout lines Chalk guidelines on the setting bed used to assist in accurate tile-setting.

Layout stick A straight, long, narrow stick marked in increments of tile widths and grout joints.

Level Tool used to check that surfaces are plumb (vertical) or level (horizontal).

Lugs Nubs or projections formed into tile edges to maintain even spacing.

Mastic Common term used for organic-based adhesives.

Mortar The mixture of sand, cement, and water used to float mortar beds.

Mosaic tile Glass or clay tile that is 2 inches square or smaller. Usually it is packaged in sheet-mounted form.

Mud Tile-setter's term for mortar.

Nonvitreous tile A very porous tile that absorbs moisture and is therefore not freeze-thaw stable.

Open time The length of time adhesive can stay on a surface before it dries out and no longer forms an effective bond.

Organic mastic Also simply called mastic. This solvent-based or water-based adhesive cures by evaporation. Mastic is generally used on walls and floors; not in places subject to heat.

Out-corner tile A trim tile used for turning a right-angle corner in a countertop or similar installation in which three adjacent planes (two vertical and one horizontal) are tiled.

Paver tile Any floor tile that is not classified as red-bodied quarry tile. Ranges from impervious porcelain to soft-bodied Mexican patio pavers.

Plumb line A long string weighted at one end with a metal plumb bob, used to determine true vertical lines.

Porosity In tiling terms, the amount of water a ceramic tile will absorb.

Pot life The maximum time that a mixed adhesive will stay flexible enough to spread and to create a good bond.

Prime coat Sealer coat of adhesive or sealant that keeps the substrate from drawing moisture out of the tile adhesive.

Quarry tile Applied to most hard, red-bodied clay floor tiles of consistent dimensions. Used indoors and outdoors.

Radiant stove A stove that encloses a fire with a single layer of metal.

Reducing strip Trim tile used to finish the edge of an installation so new and old floor levels are smoothly joined.

Reinforcing mesh Wire mesh used to strengthen a mortar bed.

Retarder additive Used to lengthen the cure time of adhesives and grouts.

Riser The vertical face of steps or stairs.

Rubber float A flat, rubber-faced tool used to apply grout.

Running bond A tile pattern in which tiles are staggered one half the tile width from the tiles in the courses above and below.

Score To scratch or etch a cutline in a glazed tile, prior to cutting. The tile will snap or break along the scored line.

Screed Straight piece of wood used to level freshly poured cement.

Sealer Liquid coating used to protect unglazed tiles and grout joints.

Semi-vitreous tile Tile that absorbs between 3- and 7- percent water.

Setup time The amount of time the tile-setter has before spread adhesive begins to cure.

Shims Thin, wedge-shaped pieces of wood, such as cedar shingles, inserted between framing gaps to prevent movement or correct sagging.

Skim coat Very thin coat of adhesive applied before the final bonding adhesive coat.

Snap cutter Hand-operated tool used to make straight cuts in tiles.

Spacers Individually inserted plastic crosses of an even thickness, used to keep grout-joint sizes consistent.

Spackling compound A powdery substance that mixes with water and is used to cover seams and nail holes in plaster and gypsum wallboard.

Spading Pushing a shovel up and down at the edges of a concrete form to eliminate air bubbles.

Spline A flat strip that fits into a groove or slot to hold the pieces of a parquet wood tile together.

Step nosing An extruded aluminum strip with a vinyl insert, installed on the front edge of stair or step treads to provide traction and prevent slips.

Striking joints Shaping concave grout or mortar joints between tiles.

Stub walls Partial walls that form the opening in a shower enclosure.

Subfloor The layer of flooring that covers joists and upon which underlayment or finish flooring is installed.

Substrate The surface or underlayment to which flooring is applied.

T-bolts T-shaped bolts that connect the toilet stool to the floor.

Tab-mounted tile A sheet of tile held together with plastic or rubber.

Tamp To pack down firmly with a series of taps or blows.

Terra cotta tiles Pavers that are available in a variety of earth tones.

Thick-bed mortar A thick layer of mortar (more than 1/2 inch) that is used to level an uneven surface for tiling.

Thin-set adhesive (mortar) Any cement-based or organic adhesive applied in a thin layer (less than 1/2 inch) for setting tile.

Tile cutter Special machine used to cut ceramic tile.

Tile nipper Plier-type tool used to make irregular-shaped cuts in tile.

Tile spacer Anything used to create consistently sized grout joints.

Tongue-and-groove (parquet) tile Wood tile cut with grooves on edges of two sides and tongues on the others; the tongue of one tile fits into the groove of the next to create a strong joint.

Tread The horizontal face of a step or stair structure.

Trim tile A specially formed tile that is used to finish off inside or outside edges and corners of tile installations.

Underlayment Smooth panels of plywood or backer board used as a base for setting tile.

Vitreous tile Nonporous tile, stronger than nonvitreous, that absorbs little water and is freeze-thaw stable.

Wainscot Wall surfacing that reaches to chair-back height.

Waterproof membrane Polyethylene film (usually 4 mil thick) or tar paper installed to prevent moisture penetration. Also called a vapor barrier.

INDEX

METRIC CONVERSION TABLES

LUMBER

Sizes: Metric cross sections are so close to their nearest U.S. sizes, as noted at right, that for most purposes they may be considered equivalents.

Lengths: Metric lengths are based on a 300mm module, which is slightly shorter in length than a U.S. foot. Check your requirements accurately to the nearest inch, and consult the table below to find the metric length required.

Areas: The metric area is a square meter. Use the following conversion factor when converting from U.S. data: 100 sq. feet = 9.29 sq. meters.

METRIC LENGTHS

Meters	Equivalent Feet and Inches
1.8m	5'10⅞"
2.1m	6' 10⅝"
2.4m	7' 10½"
2.7m	8' 10¼"
3.0m	9' 10⅛"
3.3m	10' 9⅞"
3.6m	11' 9¾"
3.9m	12' 9½"
4.2m	13' 9⅜"
4.5m	14' 9⅓"
4.8m	15' 9"
5.1m	16' 8¾"
5.4m	17' 8⅝"
5.7m	18' 8⅜"
6.0m	19' 8¼"
6.3m	20' 8"
6.6m	21' 7⅞"
6.9m	22' 7⅝"
7.2m	23' 7½"
7.5m	24' 7¼"
7.8m	25' 7⅛"

Dimensions are based on 1m = 3.28 feet, or 1 foot = 0.3048m

METRIC SIZES
(Shown before Nearest U.S. Equivalent)

Millimeters	Inches	Millimeters	Inches
16 x 75	⅝ x 3	44 x 150	1¾ x 6
16 x 100	⅝ x 4	44 x 175	1¾ x 7
16 x 125	⅝ x 5	44 x 200	1¾ x 8
16 x 150	⅝ x 6	44 x 225	1¾ x 9
19 x 75	¾ x 3	44 x 250	1¾ x 10
19 x 100	¾ x 4	44 x 300	1¾ x 12
19 x 125	¾ x 5	50 x 75	2 x 3
19 x 150	¾ x 6	50 x 100	2 x 4
22 x 75	⅞ x 3	50 x 125	2 x 5
22 x 100	⅞ x 4	50 x 150	2 x 6
22 x 125	⅞ x 5	50 x 175	2 x 7
22 x 150	⅞ x 6	50 x 200	2 x 8
25 x 75	1 x 3	50 x 225	2 x 9
25 x 100	1 x 4	50 x 250	2 x 10
25 x 125	1 x 5	50 x 300	2 x 12
25 x 150	1 x 6	63 x 100	2½ x 4
25 x 175	1 x 7	63 x 125	2½ x 5
25 x 200	1 x 8	63 x 150	2½ x 6
25 x 225	1 x 9	63 x 175	2½ x 7
25 x 250	1 x 10	63 x 200	2½ x 8
25 x 300	1 x 12	63 x 225	2½ x 9
32 x 75	1¼ x 3	75 x 100	3 x 4
32 x 100	1¼ x 4	75 x 125	3 x 5
32 x 125	1¼ x 5	75 x 150	3 x 6
32 x 150	1¼ x 6	75 x 175	3 x 7
32 x 175	1¼ x 7	75 x 200	3 x 8
32 x 200	1¼ x 8	75 x 225	3 x 9
32 x 225	1¼ x 9	75 x 250	3 x 10
32 x 250	1¼ x 10	75 x 300	3 x 12
32 x 300	1¼ x 12	100 x 100	4 x 4
38 x 75	1½ x 3	100 x 150	4 x 6
38 x 100	1½ x 4	100 x 200	4 x 8
38 x 125	1½ x 5	100 x 250	4 x 10
38 x 150	1½ x 6	100 x 300	4 x 12
38 x 175	1½ x 7	150 x 150	6 x 6
38 x 200	1½ x 8	150 x 200	6 x 8
38 x 225	1½ x 9	150 x 300	6 x 12
44 x 75	1¾ x 3	200 x 200	8 x 8
44 x 100	1¾ x 4	250 x 250	10 x 10
44 x 125	1¾ x 5	300 x 300	12 x 12

Dimensions are based on 1 inch = 25mm

For *all* of your home improvement, repair, and decorating projects, look for these and other fine Creative Homeowner Press books at home centers or bookstores...

COLOR IN THE AMERICAN HOME

Find out how to make the most of color in your American home with ideas for analyzing, selecting, and coordinating color schemes. Learn how differently light affects the colors you choose depending on where you live. Over 150 photographs.

BOOK #: 287264   176pp., 9"x10"

THE SMART APPROACH TO BATH DESIGN

Everything you need to know about designing a bathroom like a professional. Creative solutions and practical advice about space, the latest in fixtures and fittings, and safety features accompany over 150 photographs.

BOOK #: 287225   176pp., 9"x10"

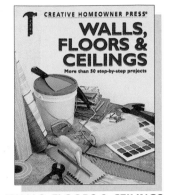

WALLS, FLOORS & CEILINGS

Here's the definitive guide to interiors. It shows you how to replace old surfaces with new professional-looking ones. Projects include installing molding, skylights, insulation, flooring, carpeting, and more. Over 500 color photographs and drawings.

BOOK #: 277697   176pp., 8½"x10⅞"

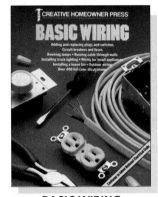

BASIC WIRING

(Third Edition, Conforms to latest National Electrical Code)

Included are 350 large, clear, full-color illustrations and no-nonsense step-by-step instructions. Shows how to replace receptacles and switches; repair a lamp; install ceiling and attic fans; and more.

BOOK #: 277048   160pp., 8½"x11"

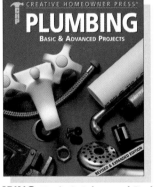

PLUMBING: Basic & Advanced Projects

Take the guesswork out of plumbing repair and installation for old and new systems. Projects include replacing faucets, unclogging drains, installing a tub, replacing a water heater, and much more. 500 illustrations and diagrams.

BOOK #: 277620   176pp., 8½"x10⅞"

MASONRY

Concrete, brick, and stone choices are detailed with step-by-step instructions and over 35 color photographs and 460 illustrations. Projects include a brick or stone garden wall, steps and patios, a concrete block retaining wall and a concrete sidewalk.

BOOK #: 277106   176pp., 8½"x10⅞"

ADDING SPACE WITHOUT ADDING ON

Cramped for space? This book, which replaces our old book of the same title, shows you how to find space you may not know you had and convert it into useful living areas. 40 colorful photographs and 530 full-color drawings.

BOOK #: 277680   192pp., 8½"x10⅞"

BATHROOMS

Shows how to plan, construct, and finish a bathroom. Remodel floors; rebuild walls and ceilings; and install windows, skylights and plumbing fixtures. Specific tools and materials are given for each project.

BOOK #: 277053   192pp., 8½"x10⅞"

KITCHENS: Design, Remodel, Build

This is the reference book for modern kitchen design, with more than 100 full-color photos to help homeowners plan the layout. Step-by-step instructions illustrate basic plumbing and wiring techniques; how to finish walls and ceilings; and more.

BOOK #: 277065   192pp., 8½"x10⅞"

For more information, and to order direct, call 800-631-7795; in New Jersey 201-934-7100.

Please visit our Web site at http://www.chp-publisher.com